D1267939

George Bernard SHAW:

A CRITICAL SURVEY

George Bernard SHAW:

A CRITICAL SURVEY · EDITED

BY LOUIS KRONENBERGER , ed.

CLEVELAND AND NEW YORK

THE WORLD PUBLISHING COMPANY

LIBRARY OF CONGRESS CATALOG CARD NUMBER: 52–5197

FIRST EDITION

The essays in this book are dated
by their publication in book form.

HC 953

CONTENTS

A SHORT CHRONOLOGY

(Plays are dated by the year Shaw finished writing them)

1856—G. B. S. born July 26, in Dublin

1871—Goes to work for a Dublin estate agent

1876—Moves to London

1879—Works for Edison Telephone Company; writes first novel, *Immaturity*

1880—Writes novel, *The Irrational Knot*

1881—Writes novel, *Love among the Artists;* grows beard; turns vegetarian

1882—Writes novel, *Cashel Byron's Profession;* turns Socialist

1883—Writes without completing *An Unsocial Socialist*

1884—Joins Fabian Society

1885—Death of Shaw's father

1886—Begins three-year stretch as art critic of *The World*

1888—Begins two-year stretch as music critic (Corno di Bassetto) on *The Star*

1889—Publishes *Fabian Essays*

1890—Begins four-year stretch as music critic of *The World*

1891—*The Quintessence of Ibsenism*

1892—*Widowers' Houses*

1893—*The Philanderer; Mrs Warren's Profession*

1894—*Arms and the Man; Candida*

1895—Begins three-year stretch as drama critic of the *Saturday Review; The Man of Destiny; You Never Can Tell*

1896—*The Devil's Disciple*

1898—Marries Charlotte Payne-Townshend; *Caesar and Cleopatra; The Perfect Wagnerite*

1899—*Captain Brassbound's Conversion*

1903—*Man and Superman*

1904—*John Bull's Other Island;* defeated as candidate for London County Council

1905—Revisits Ireland for the first time; buys house at Ayot St Lawrence; *Major Barbara*

1906—*The Doctor's Dilemma; Our Theatres in the Nineties;* meets Ellen Terry

1908—*Getting Married*

1909—*Misalliance; The Shewing-up of Blanco Posnet*

1911—*Fanny's First Play*

1912—*Androcles and the Lion; Pygmalion*

1914—*Common Sense About the War*

1919—*Heartbreak House*

1920—*Back to Methuselah*

1923—*Saint Joan*

1925—Awarded Nobel Prize for Literature

1928—*The Intelligent Woman's Guide to Capitalism and Socialism*

1929—*The Apple Cart*

1931—Visits U.S.S.R.; *Ellen Terry and Bernard Shaw: A Correspondence*

1932—*The Adventures of the Black Girl in Her Search for God*

1933—Visits America

1934—*Collected Prefaces*

1939—*In Good King Charles's Golden Days*

1943—Wife dies at 86

1950—Shaw dies, Nov. 13, at 94

INTRODUCTION

Shaw was not simply the longest-lived of modern writers and in some degree the most many-sided; he was also in a sense the most challenging and disruptive. No other writer, as a result, has been the subject of so much criticism and so much near-nonsense. In an effort to understand what Shaw "meant," a whole battery of journalists, a whole army of pundits have sadly misunderstood what he was. Some of them have wrestled in solemn social-worker fashion with Shaw as though he were entirely a writer of textbooks and tracts; some, at the other extreme, have tried to make Shaw's irreverence and iconoclasm the engine of their own craving to startle or demolish. But neither through ignoring what was most Shavian nor through trying to outdo it did much worth saying about Shaw get said. And even the wisest of Shaw's critics cannot always have known how far Shaw's showmanship concealed his serious intentions, how far it coincided with them, and how far it concealed the lack of any.

But, in whatever spirit and from whatever side, it has been notably easy to write about Shaw. Any man with a specialty or a mania must somewhere have found Shaw adverting to it; any man with a grievance must have found in Shaw an antagonist or ally; whatever a man's politics,or his God, or his denial of one, Shaw—early or late —must have had his say about it. For on however outmoded or ill-reasoned or cantankerous a basis, Shaw's collected works constitute a sort of encyclopaedia. Shaw has greeted an endless succession of events with a twenty-one-gun salute—his little innovation being to take lethal aim as well. He not only took all human activity for his province, but strongly suggested that nothing superhuman was alien to him, either—he swept Heaven clean of charm, drastically lowered the temperature of Hell, brought back the dead, landscaped and peopled the future. No matter what one's field or one's foible—God or Devil, O'Leary or John Bull, prizefighters or soldiers or poets, armament-makers or brothel-keepers, Shakespeare or Wagner, phonetics or marriage or divorce, slums or drama critics, war or revolution—Shaw may serve as a pretext for writing about it, or it as a pretext for writing about Shaw.

But exactly as his work supplies something for almost everyone to write about, it embraces too many things for any one person to write about with sufficient authority. Whoever would deal definitely with Shaw must go well beyond the writer of plays or of prefaces, the critic of plays or of music, must plunge into Marx and cross over to Ireland and turn back to Lamarck, must buy himself an atlas and burrow deep in history, must know medicine and law, the Church and many churches, the whole arena of politics, half the arcana of science, plus much miscellaneous knowledge and very much curious lore. Even where Shaw is shallow or fanciful or mistaken, the critic who would pronounce judgment cannot be. Hence the most we can really hope for is that anyone who would write with some breadth about Shaw should be a man of letters with an informed concern for ideas; should offer a literary man's verdict of Shaw's talent and a knowledgeable, however disputable, version of Shaw's "thought." No one can write comprehensively of Shaw as just a literary or dramatic critic: for again and again one must stop and explain, or digress and coordinate, or go after the facts and compare. And the difficulty isn't just how much Shaw wrote about, it is how consistently—or inconsistently—he wrote about it, in how dedicated or mischievous a spirit, with how controversial a slant, how contradictory an aim: so that one is dealing with shock tactics as well as principles, with the man who wrote for Hearst as well as for posterity, with *poseur* no less than puritan, thinker and thought-processor too, and with in some ways the most bourgeois as well as the most anti-bourgeois writer of his time.

All the same, if we are to isolate and honor what remains most vital and Shavian about Shaw we must neglect the role he assumed most vividly in his own time for the role he more and more occupies in ours; we must care less about how informed or inflammatory or even intelligent he was in favor of how supple and witty and articulate he remains. Like Shakespeare he filled his plays with historical characters, like Ibsen with social ideas, and as with them it only matters now how creatively he went about it: the problem of *Ghosts* no longer presses, the first act of *Ghosts* is a marvel of exposition still. To be sure, from the real place he occupies in history Shaw's treatment of issues and ideas has a more than usual historical interest; due tribute must be paid to such of his "thinking" as proved fruitful, or to such leadership as actually led somewhere. But equally where Shaw seemed most sound or most mistaken, his thinking side has, for our day, been too much stressed; not because of how often Shaw may have been wrong or right, but because his true genius and—as it happened—his real job lay elsewhere. Most of all and most triumphantly of all, Shaw was a showman of ideas. If it is true that intellectually he was something more, perhaps it is also unfortunate that he was; for what counts less has blurred what easily bulks largest. By a showman of ideas, I mean something big-scaled as well as admirable, I mean someone who, at his weakest, made a fashion show of all the contending issues of his age; and who, at his most trenchant, made a superb military spectacle where those issues crossed swords and drew blood and often killed one another off. His were, in many cases, sham battles and arbitrary victories and defeats: but such was his staging of them, he attracted the whole civilized world to the battlefield. This is not to deny how serious, how astute, how learned Shaw could be. There is much solid matter indeed to Shaw's encyclopaedia, as there is much to Dr. Johnson's Dictionary; but its value will rest more and more on what is Shavian about it, as with the Dictionary it is what is Johnsonian that counts. Shaw's delineation of ancient Egypt or modern England is, for vividness and bias alike, of a piece with Johnson's definition of lexicographer or excise.

So long as we have a Shaw in the role of showman, dramatist, virtuoso, entertainer; so long as his chief function is rather to exhilarate than enlighten the audience, it matters much less how often he contradicts himself, how glaringly his demonstrations nullify each other, or even how wantonly he betrays the scruples of a lifetime for the gratification of the moment. And what for me clinches the fact that Shaw is above all a showman of ideas—equally in terms of classification as of achievement—is that his is so very much more a triumph of method than of meaning—that again and again we can admire the approach while resisting, while rejecting, the arguments. T. S. Eliot once raised the point how far one can enjoy a writer whose ideas antagonize one: I don't know that he answered it, or that it is safely answerable; but the answer may well be, to the degree that he is an engaging showman. (With the pure work of art, something different —something like a willing suspension of disbelief—is involved.) In any case, write though he did on a hundred subjects, with cogency very often, with real conviction as often as not, Shaw yet never wrote so as to fuse all his contentions, reconcile all his contradictions, make some innermost quality of self light up the whole. He wears no heraldic armband, neither the *Que sais-je* of a Montaigne wise enough to doubt his own wisdom, nor the *cor laceratum* of Swift, in lifelong explosion for what deep down refused to explode, nor the *Écrasez l'infame* of Voltaire, divided by passion from Shaw however joined to him by wit and prankishness. Of dialectics, again, Dr. Johnson, like Shaw, often made a mere game, playing brusquely and unfairly to win; but the dialectics was one thing, the view of life another. When we speak of Dr. Johnson as a humane reactionary, the two words are ultimately not a contradiction but a coalescence, for to Johnson the Tory scheme of things was really at one with the tragic sense of life: inequality must needs be acquiesced in as a principle since it could not be escaped as a fact. But despite how many things Shaw espoused and militantly fought for, or exposed and fought militantly against, just where do we pierce to the heart of the matter? We all know G. B. S.; but what, precisely, is the GBessence? Possibly no symbolic heart exists because no human heart declares itself; how much gayer is a Johnson or a Mozart or a Keats for his streak of melancholy. But we no sooner seize on the gaiety of Shaw's mind than we become aware of the gaunt puritanism of his body; we no sooner respond to his anti-bourgeois laughter than we are conscious of his curiously bourgeois art. He ridicules Ireland by way of England, England by way of Ireland, he turns waggish in the pulpit, injects purpose into his pranks. Plumping for reason, he dissolves in mysticism; whooping up socialism, he lets his eye stray toward the Strong Man and worldly power. Such dazzling contradictions go far to explain Shaw's success as dramatist, but tend also to point up his untrustworthiness of mind. To put it mildly, it is all much too confusing, it is as though what one's doctor prescribed as a sedative should also prove an emetic. Were Shaw's the pervasive skepticism that frowns on all absolutes and is mistrustful of all systems, were his even the feeling that every human benefit has its price, we should know where and in what excellent company we stood. But in spite of his laughter, Shaw does deal in absolutes; in spite of snarling them up in paradoxes, he does offer solutions; and we have accordingly to reconcile a constructive program with a nihilist technique. And superbly as laughter can demolish, or paradox reinterpret, neither thing can be systematically constructive. Shaw's *modus operandi* becomes too much an end in itself; the penalty, perhaps, of diverting all who watch you is converting none of them. It is the showmanship that drapes itself in sacerdotal robes, that chants and swings incense and utters solemn proclamations— whether after Wagner's fashion, or Stanislavsky's, or Mr. Eliot's— that acquires not just audiences, but followers. The really costly thing with Shaw was not how many other people he made light of, but that—and never more than when he swaggered—he so decidedly made light of himself.

Yet we must always bear in mind two things. A man born with a genius for juggling—whether colored balls or controversial ideas— can hardly escape the role of performer, can hardly avoid ending up on the stage. So much for what Shaw was; as for what he in some measure failed to be, as for his final lack of philosophic wholeness and weight, the very thing that made him in one sense more than man—the free, volatile, unvindictive, dazzlingly gymnastic play of mind—left him not a complete man as well. He rather reversed the usual human order: in him, the animal spirits and sensual enjoyments that keep other men zestful and young were soberly dislodged or puritanically suppressed; while the philosophic doubts, the worries over the world, the concern for the good life that turn other men into split and neurotic personalities were for Shaw a source of invigoration and release. The effect, if extraordinary, is also just a little monstrous, as of someone not created but invented, as of someone marvelously, miraculously . . . two dimensional.

The masks, the pranks, the poses were in their way, of course, psychologically necessary as well as professionally shrewd. Shaw— as he himself confessed and Bertrand Russell and others quickly noted—was by nature a painfully shy man; one who compensated in print for a lack of ease in ordinary conversation; one who went still farther, and made of himself not just a dramatic figure but an almost fictional one. It doesn't matter that part of the fiction consisted in speaking the truth. Shaw's habitual joshing, moreover, bespoke not a mocking mind or witty tongue alone: the habitual josher is oftenest someone who finds the unself-conscious give-and-take of human intercourse a strain. His joshing, on the personal side, represents a kind of avoidance of conversation, while on the intellectual side it is a way, among one's inferiors, of not having to talk drivel or talk down. Something faintly mysterious, because faintly monstrous, surrounds this man in whom the mind bulks so large and the body so blatantly dwindles; whose puritan view of sex may rather signify a sexual difficulty "solved" by puritanism. But the more palpable and, I would think, serious personal difficulty was social and economic, and derives from the shabby-genteel family background, from the indigently transplanted Irishman, from the father who drank and the mother forced to work. Shaw solved the thing magnificently as a writer, but the emotions it begot he never wholly mastered or outgrew. He was one of those to whom birth wouldn't have mattered in the slightest had he only been really wellborn; he was a snob not for something he was but for something he wasn't. One thinks, if for only a moment, of Swift. Shaw, like Swift, resented his ambiguous social position, and took more than good care of his money. Like Swift again, Shaw was fascinated by men of power, and oddly evasive about women and love. But the likenesses only emphasize, in the end, the contrast between one of the most perfectly managed and one of the most tragically mishandled of all careers; between a self-regulated and smooth-functioning life and one that, deeply fissured within, ended in madness. For want of a brooding and melancholy streak, Shaw's work fails of a kind of beauty inherent in much of the finest art; but the absence of it in Shaw himself left the show-man free to shuffle his masks at will and achieve the most unlikely roles: a Savonarola who should twinkle while he thundered; a puritan man-of-the-world who, in the most Jaegerish of garments, attained to the jauntiest of styles. Consider merely the beard—by which Shaw instantly attracted attention and permanently concealed his face; by which he contrived to look flatteringly male and engagingly Mephistophelian; and by which, most of all, through seeming to part with it, Shaw permanently preserved his youth.

If in these comments of my own I have stressed a certain side of Shaw, the side that cracked a whip rather than carried a lantern, that will also explain a possible bias in my choice from the comment of others. I am not conscious of any, but it seems wise to allow for one since the whole problem of what to include in this volume was from the outset thorny. There was first of all—before deciding what to choose—the matter of what to choose from. Only someone with a fanatic's ardor and an archaeologist's skill could read all the criticism that has been written about Shaw, and even he would need to master several dozen languages, or maintain a staff of resident translators. Take Shaw's plays alone: somebody must somewhere be reviewing some one of them every day in the year; while in how many obscure and ill-fated journals dear to vegetable-eaters or élan-vitalitarians must there not have been critiques about Shaw and the flesh, or Shaw and the spirit? I can't pretend to have made even a beginning in this huge, mad, musty storehouse of provincial newspapers, crank periodicals, and privately printed brochures. Even working on a greatly restricted scale, even rooting out—from the accumulated files and stacks of nearly sixty years—what seemed reasonably promising or pertinent, proved a trifle exhausting: the more so as, among so much Shaw criticism that could be termed adequate, so little seemed really impressive.

The precise basis for choosing raised problems, too. With so many-sided a writer, should critical merit be the sole criterion, or should variety and comprehensiveness be considered also? Shouldn't there be articles on not the dramatist or drama critic, the prose-writer or pamphleteer alone, but on the Fabian, the Lamarckian, the Butler-ite, the Irishman, the Anglo-Irishman, the critic of theologians and medicos and painters and pianists and critics? Again, should there not be articles on Shaw whose writers sum up various points of view —American and English, Eire and Ulster, Tory and Marxist, religious and rationalist? And finally, should there not be a balance of opinion —or a critical spectrum, rather, ranging from eulogy to excoriation? Well—no. Other things being equal, I have wherever possible

favored variety; but since other things seldom are equal, merit for
the most part has proved decisive. If there is more here on Shaw's
writing and playwriting gifts than on what he wrote about, it is both
because they gave rise to keener criticism and because they arouse
keener interest now. If sharply defined points of view fell by the
wayside, it is because there is so little point in viewing them; the set
Tory or Marxist, the militant Churchman or anti-clerical—however
incisive at moments—will far likelier write propaganda than criticism,
much oftener exploit Shaw than examine him. Finally, a balance of
opinion cannot be achieved through using opinion unbalanced in
itself, through babbling praise or unbridled vituperation: though I
daresay I would have included a sufficiently brilliant tirade could I
have found one.

There emerges a certain range and variety withal. Along with so
much else, Edmund Wilson's essay applies socialist and Marxist
criteria to Shaw's political and social thinking. Though highly controversial, Eric Bentley's defense of Shaw's politics and political
affiliations has its expository no less than its critical merits. Joad's
discussion of Shaw's philosophy—which means his biology as well—
seems as definitive as it is lucid. There is P. P. Howe, again, on
Shaw's economics; there is Chesterton on his criticism. I would
have liked a proper piece on Shaw as art critic, and as music critic
even more; but among a handful of tries, none turned up. B. H.
Haggin, after a page or two, writes of other things; Professor Dent,
for the most part, writes memoirs of things past; Mr. William Irvine
is more descriptive than critical; and Virgil Thomson—of whom I
inquired—has written nothing at all. At the outset, too, I had hopes
of including a number of reviews, and I *have* included one or two,
notably Stark Young's valuable dissent on *Heartbreak House*. But
reviews, however sound, not only barnacle the comment with details
of the story, they befog the play with details of the production. Even
Pirandello writing, after the first New York production, of *Saint Joan*
imbeds a few bright nuggets in sandy soil. A great many of Shaw's
better-known critics have gradually lost, or perhaps always lacked,
real critical value—or so I have reacted, at least, to Archer, Walkley,
Desmond McCarthy, C. E. Montague, Havelock Ellis and a number
of others. Mencken's long out-of-print little book is mere prentice-
work in which Mencken took far more of Shaw's manner than his
measure; Mencken's later essay, "The Ulster Polonius," is one of
many articles from which, while the piece itself may be left to
perish, a line or remark should be saved. Thus Mencken ascribed
Shaw's success to his treating "the obvious in terms of the scandal-
ous." Thus—for one among many examples—W. J. Turner remarked
that "like all Puritans, Shaw feels that passion must be put to use."

And of course there is Egon Fridell's all-too-famous but more than just clever *mot*. Shaw, said Fridell, was very shrewd: always, in prescribing for the public, he coated his pills with chocolate. But the public, Fridell added, was even shrewder: it licked off the chocolate without swallowing the pills.

Of the criticism that I have included, much of the best—and this is no doubt as it should be—came reasonably early. Chesterton's book, published forty-odd years ago, was not simply a milestone; in certain of its judgments it remains a terminus as well. Dixon Scott's essay, so much admired where known (but so little known), praises and indicts, I think, with equal sharpness; and Max Beerbohm—his Tory esthetics perhaps even more outraged than his Tory politics—makes a neat blend of Shaw's gifts and his own misgivings. John Palmer brings much wit to the matter and much sense as well; while Mr. Nathan is sharp as well as blunt on the subject that Shaw most tends to sidestep and that Nathan is always enchanted to greet. Indeed, for a certain flavorsomeness, for a way of meeting Shaw on his own ground, with cognate wit or comparable weapons, the best of the Old Guard are much superior to all but the very best of the new. In general, however, the older writers sadly date, and almost as sadly— with their luxuriant literary-journalistic prose—in style as in substance.

In our time there have been some very good things written about Shaw, and some very good names indeed among the writers. Yet what stands forth glaringly is the extent to which Shaw has *not* been written about—that is to say, by the most influential of our serious critics. Though often touching on Shaw, Mr. Eliot has made no attempt to traverse him; nor, so far as I know, has a Leavis, a Blackmur, a Tate, a Trilling, a Ransom, a Winters—the list, if it is not to be lengthy, can only be suggestive. And it is of real interest to ask why so many fashionable and formidable critics have passed Shaw by, even though the answer, up to a point, seems clear enough. For one thing, of course, Shaw lived too long and, save here and there, his later work—a full twenty years of it—had almost in common decency to be ignored. More integrally, Shaw in his "art" was the kind of bourgeois writer who would antagonize today's higher criticism, and in his tactics was the kind of anti-bourgeois writer who would perhaps antagonize it even more. And not only, of course, is Shaw's method sharply didactic; his concern is not with humanity but with society. He goes at slums in terms of slum clearance, at brothels in terms of capitalist profiteers, at marriage in terms of crippling divorce laws, at the early Christians in pointed contrast to the later ones. His Caesar or his Joan is not, thanks to the creative imagination, more richly complex than in history's pages; rather each is

brilliantly simplified and straightened out, each his own most eloquent spokesman. Thus not only art in the final reckoning, but life
itself at the very outset, is too much cut to measure; everything functions mechanically, nothing breathes. Worse still, there is the fact
that Shaw, whether a poet of sorts or no poet at all or Mr. Eliot's
poet strangled at birth, quite lacks the kind of poetic sensibility that
prevails today. And indeed, even after scraping away all that is *not*
Shaw's view of Shakespeare, his insistence on the banality of Shakespeare's thinking really constitutes a misapprehension of Shakespeare's art. It is part of Shakespeare's greatness as a *creative writer*
that he avoided Shaw's mistake, that he preferred poetic truism to
scientific truth; that with such a writer ripeness is all, and ratiocination, in the end, is nothing. Shaw is indeed least poetic where he tries
hardest to be. Marchbanks is most a monster for being even less of
a poet than of a normal human being; he is quite inept when he tries
to talk like Shelley and only forceful when he begins to talk like
Shaw. And when Shaw himself aspires to poetry, as with the March
winds and frisking lambs of *Saint Joan,* his rank failure is all too
notorious.

As many critics would find no sense of poetry in Shaw, so would
they find no awareness of evil; of a troubled, darkly religious vision
of life; of the lost, or damned, or guilt-gnawed, or salvation-seeking
soul. There are no bad people, no black-hearted, God-hounded evil-
doers in Shaw; there are only corrupt classes or intolerable social
conditions or vicious laws. (Shaw's failure to understand personal
wickedness is a real deficiency.) And we have finally to reckon with
the fact that serious modern criticism has shown, quite understand-
ably, little interest in the theater, for there has been little there to
interest it. Thus, for many critics, if there has been no incentive to
discuss Shaw's own achievement as a playwright, there has equally
been no need to examine his influence—or even his lack of influence
—on playwriting.

But though one can well understand why so many critics have
failed to write about Shaw, one yet can wish that they had, or that
they would. They might nail all that on the one hand is frivolous and
on the other hand tractarian, all that is bloodless or bogus or mon-
grel or out-of-date, and contrive a sharp new formulation of where
he failed or fell short. But they might also conclude that, in violation
of his own tenets quite as much as theirs, Shaw achieved magnificent
effects; that with his verve and energy he is, time and again, nothing
less than irresistible; that for sheer articulateness and wit, he is in
modern times, all but unmatched. No one can dismiss Shaw's talent;
one can at most deplore what Shaw did with it.

LOUIS KRONENBERGER

George Bernard SHAW:

A CRITICAL SURVEY

MAX BEERBOHM

1901

A Cursory Conspectus of G. B. S.

Assuming that Mr. Shaw will live to the age of ninety (and such is the world's delight in him that even then his death will seem premature), I find that he has already fulfilled one half of his life span. Yet is it only in the past seven years or so that he has gained his vogue. One would suppose that so distinct a creature, so sharply complete in himself, must have been from the outset famous. But the fact remains that every morning for some thirty-seven years Mr. Shaw woke up and found himself obscure. Though, of course, his friends and fellow-workers recognised in him a being apart, for the Anglo-Saxon race he did not exist. I have often wondered what was the reason: was it the world's usual obtuseness, or was it that Mr. Shaw was unusually late in development? I had no means of deciding. I did not possess any of Mr. Shaw's early work. Thus very welcome to me is the reprint of a novel* written by Mr. Shaw in the flush of youth. Of the novel itself Mr. Shaw himself evidently thinks no great shakes. For on this excursion he takes with him even more than his usual armful of light baggage—prefaces, notes, appendices, quotations; he has also a new portable dramatic version of his book. And, as he bustles along the platform with these spick-and-span impedimenta in his grasp, he seems hardly to care whether or not that battered old resuscitated trunk of his be thrown into the van. Yet for me that is the real object of interest. I rush to examine it, and tears of joy well up at the sight of "G. B. S." printed on it, as on the new hand-baggage, in letters of flame.

Yes! *Cashel Byron's Profession* is quite mature. Mr. Shaw is fully himself in it, and throughout it. It tallies with all his recent work.

Reprinted from *Around Theaters* by Max Beerbohm. Copyright 1930 by the author. Used by permission of the author.
* *Cashel Byron's Profession* by Bernard Shaw. London; Grant Richards. 1901.

3

Such differences as may be found in it are differences of mere surface, due to the fashions of the decade in which it was written, not essential differences in the writer. Apart from them, it might be his latest book. It has all his well-known merits and faults, and who shall say whether his faults or his merits are the more delicious? His own quick strong brain is behind it all, darting through solid walls of popular fallacy to the truths that lie beyond them, and darting with the impetus of its own velocity far beyond those truths to ram itself against other walls of fallacy not less solid. All through the book we hear the loud, rhythmic machinery of this brain at work. The book vibrates to it as does a steamer to the screw; and we, the passengers, rejoice in the sound of it, for we know that tremendous speed is being made. As a passage by steam is to a voyage by sail, so is Mr. Shaw's fiction to true fiction. A steamboat is nice because it takes us quickly to some destination; a sailing-yacht is nice in itself, nice for its own sake. Mr. Shaw's main wish is to take us somewhere. In other words, he wants to impress certain theories on us, to convert us to this or that view. The true creator wishes mainly to illude us with a sense of actual or imaginative reality. To achieve that aim, he must suppress himself and his theories: they kill illusion. He must accept life as it presents itself to his experience or imagination, not use his brain to twist it into the patterns of a purpose. Such self-sacrifice is beyond Mr. Shaw. He often says (and believes) that he is, despite his propagandism, a true delineator of life. But that is one of his delightful hallucinations, due to the fact that his sight for things as they are is weak in comparison with his insight into himself. In fact, Mr. Shaw is not a creator. He cannot see beyond his own nose. Even the fingers he outstretches from it to the world are (as I shall suggest) often invisible to him. Looking into his own heart, he sees clearly the world as it ought to be, and sees (as I have already suggested) further still. Of the world as it is he sees a clean-cut phantasmagoria, in which every phantom is his own unrecognised self. When he describes what he has seen, himself is the one person illuded. Some novelists fail through being unable to throw themselves into the characters they have projected. They remain critically outside, instead of becoming the characters themselves. This is not the explanation of Mr. Shaw's failure. He does not stand outside his characters: a man cannot slip his own skin. Mr. Shaw fails because the characters are all himself, and all he can do is to differentiate them by "quick-changes." But these disguises he makes in a very perfunctory way—a few twists of diaphanous gauze, a new attitude, nothing more. Thus it is in *Cashel Byron*, as in his plays. Take Cashel himself. Mr. Shaw means to present him as a very stupid young man with a genius for pugilism. But soon he turns out

to be a very clever young man, with a genius for introspection and
ratiocinatory exposition. These powers are not incompatible with a
genius for prize-fighting. But quite incompatible with it are physical
cowardice and lack of any sentiment for the art practised. Mr. Shaw
makes Cashel a coward, and lets him abandon prize-fighting without
a pang at the first opportunity, in order to prove his thesis that prize-
fighting is a mere mechanical business in which neither sentiment
nor courage is involved. As usual he goes further than the truth.
It is untrue that prize-fighters are heroes and artists and nothing
else, as the public regards them. But it is equally untrue that you
can use your fists (gloved or ungloved) without courage, or that any
man with supreme natural ability can care nothing for the channel
in which it exclusively runs. Thus Cashel does not credibly exist for
us: he is the victim of a thesis. Besides, he is Mr. Shaw. So, of
course, is Lydia, the heroine, the imperturbable, strong-minded,
blue-stockinged heroine, who, like the rest of Mr. Shaw's heroines,
has nothing to do but set every one right—a sinecure, so easily does
she do it. The only characters that really illude us are the subordi-
nate characters, of whom we see merely the surfaces and not the
souls. Mr. Shaw has a keen eye for superficial idiosyncrasies, and
such figures as Mellish and Mrs. Skene are as possible as they are
delicious, though even they are always ready to dart out on us and
ratiocinate in Mr. Shaw's manner.

After all, it is Mr. Shaw *qu'il nous faut*. My analogy of the steam-
ship was misleading. Though Mr. Shaw's chief aim, indeed, is to
proselytise, we enjoy his preaching for its own sake, without reference to conviction. We enjoy for its own sake the process by which
he arrives at his conclusions. At least, we do so if we take him in the
right way. We must not take him too seriously. An eminent scholar
once said to me that what he disliked in Mr. Shaw was his lack of
moral courage. I pricked up my ears, delighted: here was a new
idea! Urged by me to explain himself, the eminent scholar said
"Well, whenever he propounds a serious thesis of his own, he does
so in a jocular vein, not being sure that he is right, and knowing that
if he is wrong he will have saved his face by laughing in his
reader's"—or words to that effect. I was disappointed. My interlocutor had betrayed simply his incapacity to understand the rudiments of Shawism. The fact that he is a Scotchman, and that Mr.
Shaw is an Irishman, ought to have forewarned me. To take Mr.
Shaw thus seriously is as inept as to believe (and many folk do believe) that he is a single-minded buffoon. In him, as in so many Irishmen, seriousness and frivolity are inextricably woven in and out of
each other. He is not a serious man trying to be frivolous. He is a
serious man who cannot help being frivolous, and in him height of

spirits is combined with depth of conviction more illustriously than in any of his compatriots. That is why he amuses me as does no one else. The merely "comic man" is as intolerable in literature as in social intercourse. Humour undiluted is the most depressing of all phenomena. Humour must have its background of seriousness. Without this contrast there comes none of that incongruity which is the mainspring of laughter. The more sombre the background the brightlier skips the jest. In most of the serious writers who are also humorous there is perfect secretion between the two faculties. Thus in Matthew Arnold's controversial writings the humorous passages are always distinct interludes or "asides" consciously made, and distinct from the scheme of the essay. They are irresistible by reason of the preceding seriousness. But in Mr. Shaw the contrast is still sharper and more striking. For there the two moods are, as it were, arm in arm—inseparable comrades. Mr. Shaw cannot realise his own pertness, nor can he preserve his own gravity, for more than a few moments at a time. Even when he sets out to be funny for fun's sake, he must needs always pretend that there is a serious reason for the emprise; and he pretends so strenuously that he ends by convincing us almost as fully as he convinces himself. Thus the absurdity, whatever it be, comes off doubly well. Conversely, even when he is really engrossed in some process of serious argument, or moved to real eloquence by one of his social ideals, he emits involuntarily some wild jape which makes the whole thing ridiculous—as ridiculous to himself as to us; and straightway he proceeds to caricature his own thesis till everything is topsy-turvy; and we, rolling with laughter, look up and find him no longer on his head, but on his heels, talking away quite gravely; and this sets us off again. For, of course, when seriousness and frivolity thus co-exist inseparably in a man, the seriousness is nullified by the frivolity. The latter is fed by the former, but, graceless and vampire-like, kills it. As a teacher, as a propagandist, Mr. Shaw is no good at all, even in his own generation. But as a personality he is immortal.

JAMES HUNEKER

1909

The Quintessence of Shaw

I

To my friend, George Bernard Shaw, the Celtic superman, critic, novelist, socialist, and preface writer, to whom the present author—*circa* 1890—played the part of a critical finger-post for the everlasting benefit (he sincerely hopes) of the great American public; and to whom he now dedicates this particular essay in gratitude for the rare and stimulating pleasure afforded him by the Shaw masques, the Shavian philosophy, and also the vivid remembrance of several personal encounters at London and Bayreuth. The announcement that Bernard Shaw, moralist, Fabianite, vegetarian, playwright, critic, Wagnerite, Ibsenite, jester to the cosmos, and the most serious man on the planet, had written a play on the subject of Don Juan did not surprise his admirers. As Nietzsche philosophized with a hammer, so G. B. S. hammers popular myths. If you have read his *Cæsar and Cleopatra* you will know what I mean. This witty, sarcastic piece is the most daring he has attempted. Some years ago I described the Shaw literary pedigree as —W. S. Gilbert out of Ibsen. His plays are full of modern odds and ends, and in form are anything from the Robertsonian comedy to the Gilbertian extravaganza. They may be called psychical farce, an intellectual *comédie rosse*—for his people are mostly a blackguard crew of lively marionettes all talking pure Shaw-ese. Mr. Shaw has invented a new individual in literature who for want of a better name could be called the *Super-Cad;* he is Nietzsche's Superman turned "bounder"—and sometimes the sex is feminine.

We wonder what sort of drama this remarkable Hibernian would have produced if he had been a flesh-eater. If he is so brilliant on bran, what could he not have accomplished on blood! One thing is certain: at the cosmical banquet where Shaw sits is the head of the table—for him.

When Bernard Shaw told a gaping world that he was only a natural-born mountebank with a cart and a trumpet, a sigh of relief was exhaled in artistic London. So many had been taking him seriously and swallowing his teachings, preachings, and *pronunciamentos*, that to hear the merryman was only shamming came as a species of liberation from a cruel obsession. Without paying the customary critical toll, Shaw had slipped duty free into England all manners of damnable doctrines. What George Moore attempted in a serious manner George Shaw, a fellow-Irishman, succeeded in accomplishing without the *chorale* of objurgation, groans, exclamations of horror, and blasts of puritanical cant. Thus Proudhon, Marx, Lassalle, Ibsen, Wagner, Nietzsche, and a lot of free-thinkers in socialism, religion, philosophy, and art, walked unmolested through the pages of critical reviews, while Mr. Moore was almost pilloried for advocating naturalism, while Vizetelly was sent to prison for translating Zola.

.After the Shaw criticisms came the novels, then the plays. The prefaces of the latter are literature, and will be remembered with joy when the plays are forgotten. In them the author has distilled the quintessence of Shaw. They will be classics some day, as the Dryden prefaces are classics. Nevertheless, in the plays we find the old Shaw masquerading, this time behind the footlights. He is still the preacher, Fabian debater, socialist, vegetarian, lycanthrope, and normally abnormal man of the early days—though he prides himself on his abnormal normality. Finding that the essay did not reach a wide enough audience, the wily Celt mounts the rostrum and blarneys his listeners something after this manner:

"Here's my hustings; from here will I teach, preach, and curse the conventions of society. Come all ye who are tired of the property fallacy! There is but one Karl Marx, and I am his living prophet. Shakespeare must go—Ibsen is to rule. Wagner was a Fabianite; the Ring proves it. Come all ye who are heaven-laden with the moralities! I am the living witness for Nietzsche. I will teach children to renounce the love of parents; parents to despise their offspring; husbands to hate their wives; wives to loathe their husbands; and brothers and sisters will raise warring hands after my words have entered their souls. Whatever is is wrong—to alter Pope. The prostitute classes—I do not balk at the ugly word—clergymen, doctors, lawyers, statesmen, journalists, are deceiving you. They speak in divers and lying tongues. I alone possess the prophylactic against the evils of life. Here it is: Plays, Pleasant and Unpleasant; and Three Plays for Puritans."

But Shaw only removed another of his innumerable masks. Beware, says Nietzsche, of the autobiographies of great men. He was thinking of Richard Wagner. His warning applies to Bernard Shaw, who is a great comedian and a versatile. He has spoken through so many different masks that the real Shaw is yet to be seen. Perhaps on his death-bed some stray phrase will illuminate with its witty gleam his true soul's nature. He has played tag with this soul so long that some of it has been lost in the game. Irishman born, he is not genial after the Oliver Goldsmith type; he resembles much more closely Dean Swift, minus that man's devouring genius. When will the last mask be lifted—and, awful to relate, will it, when lifted, reveal the secret? A master hypnotist perhaps he may be, illuding the world with the mask idea. And what a comical thing it would be to find him smiling at the end and remarking, "I fooled you, Brethren, didn't I?"

In his many rôles one trait has obstinately remained, the trait of irresistible waggery. Yet we sadly suspect it. What if this declaration of charlatanism were but a mask! What if Shaw were really sincere! What if he really meant to be sincere in his various lectures and comedies! What if his assumption of insincerity were sincere! His sincerity insincere! The thought confuses. In one of his plays—*The Philanderer*—a certain character has five or six natures. Shaw again, *toujours* Shaw!

Joke of all jokes, I really imagine that Shaw is a sentimentalist in private; and that he has been so sentimental, romantic, in his youth, that an inversion has taken place in his feelings. Swift's hatred of mankind was a species of inverted lyricism; so was Flaubert's; so may be Shaw's. Fancy him secretly weeping over Jane Eyre, or holding a baby in his lap, or—richest of all fancies—occasionally eating sausage and drinking beer! I met him, once upon a time, in Bayreuth. He spoke then in unmeasured terms of its beer drinkers, and added, without the ghost of a smile, that breweries should be converted into insane asylums.

Whether we take him seriously or not, he is a delightful, an entertaining writer. His facile use, with the aid of the various mouthpieces he assumes at will, of the ideas of Nietzsche, Wagner, Ibsen, and Strindberg, fairly dazzles. He despises wit at bottom, using its forms as a medium for the communication of his theories. Art for art's sake is a contradiction to this writer. He must have a sense of beauty, but he never boasts of it; rather does he seem to consider it something naked, almost shameful—something to be hidden away.

So his men are always deriding art, though working at it like devils on high pay. This puritanical vein has grown with the years, as it has with Tolstoy. Only Shaw never wasted his youth in riotous living, as did Tolstoy.

He had no money, no opportunities, no taste. A fierce ascetic and a misogynist, he will have no regrets at threescore and ten; no sweet memories of headaches—he is a teetotaller; no heartaches—he is too busy with his books; and no bitter aftertaste for having wronged a fellow-being. Behold, Bernard Shaw is a good man, has led the life of a saint, worked like a hero against terrible odds, and is the kindest-hearted man in London. Now we have reached another mask—the mask of altruism. Nearly all his earnings went to the needy; his was, and is, a practical socialism. He never let his right hand know the extent of his charities, and mark this—no one else knew of it. Yet good deeds, like murder, will out. His associates ceased deriding the queer clothes, the flannel shirt, and the absence of evening dress; his money was spent on others. So, too, his sawdust menu—his carrots, cabbage, and brown bread—it did not cost much, his eating, for his money was needed by poorer folk. So you see what a humbug is this dear old Diogenes, who growls cynically at the human race, abhors sentiment-mongers, and despises conventional government, art, religion, and philosophy. He is an arch-sentimentalist, underneath whose frown are concealed tears of pity. Another mask torn away— Bernard Shaw, philanthropist!

He tells us in the preface to *Cashel Byron's Profession*—which sounds like the title of a Charles Lever novel—that he had a narrow escape from being a novelist at the age of twenty-six. He still shudders over it. He wrote five novels, three of which we know, to wit: *Cashel Byron's Profession, An Unsocial Socialist, Love among the Artists*—hideous and misleading title. Robert Louis Stevenson took a great fancy to *Cashel Byron* and its stunning eulogies of pugilism. It was even dramatized in this country. With Hazlitt and George Meredith (oh! unforgettable prize-fight in *The Amazing Marriage*) Mr. Shaw praised the noble art of *sluggerei*. *The Unsocial Socialist* contains at least one act of a glorious farce comedy. He is Early British in his comedic writing. It is none the less capital fun.

This book or tract—it is hardly a novel—contains among other extraordinary things a eulogy of photography that would delight the soul of a Steichen. Shaw places it far above painting because of its verisimilitude! It also introduces a lot of socialistic talk which is very unconvincing; the psycho-physiologist would really pronounce the author a perfect specimen in full flowering of the saintly anarch. There is a rôle played by a character—Shaw?—which recalls Leonard Charteris in a later play, *The Philanderer*. All of his men are modelled off the same block. They are a curious combination of blackguard, philosopher, "bounder," artist, and comedian. His women! Recall Stevenson's dismayed exclamation at the Shaw women! They are creatures who have read Ibsen; are, one is sure, dowdy; but they interest. While you wonder at the strength of their souls, you do not miss the size of their feet. Mr. Shaw refuses to see woman as a heroine. She is sometimes a breeder of sinners, always a chronicler of the smallest kind of small beer, and for fear this sounds like an Iago estimate, he dowers her with an astounding intellectual equipment, and then lets the curious compound work out its own salvation.

He is much more successful with his servants; witness Bashville in *Cashel Byron's Profession,* most original of lackeys, and the tenderly funny old waiter in *You Never Can Tell,* a bitter farce well sprinkled with the Attic salt of irony. Otherwise Mr. Shaw has spent his time tilting at flagellation, at capital punishment, at the abuse of punctuation, at the cannibalistic habit of eating the flesh of harmless animals at Christmas, at Going to Church, extolling Czolgosz— heavens! the list is a league long. His novels as a whole are disappointing, though George Meredith has assured us in the first chapter of *Diana* that brain stuff in fiction is not lean stuff. But there are some concessions to be made to the Great God Beauty, and these Mr. Shaw has not seen fit to make. Episodes of brilliancy, force, audacity, there are; but episodes only. The psychology of a musician is admirably set forth in *Love among the Artists,* and the story, in addition, contains one of the most lifelike portraits of a Polish *pianiste* that has ever been painted. John Sargent could have done no better in laying bare a soul. Ugliness is rampant—ugliness and brutality. It is all as invigorating as a bath of salt water when the skin is peeled off—it burns; you howl; Shaw grins. He hates with all the vigour of his big brain and his big heart to hear of the infliction of physical pain. He does not always spare his readers. Three hundred years ago he would have roasted heretics, for there is much of the grand inquisitor, the John Calvin, the John Knox, in Shaw. He will rob himself of his last copper to give you food, and he will belabour you with words that assault the tympanum if you disagree with him on the subject of Ibsen, Wagner, or—anything he likes.

Beefsteak, old Scotch ale, a pipe, and Montaigne—are what he needs for one year. Then his inhumane criticism of poor, stumbling mankind's foibles might be tempered. Shaw despises weakness. He follows to the letter Nietzsche's injunction, Be hard! And there is something in him of Ibsen's pitiless attitude toward the majority, which is always in the wrong; yet is, all said and done, the majority. Facts, reality, truth—no Gradgrind ever demanded them more imperiously

than Heervater Shaw, whose red beard and locks remind one of
Conrad in *Die Meistersinger*. Earth folk do everything to dodge the
facts of life, to them cold, harsh, and at the same time fantastic.
Every form of anodyne, ethical, intellectual, æsthetical, is resorted
to, to deaden the pain of reality. We work to forget to live; our
religions, art, philosophy, patriotism, are so many buffers between
the soul of man and bitter truth.

Shaw wants the truth at all hazards; his habit of veracity is like
that of Gregers's Werle, is shocking. So he dips his subjects into a
bath of muriatic acid and seems surprised at their wrigglings and
their screams. "But I don't want to hear the truth!" yells the victim,
who then limps back to his comfortable lies. And the one grievous
error is that our gallant slayer of dragons, our Celtic Siegfried, does
not believe in the illusions of art. Its veils, consoling and beautiful,
he will not have, and thus it is that his dramas are amusing, witty,
brilliant, scarefying, but never poetic, never beautiful, and seldom
sound the deeper tones of humanity. With an artist's brain, he stifles
the artist's soul in him—as Ibsen never did. With all his liberalism he
cannot be liberal to liberalism, as Gilbert Chesterton so neatly puts
it.

The Perfect Wagnerite and The Quintessence of Ibsenism are two
supernally clever *jeux d'esprit*. As he reads Shaw and Fabianism
into the Ring of the Nibelungs, so his Ibsen is transformed into a
magnified image of Shaw dropping ideas from on high with Olym-
pian indifference. This pamphlet, among the first of its kind in English, now seems a trifle old-fashioned in its interpretation of the
Norwegian dramatist—possibly because he is something so different
from what Mr. Shaw pictured him. We are never shown Ibsen the
artist, but always the social reformer with an awful frown. He was
a fighter for Ibsen, when in London Ibsen was once regarded as a
perverter of morals. Bravery is Bernard's trump card. He never
flinched yet, whether answering cat-calls from a first night's gallery
or charging with pen lowered lance-fashion upon some unfortunate
clerical blockhead who endeavoured to prove that hell is too good
for sinners.

It is easy to praise Mozart to-day; not so easy to demonstrate the
genius of Richard Strauss. Wagner in 1888 was still a bogie-man, a
horrid hobgoblin threatening the peace of academic British music.
Shaw took up the fight, just as he fought for Degas and Manet when
he was an art critic. I still preserve with reverence his sweeping
answer to Max Nordau. It wiped Nordau off the field of discussion.

And the plays! They, too, are controversial. They all prove something, and prove it so hard that presently the play is swallowed up
by its thesis—the horse patiently follows the cart. It may not be art,

but it is magnificent Shaw. You can skip the plays, not the prefaces. *Widowers' Houses* is the most unpleasant, ugly, damnably perverse of the ten. The writer had read Ibsen's *An Enemy of the People* too closely. Its drainpipes, and not its glorification of the individual, got into his brain. It filtered forth bereft of its strength and meaning in this piece, with its nasty people, its stupidities. How could Shaw be so philistine, so much like a vestryman interested in pauper lodgings? In the implacable grasp of Ibsen, this sordid theme would have been beaten on a red-hot anvil until shaped to something of purpose and power. Shaw was not blacksmith enough to swing the Ibsen hammer and handle the Ibsen bellows. He has written me on this subject that if I were a resident of London I would see my way clearer toward liking this play. It is, he asserts, a transcript of the truth—which still leaves my argument on its legs.

The Philanderer, with its irresponsible levity and unexpected contortions, is a comedy of the true Shaw order. It is his *Wild Duck*, for in it he pokes fun at an Ibsen club, at the New Woman, and the New Sentiment, at almost everything he upholds in other plays and ways. There is a dramatic critic slopping over with British sentiment and other liquids. The women are absolutely incredible. The first act, like most of the Shaw first acts, is the best; best because, in his efforts to get his people going, the dramatist has little time to sermonize. He usually gets the chance later, to the detriment of his structure. The first act of *The Philanderer* would have made Henry Becque smile. It has something of the Frenchman's mordant irony— and then you never know what is going to happen. The behaviour of the two women recalls a remark of Shaw's apropos of Strindberg; Strindberg, who "shows that the female Yahoo, measured by romantic standards, is viler than her male dupe and slave." Here the conditions are reversed; there is no romance; the dupes are women, and also the Yahoos. The exposure of Julia's soul, poor, mean, sentimental, suffering little creature, withal heroic, would please Strindberg himself. The play has an autobiographic ring.

As to *Mrs. Warren's Profession*, it was played January 12, 1902, in London, by the Stage Society. Mr. Grein says that *Mrs. Warren's Profession* is literature for the study. The mother is a bore, wonderfully done in spots (the spots especially) and the daughter a chilly, waspish prig. The men are better; Sir George Crofts and the philandering young fellow could not be clearer expressed in terms of ink. I imagine that in a performance they must be extremely vital. And that weak old *roué* of a clergyman—why is Shaw so severe on clergymen? For the rest, *Mrs. Warren's Profession* creates a disagreeable impression, as the author intended it should. I consider it his biggest, and also his most impossible, *opus*.

You Never Can Tell, Arms and the Man, Candida, and *The Devil's Disciple* are a quartet difficult to outpoint for prodigal humour and ingenious fantasy. In London the first named was voted irresistibly funny. It is funny, and in a new way, though the framework is old-fashioned British farce newly veneered by the malicious, the roistering humour of Shaw. *Arms and the Man* and *The Devil's Disciple* have been in Mr. Mansfield's repertory for years; they need no comment further than saying that the first has something of the Gilbertian Palace of Truth topsy-turvying quality (Louka is a free paraphrase of Regina in *Ghosts,* though she talks Shaw with great fluency), with a wholly original content and characterization; and the second is perverse melodrama.

Candida is not for mixed audiences. Christian socialism is caviare to the general. In characterization there is much variety; the heroine —if there be such an anomaly as a Shaw heroine—is most engaging. Every time I read *Candida* I feel myself on the trail of somebody; it is all in the air. *The Lady from the Sea* comes back when in that last scene, where the extraordinary young poet Marchbanks, a combination of the spiritual qualities of Shelley, Shaw, Ibsen's Stranger, and Shelley again, dares the fatuous James Morell to put his wife Candida to the test. It is one of the oddest situations in dramatic literature, and it is all "prepared" with infinite skill. The dénouement is another of Mr. Shaw's shower baths; withal a perfectly proper and highly moral ending. You grind your teeth over it, as Mr. Shaw peeps across the top of the page, indulging in one of his irritating dental displays.

The Man of Destiny is a mystification in one act. Napoleon talks the purest Balzac when he describes the English, and Mr. Shaw manipulates the wires industriously. It's good sport of its genre.

Captain Brassbound's Conversion is pure force. But the joy of *Cæsar and Cleopatra* is abounding. You chortle over it as chortled Stevenson over the footman. A very devil of a play, one to read after Froude, Michelet, Shakespeare, or Voltaire for the real facts of the case. Since Suetonius, it is the first attempt at true Cæsarean history. And the stage directions out-Maeterlinck Maeterlinck with their elaborate intercalations. The gorgeous humour of it all!

Arms and the Man has been translated into German and played in Germany. What will the Germans say to *Cæsar and Cleopatra?* They take Shaw too seriously now, which is almost as bad as not taking him seriously at all. What will the doctors of history do when the amazing character of Cleopatra is dissected? If Shaw had never written another line but this bubbling study of antiquity, in which the spirit of the opera bouffe has not entered, he would be entitled to a free pass to that pantheon wherein our beloved Mark Twain sits enthroned. It is all truth-telling on a miraculous plane of reality, a reality which modulates and merges into fantasy. One almost forgets the prefaces and the notes after reading *Cæsar and Cleopatra.*

Whether he will ever vouchsafe the world a masterpiece, who can say? Why demand so much? Is not he in himself a masterpiece? It depends on his relinquishment of a too puritanical attitude toward art, life, and roast beef. He is too pious. Never mind his second-hand Nietzsche, his Diabolonian ethics, and his modern version of Car-lylean Baphometic Baptisms. They are all in his eye—that absolutely normal eye with the suppressed Celtic twinkle. He doesn't mean a word he utters. (Who does when writing of Shaw?) I firmly believe he says his prayers every night with the family before he goes to his Jaeger-flannel couch!

II

Candida is the very quintessence of her creator. Many prefer this sprightly sermon disguised as a comedy to Mr. Bernard Shaw's more serious works. Yet serious it is. No latter-day paradoxioneer—to coin a monster word, for the Shaws, Chestertons, *et al.*—evokes laughter so easily as the Irishman. His is a cold intellectual wit, a Swiftian wit, minus the hearty and wholesome obscenity of the great Dublin dean. But it is often misleading. We laugh when we should reflect. We laugh when we might better hang our heads—this is meant for the average married and bachelor man. Shaw strikes fire in almost every sentence he puts into Candida's honest mouth. After reading his eloquent tribute to Ibsen, the crooked places in *Candida* become plainer; her mission is not alone to undeceive but to love; not only to bruise hearts but to heal them.

In a singularly vivid passage in *The Quintessence of Ibsenism,* Mr. Shaw writes: "When Blake told men that through excess they would learn moderation, he knew that the way for the present lay through the Venusberg, and that the race would assuredly not perish there as some individuals have, and as the puritans fear we all shall unless we find a way round. Also, he no doubt foresaw the time when our children would be born on the other side of it, and so be spared the fiery purgation."

This sentiment occurs in the chapter devoted to a consideration of The Womanly Woman. Let us look at the phrases on the printed page of *Candida* that might be construed as bearing upon the above, or, rather, the result of the quoted passage.

Candida speaks to James, her husband, in Act II:—

> Don't you understand? I mean, will he forgive me for not teaching him myself? For abandoning him to the bad woman for the sake of my

goodness—my purity, as you call it? Ah, James, how little you understand me, to talk of your confidence in my goodness and purity! I would give them both to poor Eugene as willingly as I would give my shawl to a beggar dying of cold, if there were nothing else to restrain me. Put your trust in my love for you, James, for if that went I should care very little for your sermons—mere phrases that you cheat yourself and others with every day.

Here is one of the most audacious speeches in any modern play. It has been passed over by most English critics who saw in *Candida* merely an attempt to make a clergyman ridiculous, not realizing that the theme is profound and far-reaching, the question put being no more and no less than: Shall a married man expect his wife's love without working for it, without deserving it? Secure in his conviction that he was a model husband and a good Christian, the Rev. James Mavor Morell went his way smiling and lecturing. He had the "gift of gab," yet he was no humbug; indeed, a sincerer parson does not exist. He is quite as sincere as Pastor Manders, much broader in his views, and consequently not half so dull.

But he is, nevertheless, a bit of a bore, with his lack of humour and his grim earnestness. No doubt Shaw took his fling at that queer blending of Christianity and socialism, that Karl Marx in a parson's collar which startled London twenty years ago in the person of the Christian socialist clergyman. He saw, too, being a man with a sense of character values and their use in violent contrast, that to the rhapsodic and poetic Eugene Marchbanks, Morell would prove a splendid foil. And so he does. Between this oddly opposed pair stands on her solid, sensible underpinnings the figure of Candida. Realist as is Mr. Shaw, he would scout the notion of his third act being accepted as a transcript from life. For two acts we are in plain earthly atmosphere; unusual things happen, though not impossible ones. In the last act Shaw, droll dramatist and acute observer of his fellow-man's foibles, disappears, only to return in the guise of Shaw the preacher.

And how he does throw a sermon at our heads! The play is arrested in its mid-ocean, and the shock throws us almost off our feet. Do not be deceived. That mock bidding for the hand of Candida, surely the craziest farce ever invented, is but this author's cunning manner of driving home his lesson. Are you worthy of your wife? Is the woman who swore to love and honour you ("obey" is not in the Shaw vocabulary, thanks to J. S. Mill) worthy of you? If your love is not mutual then better go your ways—you profane it! Is this startling? Is this novel? No and yes. The defence of love for love's sake, coming from the lips of a Shaw character, has a surprising effect, for no man is less concerned with sex questions, no man has more openly depreciated the ascendancy of sex in art and literature. He would be the first to applaud eagerly Edmund Clarence Stedman's question apropos of Walt Whitman's *Leaves of Grass*: Is there no other light in which to view the beloved one than as the future mother of our children? (I trust to a treacherous memory; the meaning is expressed, though not in Mr. Stedman's words.)

Therefore *Candida* is a large exposition of the doctrine that love should be free—which is by no means the same thing as free love; that it should be a burden equally borne by both partners in the yoke; that happiness, instead of misery, would result if more women resembled Candida in candour. She cut James to the heart with the confounding of her shawl and personal purity; it was an astounding idea for a clergyman's ears. She proved to him later that she was right, that the hundredth solitary sinner is of more consequence than the ninety-nine reclaimed. Shaw, who is a Puritan by temperament, has, after his master, Ibsen, cracked with his slingstone many nice little glass houses wherein complacent men and women sit and sun their virtues in the full gaze of the world. One of his sharp and disconcerting theories is that woman, too, can go through the Venusberg and still reach the heights—a fact always denied by the egotistical man, who wishes to be the unique sinner so that he may receive the unique consolation. After a gay life, a sober one; the reformed rake; Tannhäuser's return to an Elizabeth, who awaits him patiently; dear, sweet, virtuous Penelope! Shaw sees through this humbug of the masculine pose and turns the tables by making his Candida ride the horse of the dilemma man-fashion. Maeterlinck, in his Monna Vanna and Joyzelle, enforces the same truth—that love to be love should be free.

And the paradoxical part of it all is that Candida is a womanly woman. She is so domestic, so devoted, that the thin-skinned idealist Eugene moans over her kitchen propensities. Shaw has said that "the ideal wife is one who does everything that the ideal husband likes, and nothing else," which is a neat and sardonic definition of the womanly woman's duty. Candida demands as her right her husband's trust in her love, not heavenly rewards, not the consciousness of her own purity, not bolts and bars will keep her from going from him if the hour strikes the end of her affection. All of which is immensely disconcerting to the orthodox of view, for it is the naked truth, set forth by a man who despises not orthodoxy, but those who profess it only to practise paganism. This Shaw is a terrible fellow; and the only way to get rid of a terrible fellow is not to take him seriously but to call him paradoxical, entertaining; to throw the sand of flattery in his eyes and incidentally blind criticism at the same time. But Bernard Shaw has always refused to be cajoled, and as to the sand or the mud of abuse—well, he wears the very stout spectacles of common sense.

III

What does Mr. Shaw himself think of Candida? Perhaps if he could be persuaded to tell the truth, the vapourish misconceptions concerning her terrible "shawl" speech—about which I never deceived myself—might be dissipated. It was not long forthcoming—his answer to my question, an answer the publication of which was left to my discretion. It may shock some of his admirers, disconcert others, but at the same time it will clear the air of much cant; for there is the Candida cant as well as the anti-Shaw cant. He wrote me:—

Don't ask me conundrums about that very immoral female, Candida. Observe the entry of W. Burgess: "You're the lady as hused to typewrite for him." "No." "Naaaow: *she* was younger." And therefore Candida sacked her. Prossy is a very highly selected young person indeed, devoted to Morell to the extent of helping in the kitchen but to him the merest pet rabbit, unable to get the slightest hold on him. Candida is as unscrupulous as Siegfried: Morell himself sees that "no law will bind her." She seduces Eugene just exactly as far as it is worth her while to seduce him. She is a woman without "character" in the conventional sense. Without brains and strength of mind she would be a wretched slattern or voluptuary. She is straight for natural reasons, not for conventional ethical ones. Nothing can be more cold-bloodedly reasonable than her farewell to Eugene: "All very well, my lad; but I don't quite see myself at fifty with a husband of thirty-five." It is just this freedom from emotional slop, this unerring wisdom on the domestic plane, that makes her so completely mistress of the situation.

Then consider the poet. She makes a man of him finally by showing him his own strength—that David must do without poor Uriah's wife. And then she pitches in her picture of the home, the onions, and the tradesmen, and the cossetting of big baby Morell. The New York *hausfrau* thinks it a little paradise; but the poet rises up and says, "Out then, into the night with me"—Tristan's holy night. If this greasy fool's paradise is happiness, then I give it to you with both hands, "life is nobler than that." That is the "poet's secret." The young things in front weep to see the poor boy going out lonely and brokenhearted in the cold night to save the proprieties of New England Puritanism; but he is really a god going back to his heaven, proud, unspeakably contemptuous of the "happiness" he envied in the days of his blindness, clearly seeing that he has higher business on hand than Candida. She has a little quaint intuition of the completeness of his cure; she says, "he has learnt to do without happiness."

So here is Shaw on Shaw, Shaw dissecting Candida, Shaw at last letting in light on the mystery of the "poet's secret!" There may be grumbling among the faithful at this very illuminating and sensible exposition, I feel. So thinks Mr. Shaw, for he adds, "As I should certainly be lynched by the infuriated Candidamaniacs if this view of the case were made known, I confide it to your discretion"—which by a liberal interpretation means, publish it and be hanged to you! But "Candidamaniacs!" Oh, the wicked wit of this man who can thus mock his flock! His *coda* is a neat summing up: "I tell it to you because it is an interesting sample of the way in which a scene, which should be conceived and written only by transcending the ordinary notion of the relations between the persons, nevertheless stirs the ordinary emotions to a very high degree, all the more because the language of the poet, to those who have not the clew to it, is mysterious and bewildering and therefore worshipful. I divined it myself before I found out the whole truth about it."

IV

Some day in the far future, let us hope, when the spirit of Bernard Shaw shall have been gathered to the gods, his popular vogue may be an established fact. Audiences may flock to sip wit, philosophy, and humour before the footlights of the Shaw theatre; but unless the assemblage be largely composed of Shaw *replicas*, of overmen and overwomen ("oversouls," not altogether in the Emersonian sense), it is difficult to picture any other variety listening to *Man and Superman*. For one thing, it is not a play to be played, though it may be read with delight bordering on despair. A deeper reason exists for its hopelessness—it is such a violent attack on what might be called the Shaw superstructure, that his warmest enemies and chilliest admirers will wonder what it is all about. Even William Archer, one of the latter, confessed his disappointment.

Man and Superman—odious title—is Shaw's new attempt at a *Wild Duck*, formerly one of Ibsen's most puzzling productions. Shaw mocks Shaw as Ibsen sneered at Ibsen. This method of viewing the obverse of your own medal—George Meredith would say the back of the human slate—is certainly a revelation of mood-versatility, though a disquieting one to the man in the street. It does not seem to be playing fair in the game. Sometimes it is not. With Ibsen it was; he wished to have his fling at the Ibsenite, and he had it. Shaw-like one is tempted to exclaim, Aha! drums and trumpets again, even if the cart be re-painted. (*Vide* his earlier prefaces.)

The book is dedicated to Mr. Arthur Bingham Walkley, who once wrote of his friend, "Mr. Bernard Shaw fails as a dramatist because he is always trying to prove something." In the end it is Shaw the man who is more interesting than his plays—all the characters are so many,—Shaw's winking at one through the printed dialogue.

In the pleasing and unpleasing plays, in the puritanical comedies, his "forewords" were full of meat served up with a Hibernian sauce, which produced upon the mental palate the flavours of Swift, of Nietzsche, of Aristophanes, and of Shaw. This compound could not be slowly degustated, because the stuff was too hot. Velocity is one of Shaw's prime characteristics. Like a pianoforte virtuoso whose fingers work faster than his feelings, the Irishman is lost when he assays massive, sonorous *cantilena*. He is as emotional as his own typewriter, and this defect, which he parades as did the fox in the fable, has stood in the way of his writing a great play. He despises love, and therefore cannot appeal deeply to mankind.

In the present preface the old music is sounded, but brassier and shriller; the wires are wearing. It is addressed to Arthur Bingham Walkley, by all odds the most brilliant, erudite, and satisfying of English dramatic critics. Now the cruel thing about this preface is that in it the author tries to foist upon the critic of the London *Times* the penalty attached to writing such a play as *Man and Superman*. We all cannot be Drydens and write prefaces as great as poems; and Mr. Shaw might have left out either the play or the preface and spared the nerves of his friends. He started out to make a play on Don Juan, an old and ever youthful theme. He succeeded in turning out an amorphous monster, part dream, part sermon, that will haunt its creator as Frankenstein was haunted for the rest of his days. *Man and Superman* is a nightmare.

To be impertinent is not necessarily an evidence of wisdom! nor does the dazzling epigram supply the missing note of humanity. But our author is above humanity. He would deal with the new man who is to succeed the present used-up specimen. We must freeze up, if needs be by artificial process, all the springs of natural instincts. Man must realize that in the inevitable duel of the sexes he will be worsted unless he recognizes that he is the pursued, not the pursuer. In the animal kingdom it is the male that is gorgeously bedizened for the purpose of attracting the feebler faculty of attention in the female. But in the human order the man is the cynosure of the woman. Her whole education and existence is an effort to win him— perhaps not for himself, nevertheless to win and wear him. This is biologically correct, though hardly gallant; and it is as old as Adam and Eve. Henry James once defined the situation succinctly, "It was much more the women . . . who were after the men than the men who were after the women; it was literally visible that the general attitude of one sex was that of the object pursued and defensive, apologetic and attenuating. . . ." (*In the Cage.*)

Mr. Shaw might have added that, unlike lightning, women strike twice in the same spot. Frivolity, however, is not in Mr. Shaw's present scheme of applied Unsociology.

As is the case with most reformers, he has harked back to the past for his future types. His men and women, though they go down to the sea in motor cars, converse about Ibsen, Nietzsche, and Karl Marx, affect twentieth-century modes, are in reality as old as the hills and as savage as hillmen. They are only a trifle more self-conscious. The present play—let us call it one for the sake of the argument—deals with a precious "baggage" named Ann Whitefield. She is, in the words of Ibsen, "a mighty huntress of men." She is pert, very vulgar, quite uncivilized, quite ignorant of everyday feminine delicacies; in a word, the new woman, according to the gospel of Shaw. Her pursuit of a man, unavowed, bold, is the story of the play. She is hot-footed after a revolutionary socialist, John Tanner. Every word that springs or saunters from his lips, every movement of his muscular person, betrays the breed of Daredevil Dick, of all the revolutionaries in all the Shaw plays—the true breed of which Saint Bernard is himself the unique protagonist. Tanner is rich and believes himself an anarchist. He is mistaken. He is only a Fabianite with cash, a Fabianite who has lost the "shining face" of a neophyte and talks daggers and dynamite, though he uses them not. Ann has been left an orphan. She is a new Hedda Gabler, who knows what she wants, sees it, secures it; therefore she burns no dramatic "children," sends no man to a drunkard's doom; nor will she, one feels quite certain, deceive her husband. To secure him she attempts all the deception before she marries him, and if she seldom succeeds with her white lies she nevertheless bags her game.

To supply these two pleasing persons with characters upon whom they may act and be reacted, Mr. Shaw has devised a middle-aged hypocrite, a white sepulchre and man of the world, named Roebuck Ramsden; a sap-headed young man who dotes so much on Ann that he sacrifices his own happiness that she may be happy—or humbugs himself into that belief; a self-willed young lady, his sister Violet, who conceals her marriage with evil results to her reputation; a comical low-comedy chauffeur; several pale persons; a snobbish American youth of humble Irish parentage gilded by American wealth; some brigands, a dream Don Juan, and last, but not least, the Devil, who in this case is *not* a gentleman.

The first act is promising. Mr. Shaw's little paragraphs—they are intended as a prompt-book in miniature—are more amusing than his

preface. We are deluded into the notion that a first-class comedy is
at hand. There are all the materials ready. Ramsden, an "advanced"
thinker of the antiquated Bradlaugh type, has been appointed co-
executor, co-guardian with Tanner, a thinker of the latter-day type;
that is, a man who has read Marx, Proudhon, Nietzsche, but not
Max Stirner. The fair Ann, her mother and sister are the stakes of the
game. Octavius, the sap-headed young man, is ready to sacrifice
himself, and his sister shocks all by not acknowledging the father of
her unborn child. Here is potential stuff for a tragic comedy. But
Mr. Shaw will not mould his material into viable shapes. He refuses
to be an artist. He loathes art. And so he is punished by fate—his
inspiration vanishes almost at the point of execution, and, except for
a few fugitive flashes, never burns serenely or continuously.

One telling bit is when Tanner congratulates Violet (what an
appropriate name!) on her delicate condition and is scorned by that
young person, scorned and snubbed. What—she a wicked woman!
No, she is but secretly wedded; in the fulness of time her husband
will be revealed. Tanner sneaks away, feeling that not to women
must man look for the emancipation of the sexes from conventional
notions. There are long harangues on prevailing economic evils,
social diseases—all the old Shaw grievances are paraded.

Act II is rather thin. In Act III, which recalls a Gilbertian farce,
there are cockney brigands, a bandit corporation, limited, devoted
to the robbing of automobiles that pass through Spain. The idea is
not sufficiently novel to be funny. A lengthy parabasis, written in
genuine Shavian, shows us hell, the Devil, Don Juan, and Anna of
Mozartean fame. At least the talk here is as brilliant as is commonly
supposed to prevail in the nether regions. *Inter alia,* we read that
marriage is the most licentious of human institutions—hence its
popularity. Even the Devil is shocked. "The confusion of marriage
with morality has done more to destroy the conscience of the human
race than any other single error." "Beauty, purity, respectability,
religion, art, patriotism, bravery, and the rest are nothing but words
which I or any one else can turn inside out like a glove," continues
this relentless rake and transformed preacher. Too true; but the
seamy side as exhibited by Don Juan Shaw is not so convincing as
in Nietzsche's transvaluation of all values. "They are mere words,
useful for duping barbarians into adopting civilization, or the civilized poor into submitting to be robbed and enslaved."

Admitted, keen dissector of contemporary ills; but how about
your play? In effect the author says: "To the devil with all art and
plays, my play with the rest! What I wish to do is to tell you how to
run the universe; and for this I will, if necessary, erect my pulpit in
hell!"

After this what more can be said? The play peters out; there is talk, talk, talk. Ann calls the poetic temperament "the old maid's temperament"; the brigand chief sententiously remarks: "There are two tragedies in life: one is not to get your heart's desire; the other is to get it"—which sounds as if wrenched from a page of Chamfort or Rivarol; and Ann concludes with "Go on talking, Tanner, talking!" It is the epitaph of the piece, dear little misshapen, still-born comedy. Well may Mr. Shaw write "universal laughter" at the end. Yet I am willing to wager that some critics will be in tears at this exhibition of perverse waste and clever impotency.

The Revolutionists' Handbook and Pocket Companion, which tops this extraordinary contribution, sociology masking as comedy, is its chiefest attraction. There, petrified into glistening nuggets, may be found Shaw philosophy, Shaw humour. There are maxims, too. "Do *not* unto others as you would that they should do unto you. Their tastes may not be the same." This smacks of the inverted wisdom of the late James Whistler. Marriage, crime, punishment, the beating of children, title, honours, property, servants, religion, virtues, vices—everything of vital import to thinking men and women is regarded with the charmingly malevolent eye of Shaw. He exclaims: "Property, said Proudhon, is theft. This is the only perfect truism that has been uttered on the subject." Come, come, Bernard Shaw! Proudhon said it, but the speech was not his own property. You, who know your social classics so well, should have remembered Brissot's *Philosophical Examination of Property and Theft*, only published in 1780! You also say, "Beware the man whose God is in the skies," and "Every man over forty is a scoundrel." Tut, tut! Why not add—all girls over fifty should be drowned? It is just as logical. But can one condense the cosmos in a formula?

The general impression of the book causes us to believe there is a rift in the writer's lute; not in his mentality, but in his own beliefs, or scepticisms. Perhaps Shaw no longer pins his faith to Shaw. Ibsen asserts that after twenty years a truth that has outlived its usefulness is no longer *truth*, but the simulacrum of one. Shaw's truths may be decaying. We feel sure that if they be, he will be the first to detect the odour and warn away his public. Some years ago he printed a pamphlet against anarchy and anarchist, which was to be expected from a mild, frugivorous man. Now he seems to be wearying of the milk-white flag of socialism; and yet his revolutionary maxims are maxims for children in the time of teething. The world has moved since the Fabian society scowled at the British lion and tried to twist its tail with the dialectics of moderate socialism. To use Mr. Shaw's own pregnant remark, "Moderation is never applauded for its own sake"; and: "He who can, does. He who cannot, teaches."

Fabianism taught, taught moderation! Yet to-day the real thing is not Elisée Reclus, but Michael Bakounin; not Peter Kropotkin, but Sergei Netschajew; not Richard Wagner, but his friend, Roeckel, who was sent by him across the cannon-shattered barricades at Dresden in 1849 to fetch an ice to the thirsty composer. Wagner rang the alarm bells on this opera bouffe and escaped to Switzerland, Bakounin and Roeckel remained and went to prison!

Shaw is still ringing alarm bells, but somehow or other their music is missing and carries no message to his listeners. Is it possible that he regrets the anarchy that he has never had the courage to embrace and avow? A born anarchist, individualist, revolutionist, he has always gone in for half-hearted measures of reform. Never, like Bakounin, has he applied the torch, thrown the bomb; never, like Netschajew, has he dared to pen a catechism of destruction, a manual of nihilism so terrific that advanced Russian thinkers shudder if you mention its title. It is even rumoured that the Irish dramatist serves his parish as a meek citizen should—he will be writing poetry or melodrama next. His pessimism is temperamental, not philosophical, like that of most pessimists, as James Sully has pointed out. And instead of closely observing humanity, after the manner of all great dramatists, he has only closely studied Bernard Shaw.

"Regarded as a play, *Man and Superman* is, I repeat, primitive in invention and second rate in execution. The most disheartening thing about it is that it contains not one of those scenes of really tense dramatic quality which redeemed the squalor of *Mrs. Warren's Profession,* and made of *Candida* something very like a masterpiece." Thus William Archer.

Most modestly Mr. Shaw entitles a farce of his, the celebrated drama in two tableaux and in blank verse,—*The Admirable Bashville, or Constancy Unrewarded.* It is nothing else but the story of *Cashel Byron's Profession* put into blank verse, because, as Mr. Shaw says, blank verse is so much easier to write than good prose. It is printed at the end of the second edition of the prize-fighting novel. As there has been a dramatization made—unauthorized—for a well-known American pugilist-actor, Mr. Shaw thought that he had better protect his English interests. Hence the parody for copyright purposes which was produced in London the summer of 1903 by the Stage Society at the Imperial Theatre. It is funny. It gibes at Shakespeare, at the modern drama, at Parliament, at social snobbery, at Shaw himself, and almost everything else within reach. The stage setting was a mockery of the Elizabethan stage, with two venerable beef-eaters in Tower costume, who hung up placards bearing the legend, "A Glade in Wiltstoken Park," etc. Ben Webster as Cashel Byron and James Hearn as the Zulu King carried off the honours. Aubrey Smith, made up as Mr. Shaw in the costume of a policeman with a brogue, caused merriment, especially at the close, when he informed his audience that the author had left the house. And so he had. He was standing at the corner when I accosted him. Our interview was brief. He warned me in grave accents and a twinkling Celtic eye never again to describe him as "benevolent." Half the beggars of London had winded the phrase and were pestering him at his back gate. Mr. Shaw still looks as if a half-raw beefsteak and a mug of Bass would do him a world of good. But who can tell? He might then lose some of his effervescence—that quality of humour so happily described by Edmund Gosse when he spoke of the *vegetable* spirits of George Bernard Shaw.

The new play, *John Bull's Other Island,* was first played in London by the Stage Society last November. It is said—by Shaw's warmest enemies—to be witty, entertaining, and dramatically boneless. There is no alternative now for Mr. Shaw—he must visit America, lecture, and become rich. It is the logical conclusion of his impromptu career, for it was first in America that the Shaw books and plays were successful and appreciated; the plays largely because of the bold efforts of Arnold Daly and Winchell Smith, two young dramatic revolutionists. And Mr. Shaw may rediscover America for the Americans!

G. K. CHESTERTON
1 9 0 9

The Critic

It appears a point of some mystery to the present writer that Bernard Shaw should have been so long unrecognised and almost in
beggary. I should have thought his talent was of the ringing and
arresting sort; such as even editors and publishers would have sense
enough to seize. Yet it is quite certain that he almost starved in London for many years, writing occasional columns for an advertise-
ment or words for a picture. And it is equally certain (it is proved
by twenty anecdotes, but no one who knows Shaw needs any anecdotes to prove it) that in those days of desperation he again and
again threw up chances and flung back good bargains which did not
suit his unique and erratic sense of honour. The fame of having first
offered Shaw to the public upon a platform worthy of him belongs,
like many other public services, to Mr. William Archer.

I say it seems odd that such a writer should not be appreciated in
a flash; but upon this point there is evidently a real difference of
opinion, and it constitutes for me the strangest difficulty of the subject. I hear many people complain that Bernard Shaw deliberately
mystifies them. I cannot imagine what they mean; it seems to me
that he deliberately insults them. His language, especially on moral
questions, is generally as straight and solid as that of a bargee and
far less ornate and symbolic than that of a hansom-cabman. The
prosperous English Philistine complains that Mr. Shaw is making a
fool of him. Whereas Mr. Shaw is not in the least making a fool of
him; Mr. Shaw is, with laborious lucidity, calling him a fool. G.B.S.
calls a landlord a thief; and the landlord, instead of denying or
resenting it, says, "Ah, that fellow hides his meaning so cleverly that
one can never make out what he means, it is all so fine spun and
fantastical." G. B. S. calls a statesman a liar to his face, and the
statesman cries in a kind of ecstasy, "Ah, what quaint, intricate and

half-tangled trains of thought! Ah, what elusive and many-coloured mysteries of half-meaning!" I think it is always quite plain what Mr. Shaw means, even when he is joking, and it generally means that the people he is talking to ought to howl aloud for their sins. But the average representative of them undoubtedly treats the Shavian meaning as tricky and complex, when it is really direct and offensive. He always accuses Shaw of pulling his leg, at the exact moment when Shaw is pulling his nose.

This prompt and pungent style he learnt in the open, upon political tubs and platforms; and he is very legitimately proud of it. He boasts of being a demagogue: "The cart and the trumpet for me," he says, with admirable good sense. Everyone will remember the effective appearance of Cyrano de Bergerac in the first act of the fine play of that name; when instead of leaping in by any hackneyed door or window, he suddenly springs upon a chair above the crowd that has so far kept him invisible; "les bras croises, le feutre en bataille, la moustache herissée, les nez terrible." I will not go so far as to say that when Bernard Shaw sprang upon a chair or tub in Trafalgar Square he had the hat in battle, or even that he had the nose terrible. But just as we see Cyrano best when he thus leaps above the crowd, I think we may take this moment of Shaw stepping on his little platform to see him clearly as he then was, and even as he has largely not ceased to be. I, at least, have only known him in his middle age; yet I think I can see him, younger yet only a little more alert, with hair more red but with face yet paler, as he first stood up upon some cart or barrow in the tossing glare of the gas.

The first fact that one realises about Shaw (independent of all one has read and often contradicting it) is his voice. Primarily it is the voice of an Irishman, and then something of the voice of a musician. It possibly explains much of his career; a man may be permitted to say so many impudent things with so pleasant an intonation. But the voice is not only Irish and agreeable, it is also frank and as it were inviting conference. This goes with a style and gesture which can only be described as at once very casual and very emphatic. He assumes that bodily supremacy which goes with oratory, but he assumes it with almost ostentatious carelessness; he throws back the head, but loosely and laughingly. He is at once swaggering and yet shrugging his shoulders, as if to drop from them the mantle of the orator which he has confidently assumed. Lastly, no man ever used voice or gesture better for the purpose of expressing certainty; no man can say "I tell Mr. Jones he is totally wrong" with more air of unforced and even casual conviction.

This particular play of feature or pitch of voice, at once didactic and yet not uncomrade-like, must be counted a very important fact, especially in connection with the period when that voice was first heard. It must be remembered that Shaw emerged as a wit in a sort of secondary age of wits; one of those stale interludes of prematurely old young men, which separate the serious epochs of history. Oscar Wilde was its god; but he was somewhat more mystical, not to say monstrous, than the average of its dried and decorous impudence. The two survivals of that time, as far as I know, are Mr. Max Beerbohm and Mr. Graham Robertson, two most charming people; but the air they had to live in was the devil. One of its notes was an artificial reticence of speech, which waited till it could plant the perfect epigram. Its typical products were far too conceited to lay down the law. Now when people heard that Bernard Shaw was witty, as he most certainly was, when they heard his *mots* repeated like those of Whistler or Wilde, when they heard things like "the Seven deadly Virtues" or "Who *was* Hall Caine?" they expected another of these silent sarcastic dandies who went about with one epigram, patient and poisonous, like a bee with his one sting. And when they saw and heard the new humorist they found no fixed sneer, no frockcoat, no green carnation, no silent Savoy Restaurant good manners, no fear of looking a fool, no particular notion of looking a gentleman. They found a talkative Irishman with a kind voice and a brown coat; open gestures and an evident desire to make people really agree with him. He had his own kind of affections no doubt, and his own kind of tricks of debate; but he broke, and, thank God, forever, the spell of the little man with the single eyeglass who had frozen both faith and fun at so many tea-tables. Shaw's humane voice and hearty manner were so obviously more the things of a great man than the hard, gem-like brilliancy of Wilde or the careful ill-temper of Whistler. He brought in a breezier sort of insolence; the single eyeglass fled before the single eye.

Added to the effect of the amiable dogmatic voice and lean, loose, swaggering figure, is that of the face with which so many caricaturists have fantastically delighted themselves, the Mephistophelean face with the fierce tufted eyebrows and forked red beard. Yet those caricaturists in their natural delight in coming upon so striking a face, have somewhat misrepresented it, making it merely Satanic; whereas its actual expression has quite as much benevolence as mockery. By this time his costume has become a part of his personality; one has come to think of the reddish-brown Jaeger suit as if it were a sort of reddish-brown fur, and was, like the hair and eyebrows, a part of the animal; yet there are those who claim to remember a Bernard Shaw of yet more awful aspect before Jaeger came to his assistance; a Bernard Shaw in a dilapidated frock-coat and some sort of straw hat. I can hardly believe it; the man is so much of a piece, and must always have dressed appropriately. In any case his brown woollen clothes, at once artistic and hygienic, completed the appeal for which he stood; which might be defined as an eccentric healthy-mindedness. But something of the vagueness and equivocation of his first fame is probably due to the different functions which he performed in the contemporary world of art.

He began by writing novels. They are not much read, and indeed not imperatively worth reading, with the one exception of the crude and magnificent *Cashel Byron's Profession.* Mr. William Archer, in the course of his kindly efforts on behalf of his young Irish friend, sent this book to Samoa, for the opinion of the most elvish and yet efficient of modern critics. Stevenson summed up much of Shaw even from that fragment when he spoke of a romantic griffin roaring with laughter at the nature of his own quest. He also added the not wholly unjustified postscript: "I say, Archer,—my God, what women!"

The fiction was largely dropped; but when he began work he felt his way by the avenues of three arts. He was an art critic, a dramatic critic, and a musical critic; and in all three, it need hardly be said, he fought for the newest style and the most revolutionary school. He wrote on all these as he would have written on anything; but it was, I fancy, about the music that he cared most.

It may often be remarked that mathematicians love and understand music more than they love or understand poetry. Bernard Shaw is in much the same condition; indeed, in attempting to do justice to Shakespeare's poetry, he always calls it "word music." It is not difficult to explain this special attachment of the mere logician to music. The logician, like every other man on earth, must have sentiment and romance in his existence; in every man's life, indeed, which can be called a life at all, sentiment is the most solid thing. But if the extreme logician turns for his emotions to poetry, he is exasperated and bewildered by discovering that the words of his own trade are used in an entirely different meaning. He conceives that he understands the word "visible," and then finds Milton applying it to darkness, in which nothing is visible. He supposes that he understands the word "hide," and then finds Shelley talking of a poet hidden in the light. He has reason to believe that he understands the common word "hung"; and then William Shakespeare, Esquire, of Stratford-on-Avon, gravely assures him that the tops of the tall sea waves were hung with deafening clamours on the slippery clouds. That is why the common arithmetician prefers music to poetry. Words are his scientific instruments. It irritates him that they should be anyone else's musical instruments. He is willing to see men juggling, but not men juggling with his own private tools

and possessions—his terms. It is then that he turns with an utter relief to music. Here is all the same fascination and inspiration, all the
same purity and plunging force as in poetry; but not requiring any
verbal confession that light conceals things or that darkness can be
seen in the dark. Music is mere beauty; it is beauty in the abstract,
beauty in solution. It is a shapeless and liquid element of beauty, in
which a man may really float, not indeed affirming the truth, but not
denying it. Bernard Shaw, as I have already said, is infinitely far
above all such mere mathematicians and pedantic reasoners; still his
feeling is partly the same. He adores music because it cannot deal
with romantic terms either in their right or their wrong sense. Music
can be romantic without reminding him of Shakespeare and Walter
Scott, with whom he has had personal quarrels. Music can be Catholic without reminding him verbally of the Catholic Church, which
he has never seen, and is sure he does not like. Bernard Shaw can
agree with Wagner, the musician, because he speaks without words;
if it had been Wagner the man he would certainly have had words
with him. Therefore I would suggest that Shaw's love of music
(which is so fundamental that it must be mentioned early, if not
first, in his story) may itself be considered in the first case as the
imaginative safety-valve of the rationalistic Irishman.

This much may be said conjecturally over the present signature;
but more must not be said. Bernard Shaw understands music so
much better than I do that it is just possible that he is, in that tongue
and atmosphere, all that he is not elsewhere. While he is writing
with a pen I know his limitations as much as I admire his genius; and
I know it is true to say that he does not appreciate romance. But
while he is playing on the piano he may be cocking a feather, drawing a sword or draining a flagon for all I know. While he is speaking
I am sure that there are some things he does not understand. But
while he is listening (at the Queen's Hall) he may understand
everything including God and me. Upon this part of him I am a
reverent agnostic; it is well to have some such dark continent in the
character of a man of whom one writes. It preserves two very important things—modesty in the biographer and mystery in the biography.

For the purpose of our present generalisation it is only necessary
to say that Shaw, as a musical critic, summed himself up as "The
Perfect Wagnerite"; he threw himself into subtle and yet trenchant
eulogy of that revolutionary voice in music. It was the same with
the other arts. As he was a Perfect Wagnerite in music, so he was a
Perfect Whistlerite in painting; so above all he was a perfect Ibsenite in drama. And with this we enter that part of his career with
which this is more specially concerned. When Mr. William Archer

got him established as dramatic critic of the *Saturday Review,* he became for the first time "a star of the stage"; a shooting star and sometimes a destroying comet.

On the day of that appointment opened one of the very few exhilarating and honest battles that broke the silence of the slow and cynical collapse of the nineteenth century. Bernard Shaw the demagogue had got his cart and his trumpet; and was resolved to make them like the cart of destiny and the trumpet of judgment. He had not the servility of the ordinary rebel, who is content to go on rebelling against kings and priests, because such rebellion is as old and as established as any priests or kings. He cast about him for something to attack which was not merely powerful or placid, but was unattacked. After a little quite sincere reflection, he found it. He would not be content to be a common atheist; he wished to blaspheme something in which even atheists believed. He was not satisfied with being revolutionary; there were so many revolutionists. He wanted to pick out some prominent institution which had been irrationally and instinctively accepted by the most violent and profane; something of which Mr. Foote would speak as respectfully on the front page of the *Freethinker* as Mr. St. Loe Strachey on the front page of the *Spectator.* He found the thing; he found the great unassailed English institution—Shakespeare.

But Shaw's attack on Shakespeare, though exaggerated for the fun of the thing, was not by any means the mere folly or firework paradox that has been supposed. He meant what he said; what was called his levity was merely the laughter of a man who enjoyed saying what he meant—an occupation which is indeed one of the greatest larks in life. Moreover, it can honestly be said that Shaw did good by shaking the mere idolatry of Him of Avon. That idolatry was bad for England; it buttressed our perilous self-complacency by making us think that we alone had, not merely a great poet, but the one poet above criticism. It was bad for literature; it made a minute model out of work that was really a hasty and faulty masterpiece. And it was bad for religion and morals that there should be so huge a terrestrial idol, that we should put such utter and unreasoning trust in any child of man. It is true that it was largely through Shaw's own defects that he beheld the defects of Shakespeare. But it needed some one equally prosaic to resist what was perilous in the charm of such poetry; it may not be altogether a mistake to send a deaf man to destroy the rock of the sirens.

This attitude of Shaw illustrates of course all three of the divisions or aspects to which the reader's attention has been drawn. It was partly the attitude of the Irishman objecting to the Englishman turning his mere artistic taste into a religion; especially when it was a taste merely taught him by his aunts and uncles. In Shaw's opinion (one might say) the English do not really enjoy Shakespeare or even admire Shakespeare; one can only say, in the strong colloquialism, that they swear by Shakespeare. He is a mere god; a thing to be invoked. And Shaw's whole business was to set up the things which were to be sworn by as things to be sworn at. It was partly again the revolutionist in pursuit of pure novelty, hating primarily the oppression of the past, almost hating history itself. For Bernard Shaw the prophets were to be stoned after, and not before, men had built their sepulchres. There was a Yankee smartness in the man which was irritated at the idea of being dominated by a person dead for three hundred years; like Mark Twain, he wanted a fresher corpse.

These two motives there were, but they were small compared with the other. It was the third part of him, the Puritan, that was really at war with Shakespeare. He denounced that playwright almost exactly as any contemporary Puritan coming out of a conventicle in a steeple-crowned hat and stiff bands might have denounced the playwright coming out of the stage door of the old Globe Theatre. This is not a mere fancy; it is philosophically true. A legend has run round the newspapers that Bernard Shaw offered himself as a better writer than Shakespeare. This is false and quite unjust; Bernard Shaw never said anything of the kind. The writer whom he did say was better than Shakespeare was not himself, but Bunyan. And he justified it by attributing to Bunyan a virile acceptance of life as a high and harsh adventure, while in Shakespeare he saw nothing but profligate pessimism, the *vanitas vanitatum* of a disappointed voluptuary. According to this view Shakespeare was always saying, "Out, out, brief candle," because he was only a ballroom candle; while Bunyan was seeking to light such a candle as by God's grace should never be put out.

It is odd that Bernard Shaw's chief error or insensibility should have been the instrument of his noblest affirmation. The denunciation of Shakespeare was a mere misunderstanding. But the denunciation of Shakespeare's pessimism was the most splendidly understanding of all his utterances. This is the greatest thing in Shaw, a serious optimism—even a tragic optimism. Life is a thing too glorious to be enjoyed. To be is an exacting and exhausting business; the trumpet though inspiring is terrible. Nothing that he ever wrote is so noble as his simple reference to the sturdy man who stepped up to the Keeper of the Book of Life and said, "Put down my name, Sir." It is true that Shaw called this heroic philosophy by wrong names and buttressed it with false metaphysics; that was the weakness of the age. The temporary decline of theology had in-

volved the neglect of philosophy and all fine thinking; and Bernard
Shaw had to find shaky justifications in Schopenhauer for the sons
of God shouting for joy. He called it the Will to Live—a phrase invented by Prussian professors who would like to exist, but can't.
Afterwards he asked people to worship the Life-Force; as if one
could worship a hyphen. But though he covered it with crude new
names (which are now fortunately crumbling everywhere like bad
mortar) he was on the side of the good old cause; the oldest and the
best of all causes, the cause of creation against destruction, the
cause of yes against no, the cause of the seed against the stony earth
and the star against the abyss.

His misunderstanding of Shakespeare arose largely from the fact
that he is a Puritan, while Shakespeare was spiritually a Catholic.
The former is always screwing himself up to see truth; the latter is
often content that truth is there. The Puritan is only strong enough
to stiffen; the Catholic is strong enough to relax. Shaw, I think, has
entirely misunderstood the pessimistic passages of Shakespeare.
They are flying moods which a man with a fixed faith can afford to
entertain. That all is vanity, that life is dust and love is ashes, these
are frivolities, these are jokes that a Catholic can afford to utter. He
knows well enough that there is a life that is not dust and a love that
is not ashes. But just as he may let himself go more than the Puritan
in the matter of enjoyment, so he may let himself go more than the
Puritan in the matter of melancholy. The sad exuberances of Hamlet
are merely like the glad exuberances of Falstaff. This is not conjec-
ture; it is the text of Shakespeare. In the very act of uttering his pessimism, Hamlet admits that it is a mood and not the truth. Heaven
is a heavenly thing, only to him it seems a foul congregation of
vapours. Man *is* the paragon of animals, only to him he seems a
quintessence of dust. Hamlet is quite the reverse of a sceptic. He is a
man whose strong intellect believes much more than his weak temperament can make vivid to him. But this power of knowing a thing
without feeling it, this power of believing a thing without experienc-
ing it, this is an old Catholic complexity, and the Puritan has never
understood it. Shakespeare confesses his moods (mostly by the
mouths of villains and failures), but he never sets up his moods
against his mind. His cry of *vanitas vanitatum* is itself only a harmless vanity. Readers may not agree with my calling him Catholic
with a big C; but they will hardly complain of my calling him catholic with a small one. And that is here the principal point. Shakespeare was not in any sense a pessimist; he was, if anything, an
optimist so universal as to be able to enjoy even pessimism. And
this is exactly where he differs from the Puritan. The true Puritan is

not squeamish: the true Puritan is free to say "Damn it!" But the Catholic Elizabethan was free (on passing provocation) to say "Damn it all!"

It need hardly be explained that Bernard Shaw added to his negative case of a dramatist to be depreciated a corresponding affirmative case of a dramatist to be exalted and advanced. He was not content with so remote a comparison as that between Shakespeare and Bunyan. In his vivacious weekly articles in the *Saturday Review*, the real comparison upon which everything turned was the comparison between Shakespeare and Ibsen. He early threw himself with all possible eagerness into public disputes about the great Scandinavian; and though there was no doubt whatever about which side he supported, there was much that was individual in the line he took. It is not our business here to explore that extinct volcano. You may say that anti-Ibsenism is dead, or you may say that Ibsen is dead; in any case, that controversy is dead, and death, as the Roman poet says, can alone confess of what small atoms we are made. The opponents of Ibsen largely exhibited the permanent qualities of the populace; that is, their instincts were right and their reasons wrong. They made the complete controversial mistake of calling Ibsen a pessimist; whereas, indeed, his chief weakness is a rather childish confidence in mere nature and freedom, and a blindness (either of experience or of culture) in the matter of original sin. In this sense Ibsen is not so much a pessimist as a highly crude kind of optimist. Nevertheless the man in the street was right in his fundamental instinct, as he always is. Ibsen, in his pale Northern style, is an optimist; but for all that he is a depressing person. The optimism of Ibsen is less comforting than the pessimism of Dante; just as a Norwegian sunrise, however splendid, is colder than a Southern night.

But on the side of those who fought for Ibsen there was also a disagreement, and perhaps also a mistake. The vague army of "the advanced" (an army which advances in all directions) were united in feeling that they ought to be the friends of Ibsen because he also was advancing somewhere somehow. But they were also seriously impressed by Flaubert, by Oscar Wilde and all the rest who told them that a work of art was in another universe from ethics and social good. Therefore many, I think most, of the Ibsenites praised the Ibsen plays merely as *choses vues*, æsthetic affirmations of what can be without any reference to what ought to be. Mr. William Archer himself inclined to this view, though his strong sagacity kept him in a haze of healthy doubt on the subject. Mr. Walkley certainly took this view. But this view Mr. George Bernard Shaw abruptly and violently refused to take.

With the full Puritan combination of passion and precision he informed everybody that Ibsen was not artistic, but moral; that his dramas were didactic, that all great art was didactic, that Ibsen was strongly on the side of some of his characters and strongly against others, that there was preaching and public spirit in the work of good dramatists; and that if this were not so, dramatists and all other artists would be mere panders of intellectual debauchery, to be locked up as the Puritans locked up the stage players. No one can understand Bernard Shaw who does not give full value to this early revolt of his on behalf of ethics against the ruling school of *l'art pour l'art*. It is interesting because it is connected with other ambitions in the man, especially with that which has made him somewhat vainer of being a Parish Councillor than of being one of the most popular dramatists in Europe. But its chief interest is again to be referred to our stratification of the psychology; it is the lover of true things rebelling for once against merely new things; it is the Puritan suddenly refusing to be the mere Progressive.

But this attitude obviously laid on the ethical lover of Ibsen a not inconsiderable obligation. If the new drama had an ethical purpose, what was it? and if Ibsen was a moral teacher, what the deuce was he teaching? Answers to this question, answers of manifold brilliancy and promise, were scattered through all the dramatic criticisms of those years on the *Saturday Review*. But Bernard Shaw had already dealt with these things somewhat more systematically before he began to discuss Ibsen only in connection with the current pantomime or the latest musical comedy. It is best in this matter to turn back to a previous summary. In 1891 had appeared the brilliant book called *The Quintessence of Ibsenism*, which some have declared to be merely the quintessence of Shaw. However this may be, it was in fact and profession the quintessence of Shaw's theory of the morality or propaganda of Ibsen.

The book itself is much longer than the book that I am writing; and as is only right in so spirited an apologist, every paragraph is provocative. I could write an essay on every sentence which I accept and three essays on every sentence which I deny. Bernard Shaw himself is a master of compression; he can put a conception more compactly than any other man alive. It is therefore rather difficult to compress his compression; one feels as if one were trying to extract a beef essence from Bovril. But the shortest form in which I can state the idea of *The Quintessence of Ibsenism* is that it is the idea of distrusting ideals, which are universal, in comparison with facts, which are miscellaneous. The man whom he attacks throughout he calls "The Idealist"; that is the man who permits himself to be mainly moved by a moral generalisation. "Actions," he says, "are to be judged by their effect on happiness, and not by their conformity to any ideal." As we have already seen, there is a certain inconsistency here; for while Shaw had always chucked all ideals overboard the one he had chucked first was the ideal of happiness. Passing this however for the present, we may mark the above as the most satisfying summary. If I tell a lie I am not to blame myself for having violated the ideal of truth, but only for having perhaps got myself into a mess and made things worse than they were before. If I have broken my word I need not feel (as my fathers did) that I have broken something inside me, as one who breaks a blood vessel. It all depends on whether I have broken up something outside me; as one who breaks up an evening party. If I shoot my father the only question is whether I have made him happy. I must not admit the idealistic conception that the mere shooting of my father might possibly make me unhappy. We are to judge of every individual case as it arises, apparently without any social summary or moral ready-reckoner at all. "The Golden Rule is that there is no Golden Rule." We must not say that it is right to keep promises, but that it may be right to keep this promise. Essentially it is anarchy; nor is it very easy to see how a state could be very comfortable which was Socialist in all its public morality and Anarchist in all its private. But if it is anarchy, it is anarchy without any of the abandon and exuberance of anarchy. It is a worried and conscientious anarchy; an anarchy of painful delicacy and even caution. For it refuses to trust in traditional experiments or plainly trodden tracks; every case must be considered anew from the beginning, and yet considered with the most wide-eyed care for human welfare; every man must act as if he were the first man made. Briefly, we must always be worrying about what is best for our children, and we must not take one hint or rule of thumb from our fathers. Some think that this anarchism would make a man tread down mighty cities in his madness. I think it would make a man walk down the street as if he were walking on egg-shells. I do not think this experiment in opportunism would end in frantic licence; I think it would end in frozen timidity. If a man was forbidden to solve moral problems by moral science or the help of mankind, his course would be quite easy—he would not solve the problems. The world instead of being a knot so tangled as to need unravelling, would simply become a piece of clockwork too complicated to be touched. I cannot think that this untutored worry was what Ibsen meant; I have my doubts as to whether it was what Shaw meant; but I do not think that it can be substantially doubted that it was what he said.

In any case it can be asserted that the general aim of the work was to exalt the immediate conclusions of practice against the general conclusions of theory. Shaw objected to the solution of every

problem in a play being by its nature a general solution, applicable
to all other such problems. He disliked the entrance of a universal
justice at the end of the last act; treading down all the personal ulti-
matums and all the varied certainties of men. He disliked the god
from the machine—because he was from a machine. But even without the machine he tended to dislike the god; because a god is more
general than a man. His enemies have accused Shaw of being anti-
domestic, a shaker of the roof-tree. But in this sense Shaw may be
called almost madly domestic. He wishes each private problem to
be settled in private, without reference to sociological ethics. And
the only objection to this kind of gigantic casuistry is that the
theatre is really too small to discuss it. It would not be fair to play
David and Goliath on a stage too small to admit Goliath. And it is
not fair to discuss private morality on a stage too small to admit the
enormous presence of public morality; that character which has not
appeared in a play since the Middle Ages; whose name is Everyman and whose honour we all have in our keeping.

JOHN PALMER

1915

George Bernard Shaw:

HARLEQUIN OR PATRIOT?

I

SHAW THE ENIGMA

The first fallacy is that Bernard Shaw is an immensely public person; that he is a sort of twentieth century Grand Monarch who, if manners allowed, would dine like Louis XIV in the presence of the people and receive the press in his dressing-gown. Now, it is true that Bernard Shaw has been photographed by Alvin Langdon Coburn without a stitch; that at one period of his career he almost lived upon a public platform; that he invariably tells us the private history of each of his books and plays; that, partly from a sense of fun, and partly from a determination that what he has seriously to say shall be heard, he talks and writes a good deal about himself; and that he has allowed Mr. Archibald Henderson to compile a sort of concordance to his personality.

Nevertheless, it is not true that Bernard Shaw is an immensely public person. Or perhaps I should put it this way: Bernard Shaw whom the public knows is not an authentic revelation of the extremely private gentleman who lives in Adelphi Terrace. The Bernard Shaw whom the public knows might more accurately be described as a screen. What the public knows about Bernard Shaw is either trivial or misleading. Thus the public knows that Bernard Shaw can read diamond type with his left eye at a distance of twenty-eight inches; that he can hear a note the pitch of which does not exceed 30,000 vibrations per second; that, when he sits down upon a chair, the distance between the crown of his head and the seat is 3 feet, 1.8 inches. These things are trivial. Or the public knows that Bernard Shaw is a very striking and provocative writer of plays, that he is also a socialist and a vegetarian; and these things are misleading.

That is why any satisfactory account of Bernard Shaw rendered to those who have allowed themselves to be deceived by common fame must necessarily take the form of a schedule of popular fallacies. Such a schedule will at any rate be found more useful, and certainly less hackneyed, than a personal "interview" and description of one who has been more often photographed and handled in the picturesque and familiar way of the expert pressman than the most popular member of the British Cabinet. Perhaps, therefore, I may regard myself as excused from accurately sketching the wicket-gate which leads to Bernard Shaw's private dwelling, or from telling the story of his velvet coat, or from recording the number of times he has been met upon the top of an omnibus (where he used virtually to live), or betraying what he writes to young people in confidence about the nose of a celebrated author.

Intimate revelations of this kind do not take the public far. They do not seriously disturb the inaccessible privacy which Bernard Shaw has always contrived to maintain. The truth is that the authentic author of *Man and Superman* has never really been interviewed; has never really "plucked me ope his doublet and offered them his throat to cut" to visitors who are likely to be hiding a kodak under their coat or to be surreptitiously fingering a notebook. Bernard Shaw of the interviews and the funny stories is public enough; but this Bernard Shaw is almost entirely a legend. Before this legend gets as firm a hold upon New York as it has upon London, it may be well to number some of the more striking fallacies of which it is composed. There is only one serious drawback to this method of approach, and this drawback vanishes almost as soon as it is explained. Exploding popular fallacies is disagreeable work, and it usually gives to the sentences of the author engaged upon it an air of quarreling violently with his readers and with his subject.

Such is not the intention or mood of this present article. I have an immense enthusiasm and liking for Bernard Shaw and for the greater part of most of what Bernard Shaw has written. I claim, indeed, to admire Bernard Shaw for sounder and weightier reasons than have yet occurred to Bernard Shaw himself. These reasons will be presented later in a postscript of appreciation. When the worst fallacies regarding Bernard Shaw have been briefly described and contradicted (it would require a large volume to describe and contradict them in detail), I shall be in a better position to assert, briefly again, wherein Bernard Shaw's genius truly consists; exactly how serious he is; and, more particularly, why he has just written a pamphlet about the war, and why he ought not to have done so. Meantime I hope that readers of this article will agree to digest the fallacies and to wait for the postscript; also to believe that my habitually indignant manner is simply the result of writing regularly about the British theater.

The first fallacy is already declared; namely, that Bernard Shaw is a public person. The second fallacy is that Bernard Shaw is an easy and profitable subject to write about. He is not. It is true that Bernard Shaw's interviews with the press are the best interviews, and that he invariably galvanizes the dullest of his appreciators into liveliness. Pronounce the name of Bernard Shaw in almost any company, and immediately every one perks up with an epigram or a paradox or an anecdote. Bernard Shaw like Falstaff is not only witty himself; he is the occasion that wit is in other men.

Nevertheless, Bernard Shaw is not a good subject. It is not encouraging to embark upon an enterprise with the sure knowledge that the thing has been done before and better done. Bernard Shaw is not a good subject because he has already been exhausted. There is not more than one expert upon Bernard Shaw. Every one professionally required to write about Bernard Shaw sets out under an unfortunate sense that the ground has already been covered; that the job has already been done brilliantly, thoroughly and finally.

The best essays on the work of Bernard Shaw, the most impartial authoritative, and penetrating, are by Bernard Shaw himself. The best stories about Bernard Shaw, whether they are the cruel, illuminating anecdotes which delight the envious, or the flashes of resources and honesty which are cherished by his friends and admirers, are once again by Bernard Shaw himself. Should you set out to extol or to advertise Bernard Shaw, you know that this has already been done with incomparable energy and talent, and that it has been done by one who knows. Should you, on the other hand, set out to expose or pull to tatters the reputation and character of Bernard Shaw, again you know that you are the merest amateur compared with G. B. S.; know also that, if you want to do the business effectively, and leave Bernard Shaw obviously for dead on the field of controversy, you will have to call in G. B. S. to help you. It is possible to slay Bernard Shaw; but it is possible to slay him only in alliance with himself. It is a joke of the two hemispheres that Bernard Shaw better understands his merits than any one else in the world. It is a finer joke, and not so thread-worn, that he better understands his limitations. Either way, whether you are celebrating his genius or asserting your position as the candid friend, you are

forced to acknowledge at the last that your researches into Bernard
Shaw are simply not in the same class with his own either in intimacy (which is surprising in an age when the press is often more
intimate with a man than his own toothbrush); in detachment and
absence of favor (which, again, is surprising, in an age when men
of letters take themselves very seriously); or in a severely just recognition of the subject's merit (more surprising still in an age when
public men carefully cultivate a reputation for modesty).

II

SHAW NOT AN ORIGINAL THINKER

The third fallacy is that Bernard Shaw is a profoundly original
thinker and a propagandist of absolutely new ideas. He has repeatedly told his readers and his friends that he is nothing of the
kind. His biographer somewhere quotes him as saying, "I am an
expert picker of men's brains, and I have been extremely fortunate
in my friends." Nor need we go to Bernard Shaw's biographer for
this. Bernard Shaw has spent half his life in telling the world the
exact scientific truth about himself, and of course the world has
refused to believe him. It is hardly exaggeration to say that whenever Bernard Shaw tells people soberly and honestly exactly the sort
of man he is, and exactly the kind of work he has done, they laugh
heartily, and say that Bernard Shaw is a very funny and inventive
person. Similarly, whenever he ventures into fun and fiction, his
hearers insist upon taking him seriously as they would take a
prophet.

It follows that Bernard Shaw, who is a modest, conscientious,
kindly, industrious, and well-read man of letters, is commonly regarded as a reckless firebrand who lives by the cart and the trumpet,
is up to his neck in all that is lawless and improper, is without com-
passion or shame, speaks always in paradoxes, and claims to be
greater than Shakespeare. Not fewer than fourteen years ago Bernard
Shaw told the world that he was an elderly gentleman who had
made an immense reputation by being the best of a bad lot and by
plagiarizing the English classics. He really meant what he said; but
the preface in which he said it is still supposed to be the *locus
classicus* of his claim to supersede the author of *Macbeth*. Here,
again, it is impossible to say of Bernard Shaw any true thing he has
not already said of himself. He has repeatedly urged his critics and
followers to reject utterly the legend of G. B. S. "I find myself," Bernard Shaw wrote in 1900, "while still in middle life almost as legendary a person as the Flying Dutchman. Critics, like other people, see

what they look for, not what is actually before them. In my plays they look for my legendary qualities, and find originality and brilliancy in my most hackneyed claptrap. Were I to replenish Buckstone's *Wreck Ashore* as my latest comedy, it would be hailed as a masterpiece of perverse paradox and scintillating satire."

Nothing in modern literary history is more remarkable than the reputation of G. B. S. for original and daring speculation; and no one, myself possibly excepted, more thoroughly appreciates the funny side of G. B. S. as philosopher than the man to whom this reputation is so persistently attached. Five years ago I came to London burdened with the classic wisdom of an ancient university. I had read some philosophy in one school and some economy in another. As a musician I had read Wagner for a venerable classic. As the merest Philistine in connoisseurship, I recognized in Rodin a great sculptor of the last generation, as firmly established in immortality as Michelangelo, and I saluted in the New English Art Club a thoroughly respectable academy of painting. As a playgoer destined to succeed Max Beerbohm, who himself in remote antiquity had succeeded G. B. S. on the *Saturday Review,* I had become weary of Ibsen, and had begun to wonder why Granville Barker seemed old enough to be my uncle. Now, I do not regard myself as being in the least in advance of my time; yet when I came to London I found that Bernard Shaw, who still preached Ibsen and Wagner, who spoke with Rodin as a contemporary, who preached a philosophy which was already introduced into examination-papers at a place not suspected of modernism, who talked economy out of university textbooks which it was a scholarly and pedantic exercise to confute in the lecture-rooms of Oxford—that this thoroughly safe, orthodox, and almost medieval Bernard Shaw was being received by the literary societies and the press of London as an original and revolutionary thinker. I then began to understand why Bernard Shaw has very little respect for some of his contemporaries.

III

THE "BETTER THAN SHAKESPEARE" FALLACY

This brings us to the fourth fallacy. The fourth fallacy is that Bernard Shaw has made enormous and extravagant claims for himself as a critic, philosopher, sociologist, and dramatist. Let us take a passage of Bernard Shaw's preface to the *Plays for Puritans.* It is the famous "Better than Shakespeare" passage, the foundation of a public charge that George Bernard Shaw thinks too highly of himself.

It is a conclusive proof that he does nothing of the kind. Observe also that it harks back to our second fallacy:

My stories are the old stories, my characters are the familiar harlequin and columbine, clown and pantaloon (note the harlequin's leap in the third act of *Cæsar and Cleopatra*); my stage tricks and suspenses and thrills and jests are the ones in vogue when I was a boy, by which time my grandfather was tired of them. . . . It is a dangerous thing to be hailed at once, as a few rash admirers have hailed me, as above all things original; what the world calls originality is only an unaccustomed method of tickling it. Meyerbeer seemed prodigiously original to the Parisians, when he first burst on them. To-day he is only the crow who followed Beethoven's plough. I am a crow who have followed many ploughs. No doubt I seem prodigiously clever to those who have never hopped hungry and curious across the fields of philosophy, politics and art. Karl Marx said of Stuart Mill that his eminence was due to the flatness of the surrounding country. In these days of Board Schools, universal reading, newspapers and the inevitable ensuing demand for notabilities of all sorts, literary, military, political and fashionable, to write paragraphs about, that sort of eminence is within the reach of very moderate ability. Reputations are cheap nowadays.

Who, after all, will say that Bernard Shaw has in him a particle of author's conceit? He has never claimed more than is due to him. There is not the least evidence of vanity or self-importance in the printed work of George Bernard Shaw, there is even less in his speeches, letters (the private letters of George Bernard Shaw will be his masterpiece when, and if, they ever come to be published), conversation, or general demeanor. It is true that he has frequently and vigorously claimed not to be entirely foolish, and that sometimes he has insisted that he really does know what he is writing about. But it is also true that no critic has more persistently assured the public that there is nothing really important or new in any of the ideas and devices which so curiously amazed the first audiences of his early plays. Has he not soberly assured the American public that "the novelties of one generation are only the resuscitated fashions of the generation before last"? And has he not proved this with instances out of *The Devil's Disciple?* Did he not prophesy outright in 1900 that the lapse of a few years would expose that play for "the threadbare popular melodrama it technically is"?

Nevertheless, though it is possible for anyone read in the works of Bernard Shaw to parallel these instances of self-assessment from almost any volume, pamphlet, speech, or anecdote of his life, the belief still rules that Bernard Shaw is too highly appreciated by Bernard Shaw. The truth is that Bernard Shaw has had to expend vast

stores of energy and time in reproving his friends for thinking too
much of him and in snubbing the worship of his followers. He has
had continually to explain to the superior socialists that he is not
really a great orator; to the dramatic critics that he is not really the
supreme dramatist who ever lived; to men of science that he is not
the erudite physician they have imagined from *The Doctor's Dilemma* and not the expert in acoustics they have inferred from
Pygmalion; to distracted heads of families that he is not in the least
qualified to tell them how to control their marriageable daughters.
Bernard Shaw has worked harder to escape the greatness which is
thrust upon him than many of his contemporaries have worked to
achieve wealth and a blue ribbon; and the harder he has worked,
the more convinced the public has become that he is an incorrigibly
insolent and pertinacious champion of his title to be infallible.

It is essential to get this notion of Bernard Shaw as the *miles glo-
riosus* corrected at the start, otherwise we shall never handle the key
to his achievement. You will ask how it has arisen. It has arisen simply and inevitably from the fact that Bernard Shaw was for many
years of his life a professional critic, and that he was by nature able
to regard himself and his own performances with complete detachment. Naturally, when he came to write plays, and found that the
said plays were incompetently criticized, he used his native gift for
regarding himself impartially, and his acquired skill as a professional critic, to inform his readers exactly how good and how bad
his plays really were. Hence he has acquired a reputation for vain-
glory, for it is a rooted idea with some people that a man who talks
about himself is necessarily vainglorious.

Bernard Shaw's detached and disinterested observation of his own
career and achievements is not within the power of the average man
of letters. It was accordingly misunderstood. Not every one can
discuss his own work as though it were the work of a stranger. The
self-criticism of Bernard Shaw, read as a whole, shows an amazing
literary altruism. It shows exactly how far he is from consenting to
occupy the throne into which he has been thrust. Bernard Shaw, in
his prefaces, is not a prophet claiming inspiration for his script; he
is one of the crowd that reads and judges for itself; only he reads
and judges a little more closely and severely than the rest. Bernard
Shaw's modesty—his curious aloofness from his own fame—is the
more attractive in that it is absolutely innocent of stage-manage-
ment. There are men who have made corners in retirement—men of
whom it is at once exclaimed how humble and unspoiled they are.
Shrewd observers will always suspect the man of letters who is
famous for his modesty; who seems to think it positively indecent
that his face should be seen; who has always "just left the theater"

when there is a call to be taken; who has a reputation for inaccessibility. Bernard Shaw, of course, is entirely free of this organized and blushing humility. His very real modesty consists in his being able to assess himself correctly. He is one of the few living authors who has not been taken in by his own performances. It does not occur to him to divide the literature of the day into (a) the works of Bernard Shaw and (b) other people's works. He thinks of *Man and Superman* as he thinks of *The Silver Box*. It is a play of contemporary interest and of some merit, and he does not see why he should be barred from discussing it as an expert critic just because he happens to be the author. Bernard Shaw has certainly imposed upon many of his friends and observers. He has not imposed upon himself.

IV

SHAW NOT A JESTER

The fifth fallacy is that Bernard Shaw is an incorrigible jester, that he is never serious, that he is ready to sacrifice his best friend and his firmest conviction for the sake of a really good joke. Now, the first thing to realize about Bernard Shaw is his overflowing gravity. He has taken more things seriously in his career than any living and notable person. He has taken music seriously, and painting and socialism and philosophy and politics and public speaking. He has taken the trouble to make up his mind upon scores of things to which the average heedless man hardly gives a second thought— things like diet, hygiene, vaccination, phonetic spelling, and vivisection. He has even taken seriously the English theater, unlike virtually every other English man of letters who has had anything to do with it. Compare for a moment the conduct of Bernard Shaw at a rehearsal of one of his own plays with the conduct, say, of Barrie. Barrie is happy so long as no one takes any notice of him. He has so immense a disdain for the minutiæ of theatrical production that he would rather write ten plays than control the rehearsal of one. Bernard Shaw, on the other hand, with the amazing industry of a really serious person, turns up with a closely written volume of notes, determining down to the minutest detail where, how, and when his company shall deliver their lines and do their necessary "business." It is only because Bernard Shaw is so immensely serious that he can be so tremendously casual and brilliant. He is ready for everything and everybody because he has seriously considered everything and seriously regarded everybody. A first-rate impromptu usually indicates a mind richly stored and well arranged. Bernard Shaw can extemporize on most subjects because he has seriously thought about them. The more brilliantly he sparkles upon a given theme, the more sober has been his education in its rudiments. Unfortunately, many people have come to exactly the opposite conclusion. Because Bernard Shaw has a rapid and vital way of writing, because he presents his argument at a maximum, seasons it with boisterous analogies, and frequently drives it home at the point of a hearty joke, he is suspected of sacrificing sense to sound. The dancing of his manner conceals the severe decorum of his matter. It is true that Bernard Shaw can be funny, but it is wholly false that he is in the least a flippant writer or a careless thinker. He is as serious as Praise-God Barebones and as careful as Octavius Cæsar.

v

HIS REPUDIATION OF REASON

The sixth fallacy has to do with the all-head-and-no-heart formula. It is said of Bernard Shaw by some very excellent critics that he is an expert logician arguing *in vacuo,* that he has exalted reason as a god, that his mind is a wonderful machine which never goes wrong because its owner is not swayed by the ordinary passions, likes, prejudices, sentiments, impulses, infatuations, enthusiams, and weaknesses of ordinary mankind. How the critics square this notion of Bernard Shaw with the kind friend and counselor who lives in Adelphi Terrace they alone can tell. It is probably this idea of Bernard Shaw which most heartily tickles him. Bernard Shaw greatly enjoys contemplating the motley crowd of his legendary selves; but none can please him more thoroughly—because none could be more outrageously fictitious—than Bernard Shaw the vivisector of his kind, the high priest of reason and common sense.

This last superstition has grown mainly out of the simple fact that G. B. S. as a critic of music, art, and the drama was actually a critic. He took his criticism as seriously as he took his socialism or his conviction that tobacco was a noxious weed. Being a serious critic, he found it necessary to tell the truth concerning the artistic achievements of many sensitive and amiable young people. Naturally, Bernard Shaw got the reputation of being a heartless brute for his candor, and a logical brute, owing to the soundness of his arguments. Then, when Bernard Shaw came to write plays, it was discovered that his young women behaved like reasonable creatures and that his young men appreciated the importance of five per cent. This was unusual in the soft, romantic stage creatures of the late nineties; so here was more evidence of Bernard Shaw's insensibility, of his arid and merciless rationalism, of his impenetrable indifference to all that warms the blood of common humanity.

Of course there was not the slightest real evidence of all this. If there is one idea more than another that persists all through the work of Bernard Shaw, and defines his personality, it is to be found in his perpetual repudiation of reason. Almost his whole literary career has been spent in adapting the message of Schopenhauer to his own optimism and belief in the goodness of life. Not reason and not the categories determine or create, but passion and will. Bernard Shaw has always insisted that reason is no motive power; that the true motive power is will; that the setting up of reason above will is a damnable error. Life is the satisfaction of a power in us of which we can give no rational account whatever—that is the final declaration of Bernard Shaw; and his doctrine corresponds with his temperament. Rudyard Kipling has described the rationalists as men who "deal with people's insides from the point of view of men who have no stomachs." Bernard Shaw would agree. No one, in habit or opinion, lives more remotely than Bernard Shaw from the clear, hard, logical, devitalised, and sapless world of Comte and Spencer.

VI

SHAW FAR FROM BEING AN ANARCHIST

The seventh fallacy is that Bernard Shaw is an anarchist, a disturber of the peace, a champion of the right of every man to do as he pleases and to think for himself. This idea of Bernard Shaw is so deeply rooted in the public mind, despite Bernard Shaw's serious and repeated disclaimers of its accuracy, that, if any young person in London runs away from her parents, or if any elderly gentleman abandons his wife and family, these things are not only regarded as the results of Bernard Shaw's pernicious teaching, but their perpetrators are upheld and justified by the belief that they are disciples following the lead of G. B. S. as prophet and master. These startling misconceptions have arisen from the fact that Bernard Shaw has pointed out in a popular play that children do not always agree in all points with their parents, and that he has argued in a less popular play that one or two reforms in the marriage laws of Great Britain are already overdue. Was ever a reputation won upon slenderer evidence? Why, Shakespeare told us three hundred years ago how

> The hedge-sparrow fed the cuckoo so long
> That it had its head bit off by its young,

and it is now on record in a British bluebook that a committee of the most respectable gentlemen of the British bar and church have agreed with Bernard Shaw that British divorce is unnecessarily expensive, inequitable, and humiliating. The practical extent of Bernard Shaw's anarchism coincides with the anarchism of our judges and our bishops.

Those who dig deeper than this, with the preconceived resolution to find that Bernard Shaw is an anarchist, will only be more hopelessly misled. They will find that he preaches, as we have already discovered, the ultimate supremacy of passion and will; that he sees the gods and the laws of each generation as mere expressions of the will and passion of their generation; and that he claims for posterity the right to supersede them as soon as posterity is moved by a higher will and a finer passion. But this is not anarchism. It is so far from being anarchism that side by side with these doctrines Bernard Shaw has, in *The Sanity of Art,* written down one of the best defenses of law and order—of the convenience and necessity of policemen, churches, and all kinds of public authority—that has appeared in popular form within recent years. It is true that Bernard Shaw pleads for liberty, and points out that it is better for a man to act and think responsibly for himself than to run to the nearest constable or parish priest. But it is also true that he wants people to have no more liberty than is good for them, and that he very seriously distrusts the ability of the average man to think for himself. Bernard Shaw knows that the average man has neither the time nor the brains nor the imagination to be original in such matters as crossing the road or getting married or determining whether he ought or ought not to cut the throat of his neighbor.

Nothing could be further from the mind of Bernard Shaw than the philosophic anarchy of Godwin or John Stuart Mill. Bernard Shaw is not an anarchist either in speculation or in practice. He is as sound on the question of law and order as Mr. Asquith. He is as correct in deportment and as regular in his conduct as the Vice-Chancellor of Oxford. The most pictorial way of emphasizing the difference between a real anarchist and Bernard Shaw is to compare the handwriting of Bernard Shaw and, say, of Cunninghame Graham. Bernard Shaw writes like a sensible citizen who intends his pages to be read. It is true that he asserts his individuality as one who values what is comely by writing the most beautiful hand of any author living, just as he insists that his books shall be printed in a style that proclaims him a pupil of William Morris. But he writes mainly to be read, aware that the liberty of writing illegibly is not worth the trouble it would give to a community which practised it. The writing of Cunninghame Graham, on the other hand, requires an expert in calligraphy. It has baffled half the big printing-houses in London. It is the last, insolent assertion that every man has the right to do as he pleases regardless of the discomfort and loss of time he thereby inflicts upon his neighbors. It is, in one word, anarchic, a graphic illustration of the great gulf that is fixed between two public figures of the time who, nevertheless, have impartially been described by the careless as anarchists.

VII

SHAW A PRECISION RATHER THAN A CARELESS MAN OF LETTERS

The eighth fallacy is that Bernard Shaw is a headlong, dashing, and opiniative writer, without technical equipment, who succeeds by an impudent trust in his unassisted genius, and brings off his best efforts by a happy fluke. This fallacy has stuck to Bernard Shaw all through his career as a critic of music, painting, the drama, as a playwright, as a pamphleteer, as a public speaker. When G. B. S., as Corno di Bassetto, was writing about music for a London newspaper, the public insisted that his appointment was a joke. It was the public's own joke, and the public enjoyed it immensely. Indeed, it chuckled so heartily that G .B. S. had not the malice to undeceive it. He played with this popular legend of himself, as he has so often played with a hundred others. He was thought to be merely a rude young man who knocked the professors' heads together without the least idea of what they contained. Bernard Shaw's characteristic confutation of this public error was to reduce it to absurdity. When people handed him a score, he held it carefully upside down and studied it in that position. When he was asked to play the piano, he walked to the wrong end. Bernard Shaw's conduct as a critic of music, acting under provocation, was very natural; but it was in the result unfortunate. Popularly imagined to be an irresponsible amateur with a literary knack, Bernard Shaw, in all he has undertaken, has, if anything, erred from an excessive knowledge and interest in the expert professional and technical side of his subject. Bernard Shaw knew years ago all about the enormity of exploding undiminished chords of the ninth and thirteenth on the unsuspecting ear, just as today he thoroughly understands the appallingly scientific progressions of Scriabin. Similarly he can tell you the difference at a glance between real sunshine in an open field and the good north light of a Chelsea studio, or explain why "values" are more difficult to capture when colors are bright than when they are looked for in a dark interior. As to the technic of the theater—well, the subject is hardly worth discussing. Some of his later plays are nothing if they are not technical.

The fallacy that Bernard Shaw is a happy savage among critics and artists, ignorant and careless of form, unread in the necessary conventions, speaking always at random with the confidence that only a perfect ignorance can give, is particularly deplorable, because it necessarily blinds its adherents to Bernard Shaw's most serious defect both as critic and creator. Usually Bernard Shaw knows too much, rather than too little, of his subject. He is too keenly interested in its bones and its mechanism. His famous distinction between music which is decorative and music which is dramatic is quite unsound, as I would undertake to show in nothing less than a small pamphlet; but it is not the mistake of a critic ignorant of music. It is rather the mistake of a critic too keenly absorbed in the technic of music.

If the professors in the early nineties had objected to G. B. S. because he was liable to lapse into the pedantry of which they themselves were accused, they would have been nearer the mark than they were in foolishly dismissing him as an ignoramus. Similarly, as a dramatic critic, G. B. S. erred not by attaching too little value to the forms and conventions of the theater, but by attaching too much. It is true that he did not make the absurd mistake of some of his followers, and regard Ibsen as a great dramatist on account of one or two pettifogging and questionable reforms in dramatic convention, such as the abolishing of soliloquies and asides and extra doors to the sitting-room. But he certainly attached too much importance to these things, mainly because he knew so much about them; and this critical insistence of his as a Saturday Reviewer has had its revenge in some of his own plays, where his purely technical mastery of theatrical devices, his stage-cleverness, and craftsman's virtuosity have led him into mechanical horse-play and stock positions unworthy of the author of *John Bull's Other Island* and *Major Barbara*. Bernard Shaw has continually suffered from knowing his subject too well from the angle of the expert, and he has frequently fallen into the mistakes of the expert. Far from being the happy and careless privateer of popular belief, he is usually to be found struggling for freedom under the oppression of things stored for reference in his capacious memory. The great critic, like any ordinary, unskilled spectator, should be able to look at a work of art without prejudice in favor of any particular form or fashion. It should not matter to him a jot or influence his judgment in the slightest whether the music he hears is symphonic or metrical, whether the thirteenth is exploded as a thirteenth or prepared as a six-four chord. He should be similarly indifferent whether a dramatist talks to him in blank-verse soliloquy or in conversational dialogue. Preoccupation with manner, *apart from matter*—usually implying an *a priori* prejudice in favor of one manner over another—is the mark of pedantry; and of this pedantry—always the pedantry of a man who is expert and knows too much—Bernard Shaw is not always free, though he is far too good a critic to be often at fault.

VIII

THE REAL SHAW

We have not yet exhausted the popular fallacies about Bernard Shaw, but as most of my readers will already be wondering what is left of the man who has just described Sir Edward Grey as a Junker, I will turn now from George Bernard Shaw, who is as legendary as the Flying Dutchman, to the very positive and substantial author of *Common Sense About the War*. I have yet to explain why Bernard Shaw, stripped of his professional masks, and rescued from the misconceptions of his admirers, remains one of the most striking public figures of our day, and must fairly be regarded as the most important apparition in the British theater since Goldsmith and Sheridan. We have seen that Bernard Shaw is not original in what he preaches, is erudite rather than adventurous, is in no sense revolutionary or anarchical, is extremely serious, and is far from being an orgiastic and impudent rationalist for whom drifting humanity is stuff for a paradox. Bernard Shaw has not won the notice of mankind because he has thought of things which have hitherto occurred to no one else; nor has he won the notice of mankind because he has a native gift of buffoonery and a talent for the stage. The merit of Bernard Shaw has to be sought outside his doctrine. The secret of his genius lies deeper than his fun, and has scarcely anything to do with his craft.

It ironically happens that Bernard Shaw as a critic has virtually made it impossible for those who accept his criticism to allow that Bernard Shaw as a dramatic author has any right to be really famous. We have seen that Bernard Shaw as a critic repeatedly fell into the grievous error of separating the stuff he was criticizing into manner and matter. Thus, confronted with the Elizabethan dramatists, Bernard Shaw always maintained that they had nothing to say and that they were only tolerable because they had an incomparably wonderful way of saying it. Comparing Shakespeare with Ibsen, for example, he would point out that, if you paraphrased Ibsen's *Peer Gynt*, it still remained good intellectual stuff, and that, if you paraphrased Shakespeare's "Life's but a walking shadow," it became the merest commonplace. Bernard Shaw thence proceeded to draw the moral that Ibsen, apart from mere favor and prettiness, was the

greater and more penetrating dramatist. Fortunately for Bernard
Shaw, as we shall shortly realize, this criticism of his is not only false
in fact, but it is also nonsense in theory. It is false in fact, because it
is quite untrue that Shakespeare paraphrased is commonplace
whereas Ibsen paraphrased is an intellectual feast. It would be more
to the point if Bernard Shaw had said that Shakespeare paraphrased
is commonplace for all time and that Ibsen paraphrased is commonplace for only the nineteenth century. It would be still more to the
point if Bernard Shaw had said that it is quite impossible to paraphrase any work of genius in so far as genius has gone to its making.
It is absurd to talk of paraphrasing Shakespeare, because Shakespeare is of genius all compact; and it is as true of Ibsen as of Shakespeare that, so far as he is a genius and not merely a scientific
naturalist, it is absurd to separate what he says from his way of
saying it. When Shakespeare has written:

> . . . Out, out, brief candle!
> Life's but a walking shadow, a poor player
> That struts and frets his hour upon the stage
> And then is heard no more: it is a tale
> Told by an idiot, full of sound and fury,
> Signifying nothing.

he has written more than the equivalent of "life is not worth living."
If Bernard Shaw will not admit that Shakespeare in this passage is
no more than an utterer of a universal platitude for pessimists, he
will have to agree that Ibsen is no more than an utterer of parochial
platitude for the suffragette platform. Probably, however, now that
Bernard Shaw has himself become a classical author, he has realized
that to distinguish between the ideas of a literary genius and the language in which they are expressed is as absurd as to distinguish
between the subject of a painter and the way in which it is painted,
or between the themes of a musician and the notes in which they are
rendered.

At any rate, Bernard Shaw must realize how very badly he himself would fare under such a distinction. We have seen that Bernard
Shaw *in doctrine and idea* is in no sense original. His celebration of
the state is as old as Plato. His particular sort of puritanism is as old
as Cromwell. His particular brand of socialism is as old as Owen.
A paraphrase of Bernard Shaw—a reduction of Bernard Shaw to the
bare bones of his subject matter—would be as intolerable as the
speeches of his disciples and some of his masters usually are. In a
word, if Bernard Shaw is a genius, he is a genius for the same reason
that Shakespeare is a genius. He is a genius not because he has anything new to say, but because he has a passionate and a personal

way of saying it. If I had the time to go deeper into this matter, I should like to ask whether it is really possible to get hold of a new idea as distinguished from a new way of presenting an old one. But, at all events, I have already said enough to justify the assumption that, if Bernard Shaw can claim an immortality, however brief, it will not be by virtue of his original, novel, and startling opinions, but by virtue of his literary presentation of them in a manner entirely his own. The equations read:

The ideas of Bernard Shaw = the commonplaces of his time.

The ideas of Bernard Shaw + his way of presenting them = G. B. S.

IX

PASSION AND STYLE THE SECRETS OF SHAW'S SUCCESS

Bernard Shaw, then, has won the attention of the present generation, and he will hold the attention of posterity not because he has new theories about the world, but because, by virtue of strictly personal and inalienable qualities, he is able to give to the most "hackneyed clap-trap" (Bernard Shaw's own description) an air of novelty. Were he baldly to tell us that incomes should be equally divided, and that interest is an inquitous and profoundly unsocial device invented by those who have too much money for the purpose of levying blackmail upon those who have not enough, we should simply remember that we had read all this years ago in an old book and turn to something rather more worth our time and attention.

But when Bernard Shaw writes *Widowers' Houses* or *Socialism and Superior Brains,* it is quite another matter. Here we have original work of the first quality. The ideas are common to us all; but Bernard Shaw's presentation of these ideas thrills us with a conviction that nothing quite like it has ever come within our experience. We realize that we have never before encountered just this blend of wit and sense, this intellectual wrestle and thrust, this fervor and fun, this argumentative and syllabic virtuosity, this apparently impudent disregard of style that only the more piquantly emphasizes a perfectly individual and highly cultivated literary art. Then we begin to wonder what is the inspiration of this rapid Jehu; whence does he get his impulse to drive all these ancient ideas so furiously through the modern world. How are we to explain the passion that fills him and lifts his work to levels higher than the platform he undertakes to fill? We are sensible in Bernard Shaw's best work of a horsepower, of a spiritual energy, which is no more the product of his doctrinal prejudice against rent and interest than the energy which drove Wagner to compose the *Nibelung's Ring* was the product of his desire to justify his revolutionary principles or to improve the operatic stage scenery of his generation. We know that the inspiration of Bernard Shaw must be something deeper than a dislike of Roebuck Ramsden or a desire to abolish Mr. Sartorius. We know, in fact, that Bernard Shaw, like every man of genius, is the happy agent of a power and a passion which uses his prejudices, memories, and doctrines in a way he is intellectually powerless to resist.

The real thrill of his work is conveyed in some sentences of his preface to *Man and Superman*—sentences used by him in quite another connection:

> This is the true joy of life: the being used for a purpose recognised by yourself as a mighty one; the being thoroughly worn out before you are thrown on the scrap-heap; the being a force of nature, instead of a feverish, selfish little clod of ailments and grievances, complaining that the world will not devote itself to making you happy.

To apply this passage to the work of Bernard Shaw is again to destroy the popular conception of him as merely the acute *raisonneur,* the intellectual critic of his kind, with a wallet of revolutionary propaganda whereby his reputation lives or dies. Not his doctrine and not his deliberate pulpiteering make Bernard Shaw a vital influence in modern literature. The real secret of his influence can be explained in a sentence. Bernard Shaw has passion and he has style. Therefore, like every man of genius, he is driven to say more than he intends, and to say it in an arresting voice.

It remains to ask what is the prime irritant of this passion in Bernard Shaw. Where are we to look for the catfish which keeps his mental aquarium alive and astir? First, without preliminary, let us dart on that preface "Why for Puritans," which more than any other gives us the key to Bernard Shaw's work and character. Bernard Shaw writes as follows:

> I have, I think, always been a Puritan in my attitude towards Art. I am as fond of fine music and handsome buildings as Milton was, or Cromwell, or Bunyan; but if I found that they were becoming the instruments of a systematic idolatry of sensuousness, I would hold it good statesmanship to blow every cathedral in the world to pieces with dynamite, organ and all, without the least heed to the screams of the art critics and cultured voluptuaries.

Bernard Shaw's primal inspiration, that is to say, is not esthetic or intellectual, but moral. We have to reckon with a moral fury where he most individually rages. The demon which seizes his pen

at the critical moment, and uses him for its own enthusiastic purpose, is the demon which drove Milton to destroy Arminius. When
Bernard Shaw imagines that he coolly and reasonably desires, simply as a practical socialist and in the name of common sense, to
nationalize land and capital, and give to everybody as much money
as he requires, he is mistaken. Like every other prophet who has
succeeded in moving his generation, Bernard Shaw begins with a
passion and a prejudice, and afterward manufactures and systema-
tizes the evidence. That Bernard Shaw is a socialist is an accident of
the time. The essential thing is that Bernard Shaw passionately hates
all that is complacent, malevolent, callous, inequitable, oppressive,
unsocial, stupid, irreligious, enervating, narrow, misinformed, unim-
aginative, lazy, envious, unclean, disloyal, mercenary, and extravagant. Hating all this with the positive, energetic, and proselytizing
hatred of an incorrigible moralist, he has naturally seized on the biggest and most adequate stick in reach with which to beat the nineteenth-century sinner. This stick happened to be the socialist stick.
If G. B. S. had lived with Grosseteste in the thirteenth century, it
would have been the no-taxation-without-representation stick. If
he had lived with Star Chamber in the sixteenth century, it would
have been the Habeas Corpus stick. If he had lived with Rousseau
in the eighteenth century, it would have been the social-contract-
and-law-of-nature stick. Bernard Shaw's socialism stick is simply his
weapon—the most convenient weapon to hand—with which to convict a society founded upon capitalism of the greatest possible
amount of sin with the least possible opportunity of an overwhelming retort from the sinner. The important thing is not that Bernard
Shaw preaches socialism, but that he uses the doctrines of socialism
as Cromwell's troopers used the psalms of David or as Tolstoy used
the gospels of Christ—namely, to put the unjust man and his evil
ways out of court and countenance. To this end he employs also his
craft as a dialectician, his gift as a stylist, his clear exposition and
wit, his fun, irony, observation of men, genius for mystification and
effective pose—all, indeed, that enters into the public idea of G. B. S.
These things are merely auxiliary; any moment they are likely to be
caught up in the service of his passionate mission—a mission of
which Bernard Shaw is often himself aware when he is most firmly
under its dominion.

X

OUR MODERN TREATMENT OF PROPHETS

This brings us within view of Bernard Shaw's pamphlet on the war.
It is natural in a preacher that the most unpardonable sin of the

many he is called to denounce should be the sin of complacency; for the sin of complacency virtually amounts to the sin of refusing to hear what the preacher has to say, or, at all events, of refusing to take it seriously. Bernard Shaw has said continuously for many years that the average man is an unsocial sinner; and the average man, instead of hanging his head and mending his ways, has smiled in the face of the prophet. At one time the prophet was stoned, and at another time he was poisoned or ostracized or pelted in the pillory. But we have lately learned a more effective way of dealing with a prophet: either we turn him into a society preacher and enjoy his denunciation of what our neighbors do, or we pay him handsomely to amuse us in the theater. We have thus improved immensely on the methods of the scribe and the Pharisee; for where the scribe and the Pharisee destroyed only the bodies of their prophets, we, with an even more thorough complacency, aim also at destroying their souls—usually with some success.

But the British public has not succeeded with Bernard Shaw, who continues to be periodically stirred to frenzy by his inability to make everyone realize that he or she is directly responsible for all the crimes and miseries of modern civilization. Moreover, because Bernard Shaw has lived most of his life in England, and has therefore been less seriously taken in England than elsewhere, he has concluded that the English are more complacent than any other people in the world. More and more he has come to regard it as his special mission to humble this complacency, to convict the Englishman, above all men, of sin, and of the necessity for humility and repentance. Therefore, whenever the British public becomes, in the view of Bernard Shaw, unduly exalted,—whenever, in fact, it thinks it has a reason to be proud of the British name,—Bernard Shaw is at once suspicious and usually incensed. Latterly he has been unable to resist any occasion of pricking the inflation, real or imagined, of the British spirit; and latterly, misled by habit, and exaggerating the sins he was born to chastise, Bernard Shaw has made some serious mistakes.

Thus when, more than two years ago, the whole British nation was struck with grief at the loss of the *Titanic*, and was reading with a reasonable pride of the splendid behavior of her heroic crew, Bernard Shaw rose in his robe of the prophet and told the public not to exaggerate its vicarious gallantry. Then in August, 1914, when Great Britain was straining every nerve to get her army to the Continent in time to save Belgium from the worst of war, Bernard Shaw published an article in the British press virtually to the effect that Great Britain was not fighting for the sanctity of treaties or the rights of a little nation, but for British homes and British skins.

Maliciously he chose for the publication of this assault upon British complacency the most obstinately and hatefully complacent British newspaper at his disposal.

Finally there came the celebrated pamphlet *Common Sense About the War*. This must be read as Bernard Shaw's most audacious effort to puncture the self-esteem of the British public. It has caused much brain-searching among those who have simply regarded George Bernard Shaw as a very discreet and financially successful mountebank; for Bernard Shaw, in writing this pamphlet, has done a clearly unpopular thing. Undoubtedly he has angered and estranged many of his admirers. Some regard the pamphlet as an obscure attempt to discredit the allied cause. Others regard it as an escapade of revolting levity, inexpedient from a patriotic point of view and essentially wrong in its conclusions. The real point that concerns us here is that the pamphlet is not a new, unexpected, or isolated performance of Bernard Shaw, but a natural sequel of all he has hitherto written. Those who have followed Bernard Shaw to the threshold of his pamphlet on the war have no right at this time to be astonished or to refuse him their applause. *Common Sense About the War* is simply a topical and a later edition of *Widowers' Houses*. That is to say, it is a tract in which the case against British complacency is put at a maximum by a fearless and passionate advocate for the prosecution.

Not Bernard Shaw, but the time, has changed. Here we strike at the root of Bernard Shaw's mistake. Hitherto, he was doing salutary work in his campaign against the silent self-assurance of the mean, sensual man. There are as many complacent persons in Great Britain as elsewhere, and so long as Great Britain was at peace with her neighbors, it was beneficial that Bernard Shaw should imagine that the British, among whom he lived, were more guilty in this respect than any other extant community, and that he should lose no opportunity for satirical, ironical, comic, or didactic reproof. But when Great Britain and her allies had their back to the wall, when there were opponents to be countered and met, Bernard Shaw's insular mistake that the British as a nation are any more complacent than any other nation with a past to be proud of and a future to believe in became a really injurious heresy. It began, indeed, to look rather like giving away his people to the enemy. Of course it was nothing of the kind. *Common Sense About the War*, intelligently read, vibrates with patriotism, and it proudly proclaims the essential rightness of the struggle in which Great Britain is now engaged. But the patriotism of *Common Sense About the War* is less apparent to the audiences which laugh at Bernard Shaw in the theater and outrageously regard him as a privileged fool at the court of King Demos, than the fact that it begins by asserting that Sir Edward Grey is a Junker, and goes on to examine very particularly whether we really have the right to condemn our enemies without a preliminary inquiry into our own consciences and affairs.

Bernard Shaw has made a mistake, but it is a natural, not an ignoble, mistake. It will have no permanent effect upon those who are sensible, even in Bernard Shaw's most special pleading, of the passionate moral sincerity which gives consistency and fire to all he writes. *Common Sense About the War* was a blunder; but it was also an act of disinterested courage. It was not dictated by any wish to stand in front of the picture or to splash in a sea too deep for purposes of exhibition. Bernard Shaw, in writing *Common Sense About the War*, is simply the priest who insists upon sacrifice before going into battle, or believes that every good fight should be preceded by confession, absolution, and high mass.

One word more. Bernard Shaw, the prophet and the puritan, lives in his work. But the passion which gives him uniformity and purpose as a public figure has not impaired his personal humor, his tolerance for all that is sweet and commendable, his broadness of view and eagerly inquisitive outlook upon life, his candor and honesty of mind, his generous welcome of new ideas, his love of beautiful things, his ability to appreciate and sympathize even with those forces which are banded to destroy him. These are the qualities which have obscured from contemporaries the essential simplicity of his mind, and have warmly endeared him to the younger generation of authors and critics who have learned from their master how profitably they may supersede him. This younger generation, though it very frequently turns the weapons of Bernard Shaw against himself, will never forget or neglect the debt it owes to the helpful, patient, and wise counselor it has been privileged to observe and know.

P. P. HOWE

1915

Shaw's Economics

If we turn in this section of this study to the consideration of Mr. Shaw as political economist, it is with no wish to surprise that we do so. For if we come to think about it, it was to political economy that Mr. Shaw himself turned first, if we neglect for the moment (but only for the moment) his almost but not entirely negligible novels. And if we do not think about it, if we have not, that is to say, the sequential order of our subject's career as clearly before us as we should have if it were his biography we were engaged on, do we not then with equal ease deduce the economist from the dramatist? It will be some part of the purpose of this study to do so. We shall find that Mr. Shaw, in his capacity as dramatist (and that, after all, is only one of his capacities), has built, not on the human heart, as Browning's Sordello exhorted the poet to do, but on the "economic man" of the economists. And if my word is not conclusive, as, at this stage, it can hardly be expected to be, we have the word of Mr. Shaw himself, who wrote in a letter to Professor Henderson, "In all my plays my economic studies have played as important a part as a knowledge of anatomy does in the works of Michael Angelo."

II

There is no man who prides himself more on the normality of his vision than the economist; indeed, he is often a man who thinks that no other men have any vision at all. Political economy is the only game you may engage in (except perhaps politics) with forty-eight million pawns, and have for your board the national exchequer. At the same time it is one of the most secret of vices; more secret than

Reprinted from *Bernard Shaw: A Critical Study* by P. P. Howe. Used by permission of Dodd, Mead & Company, publishers.

politics, in which you have occasionally to meet your opponent at the poll, although you need never meet his arguments. But the political economist may go on playing his own game in his own corner, awarding us our income under his pet law of wages, which he terms an "iron" law, and disposing of it to his own satisfaction; and we, who make our living and spend it—or who spend it without making it—may not be aware of his existence. I suppose there are not ten men at this moment in the City of London, engaged in bringing us our bread, who have the smallest grasp of the economic theory, as distinct from the business principle, of what they are doing. This is neither to their credit nor their discredit; the unreality of the economist is almost a point of faith in England. Partly the reason is that the orthodox economists have contented themselves with "explaining" the system by which we live, and as their explanation has always amounted to one hundred good reasons why that system cannot possibly be different in any respect, it is no surprise that we have not taken the trouble to read them. For the system by which one lives, the iron laws, that is to say, which govern the fact that one's particular slice of bread and butter is no bigger, is not a thing one wants to read about—merely to learn that one's slice *can* be no bigger. It is not a thing like the theory of music, without some study of which one cannot be a musician; or the theory of literary technique, without which one cannot write good novels (despite a very general belief to the contrary). By the sweat of one's brow to earn one's bread is partly an instinct and partly a stern necessity; and there is small blame to the plain man if he think neither his instincts nor his necessities a proper subject for theoretic study.

But the Socialist altered all this, because they said to the plain man *if* you study the theory of the system by which you live you will see that your slice may be, nay ought to be, bigger. The Socialists thus provided the first definite inducement in the history of the world (for the study is as old as Aristotle) for the plain man to read the economists. He would read the orthodox economists, that is to say, to find them out; to detect in their writings what Bentham called the sinister interest—to convict them of canonizing a system merely because it was the system that was current. The Socialists he would read to obtain a glimpse of an ideal system; or to learn how, by a catastrophic upheaval of the simplest kind, he might increase the size of his own slice of bread and butter. Unfortunately the Socialists, when they were economists, were not very good artists, and when they were artists, were not very good economists; and frequently they were neither. How charming a picture Fourier might have made of the phalanstery, if he had had one quarter of the art of Sir Thomas More; but he had not any at all, merely the vocabulary of his calling, which was that of a commercial traveller. How persuasive Marx might have been, if his explanation that all values are only definite masses of congealed labour-time, and therefore the sole property of the plain man, had not been more positively unreadable than the explanations of the orthodox economists, in addition to being less accurate. With what eagerness we should have thrown ourselves into the Utopia of Morris, if the limpid and beautiful book had contained any more precise instructions for its attainment than the conversion of the Houses of Parliament into a municipal dung-heap. But it didn't; and even though England for once had grown a Socialist, instead of importing him—Fourier, Saint-Simon, Engels, Marx—the system went on working, and the orthodox economists went on explaining it to the entire satisfaction of themselves and of the very few people who wanted to listen.

III

That was the position when our subject made his double discovery, that his eyesight was normal and that the population of these islands were mostly fools. (Both these discoveries are undated, but I think we may take them as occurring not long after 1856, in which year Mr. Shaw was born in Dublin. I am aware that *News from Nowhere* did not make its appearance until 1890, fourteen years after Mr. Shaw came to London, and a year later than *Fabian Essays*.) I think it probable that a third discovery antedated these two by a little, and that was our subject's discovery that he was a good hand at an explanation; indeed, if it were the custom to record as religiously the first words of great men as it is their last—a custom which presents unfortunate difficulties since there is no way of knowing a great man in his cradle—we may be pretty sure that the first words of our subject would prove to be, "Let me explain." Once more, whether this were so or whether this were not so (and it is a domestic scene which, if it occurred, Mr. Shaw has omitted unaccountably from his so carefully presented reminiscences), we should be inclined to deduce it from our subject's work in general; in which, whether dramatic or extra-dramatic, no three words have enjoyed more frequent recurrence. For every reason, then, of destination and of choice, the field of the political economist was open to our subject. He found it for the first time in the history of English letters, an arena in which a man who was bent upon catching the eye of his generation might seriously think of succeeding. Ruskin had Thackeray to thank for a good deal when he found Unto this Last too shocking for the Cornhill; but Ruskin wrote before the Socialists had rendered the explanations of the orthodox economists really interesting to the general public, and he had made his name in other fields before he turned to teaching political economy to young ladies' academies and to long-suffering and hypothetical working men. It is impossible to assert that the physiocratic sentimentalism of Ruskin, in spite of the eloquence of its expression, has very much influence in England at this moment. But our subject found in the orthodox economist a prime instance of the "hopelessly private person" for whom, doubtless by nature, he had an antipathy. He found a sufficient number of persons—shall we say that he found the newspapers?—willing to give their attention to the phenomenon of the Socialists turning upon the system of society the guns they had wrested from the hands of its trusted if neglected defenders, the economists. He found within his own person an exceptional brain, quite equal to doing rather better in any field of public activity that it chose than most of its contemporaries. Add to this a severe and dutiful sobriety of character which religiously kept that brain working when the nearest rivals among those contemporaries happened to be taking a holiday; and a gift of "effective assertion" (which is our subject's definition of style), a gift already disciplined to the writing of his quartette of voluble novels. And add to this again the artless pleasure of the undergraduate in mere ratiocination. What better field for these things to cut a figure in, in the English 'eighties at any rate, than that of the economists? Our subject soon was busy cutting it. Within a very small number of years he was delivering an address to the Economic Section of the British Association—putting them into their own corner, as it were, and saying, "Let me explain."

IV

It is not without significance that what Mr. Shaw undertook to explain to the economists was The Transition to Social Democracy, for that is what the members of The Fabian Society have been explaining to one another ever since. I do not wish, in saying this, to be misunderstood. The Fabian Society, a body of persons of both sexes who have met together once a fortnight for a quarter of a century to listen to Mr. Shaw, and have left before his speech was over if the duration of its interest conflicted with the departure of their train for the suburbs, are only of significance to the subject of our present study in so far as their history is his history. In themselves, and apart from the admirable special activities of Mr. and Mrs. Sidney Webb and others of the platform figures, they may be described as the passionate friends of the unreality of the economist. For a quarter of a century they have discussed how they will behave, how we shall all behave, how they will allow us to behave, "under Social-

ism.". It is an amiable hobby, like another, and they have pursued it
with the diligent single-mindedness with which another body of
persons might discuss how vegetables behave under glass. I propose
to assert that Mr. Shaw the borough councillor, the apostle of the
cart and trumpet, the cogent advocate of municipal trading, has all
the time been a sufferer from the unreality of the economist. He
cleared the economists out of their corner just as, later on, he cleared
the dramatists out of the theatre, and for the same reason—to make
room for some goods of his own which he had all ready for delivery.
For the unreality of the orthodox economists he substituted, in the
name of reality, a new unreality; just as for the unreality of the
orthodox dramatists he went on to substitute, in the name of reality,
a new unreality again. But we must not get on too fast.

What is, in actual fact, the outcome of our subject's series of
treatises—the *Fabian Essays* of 1889, *The Impossibilities of Anarchism, Socialism for Millionaires, Socialism and Superior Brains, Fabianism and the Empire, Fabianism and the Fiscal Question, The
Commonsense of Municipal Trading, The Case for Equality* of 1914?

It is a very delightful series, displaying at every point the tongue
of the ready debater as well as the pen of the ready writer. In the
series, one would say, lives the athletic charm of our subject's public
figure, as it has talked down to its generation from a hundred platforms. That, in itself, is very delightful. One is sure that the series
has been read by very many people who have not read any other
kind of economist at all. They have imbibed a very great deal of
perfectly sound economic theory, and they have not imbibed any
nonsense. Our subject's first effort in this particular field was to offer
a pronounced opposition to the theory of Marx; partly, no doubt,
moved by an instinct to throw out of the field the biggest occupying
figure he found in it; partly because our subject has at any time
given really very little quarter to other people's nonsense. On the
subject of Value, he threw out Marx and allied himself to the late
Mr. Stanley Jevons, an orthodox economist. This annoyed the Socialists; but Mr. Shaw has always delighted in annoying those people
whose attachment to an idea is by means of a sentiment. Along this
line, if it were any part of our immediate business, we might discover in him a great deal of æsthetic as well as intellectual integrity.
He annoyed the friends of the little peoples by his advocacy, because of its superior efficiency, of British ascendancy in South
Africa; when the Americanized trust then known as the Times Book
Club promised superior efficiency, he annoyed the friends of the
freedom of letters by giving the enterprise his support. In fact, I
suppose our subject has always been more than anything else in love
with efficiency. "Become efficient at your own particular trade or

profession," has been his advice to the young Fabians, "and then tell everyone you are a Socialist." That has been his policy of peaceful permeation; in contradistinction to the jolly umbrella-shaking of Mr. Hyndman amongst the lions in Trafalgar Square, and the distinguished hidalgoism of Mr. Cunninghame Graham in the same setting. It is advice with which it is not possible to quarrel.

And our subject's love of efficiency is the real reason why he dislikes the poor so much. The one actual outcome of all these treatises —oh yes, and of a round dozen of prefaces which I haven't forgotten —is our subject's intense dislike for the poor. That is something new in the science of political economy. Because it is a very early utterance which remains absolutely personal and characteristic, I propose to quote here a fairly long passage from the *Fabian Essays:*

> But indeed the more you degrade the workers, robbing them of all artistic enjoyment, and all chance of respect and admiration from their fellows, the more you throw them back, reckless, on the one pleasure and the one human tie left to them—the gratification of their instinct for producing fresh supplies of men. You will applaud this instinct as divine until at last this excessive supply becomes a nuisance: there comes a plague of men; and you suddenly discover that the instinct is diabolic, and set up a cry of "over population." But your slaves are beyond caring for your cries: they breed like rabbits; and their poverty breeds filth, ugliness, dishonesty, disease, obscenity, drunkenness and murder. In the midst of the riches which their labour piles up for you, their misery rises up too and stifles you. You withdraw in disgust to the other end of the town from them; you set your life apart from theirs by every class barrier you can devise; and yet they swarm about you still: your face gets stamped with your habitual loathing and suspicion of them: your ears get so filled with the language of the vilest of them that you break into it when you lose your self-control: they poison your life as remorselessly as you have sacrificed theirs heartlessly. You begin to believe intensely in the devil. Then comes the terror of their revolting; the drilling and arming of bodies of them to keep down the rest; the prison, the hospital, paroxysms of frantic coercion, followed by paroxysms of frantic charity. And in the meantime, the population continues to increase!

And to place against that passage, for your edification, I give you another from the preface to the *Major Barbara* of nearly twenty years later:

> Now what does this Let Him Be Poor mean? It means let him be weak. Let him be ignorant. Let him become a nucleus of disease. Let him be

a standing exhibition and example of ugliness and dirt. Let him have rickety children. Let him be cheap and let him drag his fellows down to his price by selling himself to do their work. Let his habitations turn our cities into poisonous congeries of slums. Let his daughters infect our young men with the diseases of the streets and his sons revenge him by turning the nation's manhood into scrofula, cowardice, cruelty, hypocrisy, political imbecility, and all the other fruits of oppression and malnutrition. Let the undeserving become still less deserving; and let the deserving lay up for himself, not treasures in heaven, but horrors in hell upon earth. This being so, is it really wise to let him be poor? Would he not do ten times less harm as a prosperous burglar, incendiary, ravisher or murderer, to the utmost limits of humanity's comparatively negligible impulses in these directions? Suppose we were to abolish all penalties for such activities, and decide that poverty is the one thing we will not tolerate—that every adult with less than, say £365 a year, shall be painlessly but inexorably killed, and every hungry half-naked child forcibly fattened and clothed, would not that be an enormous improvement on our existing system, which has already destroyed so many civilizations, and is visibly destroying ours in the same way?

Now the voice of those two utterances is demonstrably the same voice, which has gone on saying the same things with an iteration which cannot possibly be condemned. It is the voice, I think, of a man who does not like our old world at all, who pushes it away with the tips of gloved fingers, with the request that it will kindly make itself clean and tidy before presenting itself again for attention. It is a voice that is attenuated, almost into shrillness, by its burden of æsthetic disgust. How enormously (we may conceive that voice saying) how enormously much more I should like you people if you presented a uniform face; a face, above all, that was uniformly clean! Blanche Sartorius, in Mr. Shaw's first play, spoke in much this tone when she said: "Oh, I hate the poor. At least, I hate those dirty, drunken, disreputable people who live like pigs." And in one of the latest of Mr. Shaw's plays—the play which was on no longer ago than the other day—one of the statements of a quarter of a century earlier was illustrated: the statement that our ears get so filled with the language of the vile that we break into it when we lose our self-control.

But it is the message, and not the tone, of the voice which is to the point for the moment. The way to a uniform cleanness of face and of character is by means of a uniform income. That is Mr. Shaw's economico-psychologic discovery. That is the actual outcome of our subject's series of treatises. It is hinted at in *Fabian*

Essays*; it is presented for Mr. Mallock's consideration in *Socialism and Superior Brains;* it is affirmed in the preface to *Major Barbara;* it is reaffirmed in *The Case for Equality.* Incomes for All is the one positive contribution to the science of political economy made by our subject. It is the Shavian theory of distribution, as you might say the Jevonian theory of value or the Ricardian theory of rent. It is the categoric alternative to Let Him Be Poor. It is the means by which "all the detestable fruits of inequality of condition" (see *The Impossibilities of Anarchism*) are to be nipped off in the bud.†

V

What the Fabians discovered, in actual fact, was that it was much more amusing to talk about Socialism than to achieve it. That has very little to do with Quintus Fabius; but we need not trouble ourselves about that. I think it was Mr. Chesterton who, having taken off his hat to our subject's superior brain, took it off again to the fact that our subject had devoted his superior brain to talking about drain-pipes. Now we may be all for taking off our hats to our subject, and yet not be unaware that he has enjoyed himself talking about drain-pipes. Mr. Shaw has enjoyed talking about everything. It is not as though Mr. Shaw particularly promised himself the pleasure of talking about something else, and gave it up in order to talk about drain-pipes from a stern sense of duty. The stern sense of

---

* At that point in Mr. Shaw's second essay at which it is suggested that "rent of managerial ability might in course of time become negative," that is to say that the manager should receive *less* for his work than the artisan, the captain less than the cabin boy, because, "under Socialism," of the honour of superior service. That, in the precise spirit of the undergraduate who suggests to his tutor in political economy that interest should be negative—that is to say, a payment demanded for capital conserved instead of a payment conceded for capital used—is the genesis of Mr. Shaw's discovery.

† If this were primarily an economic study we might pause to see how Mr. Shaw has proved himself to be, with this single exception, an orthodox economist; or rather, an orthodox economist with a Socialist bias—with the orthodox Socialist bias. For example, we might read in our Mill: "To make the public pay much that the treasury may receive a little, is not an eligible mode of obtaining a revenue. In the case of manufactured articles the doctrine involves a palpable inconsistency. The object of the duty as a means of revenue, is inconsistent with its affording, even incidentally, any protection. It can only operate as protection in so far as it prevents importation; and to whatever degree it prevents importation, it affords no revenue." Now that is precisely what Mr. Shaw himself has put forward from one thousand platforms; it has been taken to be one of his daringly sudden simplifications. That, for example, among other things, is *Fabianism and the Fiscal question.* . . . But this is not primarily an economic study. It will not be irrelevant to have noted here our subject's pleasure in making any kind of a point, whether it is his own or another's; for that, in its essence, is the debater's pleasure. He has done nothing as a constructive economist to be compared with Mr. J. A. Hobson's analysis of the industrial system, for example.

duty is there plain enough in our subject, but I do seriously suggest that we see it in a better perspective if we admit that a drain-pipe is a peculiarly pleasant thing to juggle with to a man of Mr. Shaw's temperament. In the first place a drain-pipe is "real," a real solid fact, with no nonsensical romance about it; and in the second place there are very few men who can balance a drain-pipe. No one would have expected the late Oscar Wilde, for example, to make a very good performance with a drain-pipe; and sure enough when at one point in his career he too caught the Fabian fever (for he was particularly impressionable, far more so than our subject), it was not drain-pipes that he wrote about, but the soul of man, "under Socialism."

The Soul of Man under Socialism has not hitherto, so far as one is aware, been regarded as a Fabian essay; but that is what it is in reality. For the moment, Wilde permitted himself the amusement of granting that Utopia had, indeed, been added to our dominions; and he made for himself in it, along with the other artists, a haven of artificial seclusion in which, with beautiful pens and fair white paper before him, the artist would sit down and would look out over a garden at the high wall which saved him from the rude stresses of a competitive world, and would produce—one may be quite sure, nothing. Now if Mr. Chesterton meant that Mr. Shaw would rather have written about the place of the artist "under Socialism" than about drain-pipes, I think he made a mistake. Did not Mr. Shaw himself write, as we shall find in the next chapter, an exposure of the current nonsense about artists being degenerate? If artists were not degenerate in the highly competitive and distressing year 1895, after having to put up with all but five years of what Mr. Shaw has asserted posterity will call "the wicked century," it is surely a fair inference that in our subject's opinion Utopia is not necessary on their account. As a matter of fact, our subject has steadfastly refused to talk any of the current nonsense about artists; he has worn his hygienic mantle with the most complete absence of affectedness, and that is one of the most charming things about him. He has put on his gloves and balanced a drain-pipe, because—as he has said of the writing of prefaces—he *can*. And when he came to the writing of plays, he did not immediately drop his drain-pipe, as Wilde dropped his Utopiaism and submitted himself to the impress of the highly competitive West End managers—he wrote plays about drain-pipes.

Our subject, then, has been happy with his drain-pipe: that is the precise spectacle presented by, let us say, *The Commonsense of Municipal Trading*. If he had not been happy, we should not have read it; and I suppose we all have done that. But while Mr. Shaw has been busy explaining—with the aid of a great deal of sound economic theory, with a wit which refuses to be frowned off the field of the dullards, and with an incurable zest in the mere processes and triumphs of debate—the precise advantages of the fact that our drain-pipes have been municipalized, he has talked himself into a curious delusion. He has talked himself into the delusion that all this time he has been "pointing out" and "clearing up" he has escaped the unreality of the other economists. Of Life he has said, "Only by intercourse with men and women can we learn anything about it"—with the obvious implication that it is by this means that he himself has learned all about Life. And yet it is the hard fact that the Fabian Society and the cart and trumpet are not intercourse with men and women in the completest of possible senses. If we were to take our subject at his own valuation, he would appear as one of those who, in Plato's phrase, "have gained a knowledge of each thing in its reality." By becoming elected to a Borough Council one gains a knowledge of a Borough Council in its reality, and that is admirable; but one does not of necessity gain a knowledge of men and women other than Borough Councillors. I propose to point the reader to those passages quoted on pp. 64-65, and to assert that they do not betray a knowledge of life gained primarily by intercourse with men and women. I will even go so far as to say that they are the words of a man to whom any kind of ordinary mixed public intercourse—say, at the Oval, or at a Socialist meeting, unless he were on the platform—would be extremely distasteful. The fact is that our subject is a platform figure, whose principal intercourse with men and women, we should say from his works, has been by means of talking about them.

VI

We shall find when we come to Mr. Shaw's plays, with their machinery of the preface, that his procedure is just what we should expect. It is an *a priori* procedure, from the general to the particular; from "the millions of poor people, dirty people, abject people," for example, of whom one reads in the preface to *Major Barbara*, to West Ham, and not vice versa. It is as though Mr. Shaw, having written a letter to The Times establishing that poverty is a crime, had then paid a visit to a Salvation Army shelter, and found there everything which he had expected to find. His observation, that is to say, does not begin with Rummy Mitchens, and Snobby Price, and Bill Walker; it begins in the economist's own corner, and only condescends, in a humorous and delightful manner, to make itself concrete

in Rummy and Snobby and Co. And now perhaps it will be as well
to substitute for the word "economist" the word "publicist." Our
subject has only sometimes been the economist, he has been the
publicist all the time. In one sense, of course, every artist is a publicist; if he does not find his matter in what people happen to be
interested in, he hopes that people will happen to be interested in
his matter. But the true publicist, whether he is an artist or not,
wants to be interesting people in his own particular brand of goods
all the time. If he is an artist, he will interest them by means of his
art, and he will want to interest them outside of his art as well—by
means of his opinions on every conceivable subject, by means of his
personality and person, by means even of the fact that his tele-
graphic address is "Socialist, London." We may as well sum it all up
by saying, as our subject has done, "I want to change the ideas of the
people of this country." How that desire and aim consorts with
artistic principles, how, indeed, it conditions them, we shall better
understand when we have devoted a chapter to the æsthetics of our
subject. But the difference between Mr. Shaw and, let us say, Mr.
Conrad, is apparent; Mr. Conrad who, when his books have spoken
for him, really has nothing else that he particularly wants to tell us,
or Mr. James, who has no views at all, positively no views at all that
any reader ever discovered, but only a view of the world. The first
kind of artist (he who is not consciously a publicist) does not understand the second kind of artist; Mr. Conrad has expressed this mistrust in his ironic tale of *The Informer*. "Does a man of that—of that
—persuasion still remain an anarchist when alone, quite alone and
going to bed, for instance? Does he lay his head on the pillow, pull
his bedclothes over him, and go to sleep with the necessity of the
chambardement général, as the French slang has it, or the general
blow-up, always present to his mind? And if so, how can he?" Our
subject is not an anarchist—has he not pointed out, and explained,
and generally and sufficiently cleared up, the impossibility of being
one? But our subject is all for the *chambardement général*—oh yes,
a purely intellectual blow-up, a change of ideas. For he is a humane
man, who even though he wishes that the adult poor might be "inexorably" killed, is yet careful to explain that the thing should be
"painlessly" done, and the orphans forcibly fattened. . . . That is the
kind of thing we must conceive our subject as taking to bed with
him, and giving voice to, with pathos, with humour, and with a
variety of effective assertion, the next morning. He is a man "of that
—of that—persuasion."

There is a penalty for being a publicist, and that penalty is the
publicist's unreality. It would be perfectly easy to define the un-

reality of the publicist, to go on defining it (for that is what, if it amounts to anything, this chapter amounts to); but what is the use, since Hazlitt has done it already, far better than anyone else could possibly do it, in his character of Mr. Cobbett? That passage from On Knowledge of the World may well stand at the end of this chapter:

> As I have brought Mr. Cobbett in here by the neck and shoulders [says Hazlitt], I may add that I do not think he belongs properly to the class, either of philosophical speculators, or men of the world. He is a political humorist. He is too much taken up with himself either to attend to right reason or to judge correctly of what passes around him. He mistakes strength of purpose and passion, not only for truth, but for success. Because he can give fifty good reasons for a thing, he thinks it not only *ought* to be, but *must* be. Because he is swayed so entirely by his wishes and humours, he believes others will be ready to give up their prejudices, interests and resentments to oblige him. He persuades himself that he is the fittest person to represent Westminster in Parliament, and he considers this point (once proved) tantamount to his return. He knows no more of the disposition or sentiments of the people of Westminster than of the inhabitants of the moon (except from what he himself chooses to say or write of them), and it is this want of sympathy which, as much as anything, prevents his being chosen. The exclusive force and bigotry of his opinions deprives them of half their influence and effect, by allowing no toleration to others, and consequently setting them against him. . . .
>
> A knowledge of mankind . . . is less an intellectual acquirement than a natural disposition. . . .

I do not know whether that gave the picture of Mr. Cobbett to his contemporaries: it most certainly gave, and gives, the picture of one kind of man. It gives the picture of the publicist. One would not wish to make too much of the comparison; when one thinks of the subject of this study as a kind of social institution, as it were, one thinks of Godwin at least as often as one thinks of Cobbett. But perhaps he is, as near as we can get to him, the Mr. Cobbett of his age —that Mr. Cobbett of the pure and trenchant English style who wondered how Paradise Lost could have been tolerated by a people conversant with astronomy, navigation, and chemistry, and who found some things in Shakespeare to please him but much more that he did not like; that Mr. Cobbett who was as well known as any man in England, down to the minutest circumstances in his character, habits, and opinions, including the colour of his waistcoat. Mr. Shaw has never stood for Westminster, but he has stood for St. Pancras for the County Council. And if one searched one's mind and heart for a phrase to cover those activities of our subject which this present chapter has feebly and hopelessly limped after, "political humorist" would be the phrase one would come back to. "Because he can give fifty good reasons for a thing, he thinks it not only ought to be, but must be."

DIXON SCOTT

1916

The Innocence of Bernard Shaw

"*Let him beware of his damned century; his gifts of insane chivalry and animated narration are just those that might be slain and thrown out like an untimely birth by the Dæmon of the Epoch.*"—ROBERT LOUIS STEVENSON, *in a Letter.*

"*He is perhaps a 'fraud,' as the Americans put it; but the first victim of Bernard Shaw's charlatanism is Bernard Shaw himself. Susceptible to impressions (as are all artists) and a philosopher at the same time, he cannot do otherwise than deceive himself.*"—AUGUSTE RODIN, *in a Conversation.*

When part of this impression first appeared (in a special number of *The Bookman*) it was hailed as "a brilliant attack." I want to say at once that it is only a diffident defence. Quite simply and sincerely, with a strong sense of presumption, it comes forward to make excuses for our most mordant accuser; it is an honest attempt to discover the cause of the disparity between Mr. Shaw's superb powers and his performances, between the work he might have done for us—the work he wanted to do for us—and the work he has actually done; and as it gropes and taps sympathetically it does come delightedly on evidence which seems to prove overwhelmingly that the real villain of the piece is—not the author of *Androcles*—but that wasteful, wanton mocker whose present alias is The Life Force, which actually completed its frustration of Mr. Shaw's career by sardonically setting him to work to sing its praises. There is something positively conspiratorial in the cunning logic of events which drove this splendid Irishman astray; he was plucked about like a puppet—torn out of his true place—crammed when still young and tender into an inappropriate mould, and held there while circumstances, with a diabolical deftness, screwed the die down on his features ineffaceably; and his very air of arrogance, which makes this description sound absurd, was but one of the imprints received in that hour. That the man whose deepest desire is to heal and help humanity should have become a kind of byword for mockery; that his altruism should seem egotism, his earnestness insolence, his mysticism materialism, his refusal to have living creatures slaughtered for his food a symptom, not of warm-heartedness, but of cold-bloodedness; that the man whose only quarrel with Christianity is its acquired element of cruelty, and who has preached and practised constantly an absolutely saintly code of private conduct and the strictest obedience to the Church's hardest rules, should yet be regarded as a dangerous enemy of morals and reproved (as he was by *The Times* itself in a leader on *Androcles and the Lion*) for ribaldry and irreverence in regard to sacred things: all these and their hundred kindred contradictions are explained when we watch his career from the beginning and perceive the frightful dexterity with which fate has always employed his best qualities to drive him along a road that must distort them. We shall find the essential Shaw to be eager, idealistic, impulsive, romantic. We shall see him flung, at exactly the most impressionable hour of his life, into the peculiarly priggish and self-assertive little world of the intellectual London of the eighties. We shall see how his native eagerness and inexperience idealized that environment; and how his wit and his vividness and his love of picturesqueness urged and enabled him to reproduce all its elements in a single concentrated pose; and how the accent he then adopted, the attitudes he struck as he hectored the world from rebel platforms, ate back into his instincts and affected his habit of mind, until at length intolerance, arrogance, contentiousness, contradictiousness, became instinctively his imagination's weapons. And finally we shall see how his very earnestness and craving for consistency forced him on to the concoction of a philosophy which would justify his policy of pert exasperation; and how he gradually perfected a theory which represented irritation as the only open sesame to men's consciousness, and cold clear thinking as the weapon now most needed to cut us free from our pampering illusions, and which therefore laid on the man of genius as his deepest duty this thankless task of challenge and contempt. And we shall watch this adventitious creed drinking up vitality from his veins, dilating till at last it shut *him* in—trapped in a dense grove of ideas that slowly altered him until he matched them—as dungeon walls will do a captive. . . .

I

The whole thing, put abruptly, is another example of the tyranny of technique over temperament—of the way an instrument invented for too narrow a need will react on the fingers that use it, stiffening and striking back till it fatally deforms them, wrenching their special talent awry. The "tyranny of technique over temperament" may sound, indeed, just at first, a predicament as purely academic as the famous "deduction killed by a fact"; but really it is far fuller of ringing human comedy, of thrills, and alarums and poetry, than even the most dramatic of all the existing portraits of Shaw, the most exciting of the alternative estimates. The man's contradictions—his literary licentiousness and his personal restraint—his intellectual voracity and physical vegetarianism—the intense earnestness and benevolence of his real aims and ideals and the daft capers he cuts as he preaches them—have inspired any number of vivid interpretations, all of them with at least the life of paradox; but the best of them by far, much the noblest and the neatest, is the one which seizes all these contrasts—the austerity and the perversity, the inverted altruisms, the harangues and the humility, the general wild lack of all resemblance between reputation and reality—and thereupon presents him as a martyr who twice over and more has sacrificed the hard-won crown of martyrdom, its impressiveness, its reward of dignity—a prophet who has disguised himself as a jester to gain an audience for his message, staining his sackcloth to look like motley, only to find that his frantic jokes, invented so feverishly, simply exasperate his listeners instead of luring them—that they regard his levity as ill-timed, his solemn touches as sacrilegious, and the texts which they feel his pranks profane, and which they had hitherto accepted unsuspiciously, as being rendered henceforward and for ever quite unfitted for respectable family consumption. This conception of his last martyrdom, as might be expected, is naturally the one Mr. Shaw favours himself. "My case is really that of Rabelais over again," he has said. "In order to gain a hearing it was necessary for me to attain the footing of a privileged lunatic, with the licence of a jester. My method has therefore been to take the utmost trouble to find the right thing to say and then say it with the utmost levity. And all the time the real joke is that I am in earnest."

But there is a realler joke than that, and a very much richer. That's the merest drop-scene: the true Comedy lies behind. Another second and we will ring the curtain up. Your deliberate martyr, after all, no matter how he fails, has a certain splendour that makes the Comic Spirit feel respectful; and the more undignified Shaw became for the sake of a high purpose, the more dignified would he actually appear. It is not futility, it is fatuity, that legitimates laughter; and in Shaw's case the fun only really begins when we see that this self-sacrifice was quite unintentional, that the martyrdom which he now mentions with such a brave lightness and sad pride was not only a mistaken policy, but actually quite a mistake. It was to cook his own dinner that he kindled the fire that turned and tortured him. He went to Smithfield because he thought it a good market-place. The entire proceeding was a practical joke lazily played on an overeager young innocent by the world he imagined he was taking firmly in hand. His "disguise" was a dress he slipped on as unsuspectingly as a man whose clothes have been changed overnight; and when he began to skip about in it like "a privileged lunatic" (a mad mixture of harlequin and hermit), it was he who was the dupe, not society. . . .

And if someone suggests (as someone ought to do) that no practical joke fails so wretchedly as the one that entirely succeeds, we can still defend, with quiet dignity, our present proposal for a few minutes' mirth. It is true, indeed, that the game *has* gone rather far —that the joke of Shaw thinking of himself as the joker when he was actually the victimized jokee, proves after all to have been made at our expense. If it had been merely a case of a mediocrity smirking self-satisfied when he ought to be feeling subdued, like an actor persuading himself that his involuntary tumble was a brilliant impromptu, then we might chuckle unchecked, undeterred by any danger of hurting the hero's complacency, and thankfully accepting his absurdity as his real contribution to the play. But this performer is such a fine one, his powers are so extraordinary, that any illusion he may suffer from, any mistake he may make, is immeasurably our loss. Our damned century has tripped him up, as Stevenson foretold, and that is, no doubt, very clever of our century. But it is surely a pretty silly sort of cleverness that hoodwinks its own children, fooling the very cleverest of them all to show its strength.

True—but listen further; there is one thing more. How would it be if the benefits of Shaw's work were actually increased by the discovery that their author was a dupe? That is precisely what happens. There are several reasons. It removes the venom from his virulence, for one thing, reduces our resentfulness, leaves him, immensely more likable, just a poor puzzled creature like ourselves. And it also provides the perfect complement and corrective to his contribution of ideas. There is only one way to give Shaw's work any adequacy, to make his utility at all proportionate to his powers, and this is to see him as a gull. To watch the man who supremely prides himself on his freedom from illusions, and on the irresistible power of pure thought, being used as an idle toy by superior powers at the very moment he is triumphantly proving their non-existence, is to be the spectator of something far more than a mere final farce to send us away in good humour; it is to watch an integral scene that entirely alters and immensely deepens the meaning of those that go before. Add Shaw himself to his *dramatis personæ*, and the latter begin to kindle and grow human; make the story of his deception an extra act to all his plays, and they begin to teach a genial tolerance and to breathe a smiling wisdom which, it must be admitted, they do not otherwise exhale. They lose that bitterness and barrenness, that hard and cruel angularity and bleak glitter, which has led to their author being denounced for inhumanity. To the array of stabbing truths with which they bristle, thrusting out at us like spears, there is added yet another, perhaps the only one omitted, which transforms the fierce attack into a rescue. It sets them wavering and faltering, as in a blur of mist; and that was all they needed to make them noble and reliable. We can trust them after that, for they have lost the hard exactness which has hitherto always made them so unreal. All Shaw's work hitherto has been too precise to be accurate; it has been too exact to be true.

One point more. A glance back at the quotations at the beginning of this article will show the reader that two other great minds have been before us in this suspicion of a stage behind the drop-scene. The fact will reassure some; but others it may damp: a word of comment will satisfy both. It is true that both Stevenson and Rodin pushed the curtain aside—saw the performance going on secretly behind it; but the old Frenchman went no further than that cryptic phrase about the "fraud," and the young Scotsman was compelled to leave the house abruptly before his little forecast was fulfilled. We may therefore enjoy both the sense of their patronage and the prouder one of being pioneers. We still occupy the enviable position of first-nighters. And for my own part I confess that it is with a thrill of real excitement that I now stretch out my hand and press the prompter's bell. . . .

II

And instantly there vanishes, whipped away forever, that striking picture of St. Bernard, the austere Irish eremite, staining his sackcloth to make it look like motley, and turning his staff and scrip, sublimely sacrilegious, into a fool's bladder and wand. It simply will not do. History won't have it. Mr. Chesterton, to be sure, has spoken, with much pathos, of Mr. Shaw's "narrow Puritan home"; Mr. Huneker, with pride, has enlarged on his "humble peasant birth"; and to listen to these phrases and then turn to any of the portraits and caricatures, from Max's to Coburn's, from Rodin's to Elliott & Fry's—which have made his face more familiar to the average English reader than that of any personage alive—is really to feel that one discerns the harsh features of the fanatic, that one can recognize in the fierce eyebrows, the aggressive beard, and the scowl, the face of a merciless fanatic, austere as the stony soil from which he sprang, ablaze with the bitter passion of the protestant. Sheer hallucination, I assure you! We are being hoaxed by the beard. It conceals a soft and charming chin. And Chesterton and Huneker are a pair of sentimental humbugs. For absolutely the first and most fundamental thing about Bernard Shaw biographically is—that he was the son of Lucrezia Borgia!

Of Lucrezia Borgia and of the Margaret of *Faust,* and of the Donna Anna of *Don Giovanni.* For Shaw's mother was a young and beautiful Irish opera-singer (she was only twenty years her son's senior), who carried on a "blameless *ménage à trois*" with a famous musical genius on the one hand and the feckless second cousin of a baronet (Bernard Shaw's father) on the other; and Lucrezia (Donizetti's), Donna Anna, and Margaret were her three favourite parts.

It is astonishing how adroitly these romantic facts have been mingled in all the current accounts of his life. "His family was a middle-class one," says one well-known critic, "with all the prejudices and habits of that class." "L'écrivain a peut-être évoqué des souvenirs d'enfance," writes M. Charles Cestre, "quand il a décrit, dans le *Disciple au Diable,* les affranchements et les indignations d'une famille puritaine dont le chef, le bonhomme Dudgeon, a conservé quelques faiblesses humaines au milieu de l'austérité aigre et hargneuse des siens," and goes on to speak impressively of the youth practising "sans effort une sorte d'ascétisme inné." "Austérité aigre et hargneuse" be hanged! The lad's life was a voluptuous revel. He dreamed and dawdled at school, where he was only a desultory day-boy, and where, as he has owned himself, he learned nothing whatever—not even (more's the pity) fives or footer; and at home, the less distracted, he simply soaked himself lusciously in the licensed orgies and ecstasies of music. Melody, grand opera melody, not only, for him, took the place of the prose of real life, he even dissolved all his books in it, making it a vehicle for absorbing Scott and Victor Hugo and Poe, in an absolutely sensuous physical form. "In music," he once wrote (in an article we ought to have reprinted—an early article describing these indulgences):

In music you will find the body of and reality of that feeling which the mere novelist could only describe to you; there will come home to your senses something in which you can actually experience the candour and gallant impulse of the hero, the grace and trouble of the heroine, and the extracted emotional quintessence of their love.

I gained penetrating experiences of Victor Hugo and Schiller from Donizetti, Verdi, and Beethoven, of the Bible from Handel, of Goethe from Schumann, of Beaumarchais and Molière from Mozart, and of Mérimée from Bizet, besides finding in Berlioz an unconscious interpreter of Edgar Allan Poe. When I was in the schoolboy adventure vein, I could range from Vincent Wallace to Meyerbeer; I could become quite maudlin over Mendelssohn and Gounod. . . .

Enrich these orgies still further with emotions insatiably sought for in the Italian rooms of the Dublin Art Gallery—rooms which he admits he haunted hungrily, weeks at a time, all through his romantic adolescence, and you have a faithful impression of the way this young man began to "pratiquer" his "ascétisme inné." When Oscar Wilde's mother, in Merrion Square, was posing languishingly in her drawing-room as Speranza, Mrs. Shaw, in a Dublin theatre, a few streets away, was flinging herself passionately into the part of Azucena; and before the son of the latter was out of his teens he had drained dizzier delight from the coloured lines of the world's greatest painters, and had absorbed far more heady music, than the son of the former did all the days of his life. Nor is the "narrow puritanism" of the picture very markedly increased if we complete it by putting in the figure of Shaw's father—an amiable weak tippler and rather lovable snob, helplessly haughty about his kinsman the baronet; or if we extend it to include the figure of that favourite uncle who (as Mr. Shaw somewhere mentions) used to go about declaring that the revival of Lazarus was a pre-arranged job, done on the basis of a bribe.

No, no! London, a little later, may have partly cemented G.B.S., made a sterner and a sourer, and in some ways a stricter man of him; but, when he reached it, in his twenties, he was an out-and-out romantic—as little like a preacher as Bunyan before Bedford Gaol or St. Francis in the gallant days of his youth. Soaked in Gounod and Mendelssohn, dreaming of Mozart and Michelangelo, hugging a vague idea of becoming "a wicked baritone in opera," he was still (as he has owned) "chronically ashamed and even miserable," simply because "I felt I couldn't do anything." "What was wrong with me was the want of self-respect, the diffidence, the cowardice of the ignoramus and the duffer." "My destiny was to educate London, but what I knew was exactly what the educated Englishman did not know, and what he knew I either didn't know or didn't believe." He came up to London, in short, as young poets always have come;

with a knowledge of life, of human nature, including their own, limited to the information supplied by opera libretti and the hydrogenous prose of De Quincey and Shelley; agonized by their own awkwardness, shamed by their own innocence, desperately troubled by their unpreparedness for destiny, but beautifully upheld through it all by the dim, golden conviction that a Destiny of some distinction does await them, and that London, the wise alchemist, will know the very drop to add to send their dreams showering down in a shining precipitate of definite tasks and high resolutions.

In fact, just exactly the usual glorious mixture of prig, blushing schoolgirl, and god. And the year (this is very important indeed) the year was 1876.

III

Now let the game softly begin. London, deft, crimp, has one regulation ruse which she tries on all such shy new-comers: she feigns lethargy, indifference, a bored kind of nonchalance, a composure that looks exactly like incapacity—and so, with one stroke, restores the novice's self-confidence and sets his indignation briskly sparking. Apathy, a wasteful apathy—that is invariably the personal quality the place seems to present to the aspirant: a smooth, maddening indifference, not to his own entrance merely (that indeed might have proved his superiority—for that he was humbly prepared), but to her own powers and opportunities, her duties and beauties—to the general dazzling adventurousness and terrific irrevocableness and tormenting possibilities of Life. Actually, to be sure, this languor is merely a mask; it is the disguise adopted by good nature, good form; the quiet is that of wisdom, not woodenness—the composure is not of torpor, but of powers tested and serene because sure; but the debutant doesn't find this out till much later on. What he does do is to compare this bland calm with his own keenness, and to feel that his prevision of a Destiny was sound. He *is* different from these people, with their small talk and trifling; excitedly he sets his teeth and squares his jaw. Reassured at the very moment he expected to be abashed, he buckles to with his book, picture, play. London has set him to work, very neatly, by pretending to be incapable of commands.

Nine times out of ten, therefore, the trick works to admiration. But Shaw happened to come tenth. Remember the hour; it was the eve of the eighties, when the arts joined the isms. And Carlyle begat Ruskin, and Ruskin begat Morris, and Morris begat Cunninghame-Graham, and the Carpenters, and the Cranes and the Salts: instead of velvet packets and a slap-dash joviality, young artists took to

sæva indignatio and sandals. It was really very interesting. Just why
poetry and proteids should suddenly seem natural affinities; just
what there was in the atmosphere to make Jaeger and Ibsen and
Esoteric Buddhism appear inevitable associates; and why to eat the
leek, loudly declaring it to be the only pure and blameless form of
food, should suddenly become the accepted sign of independence—
these profound problems have never yet been adequately explained,
for we are still doubtless too much involved in the traditions then
set on foot to get the full effect of this fearsome abnormality. But
though the origins were intricate, there was one plain and large
result—the arts went over with a rush to their traditional enemy.
They joined the majority. They made friends with the mob. Sculp-
tors, painters, and poets, for the first time in English history, deserted
the aristocrats and lined up with the proletariat. Instead of adoring
the graces they began denouncing disgraces. In place of priding
themselves on their immunity from the vulgar hobby known as politics, they began to boom and bleat like a lot of leading articles. And
they had a thoroughly enjoyable time. For the new game gratified
the vanity which is the curse of all their tribe by its flattering sense
of putting everybody right; and it satisfied the disrespectfulness
which is the chief of all their charms by giving them for target every
rule, religion, creed, convention which had lent its countenance to
civilization by forming part of it. They became infidels, atheists,
anarchists, cosmogonists, vegetarians, anti-vivisectionists, anti-vac-
cinationists. They revelled in a fresh field of topics—they founded
numberless societies to listen to their oratory and countless papers
that would print their verse and prose: it was canvas and model
combined. The big men liked the feeling of doing practical spade-
work at last; the little ones (and there seemed to be such a dreadful
lot of these) simply loved being ranked as "intellectuals." It gave
humble giants, like Morris, a chance to stoop and be chivalrous. It
hoisted the pigmies on to platforms where they could hector and
strut. It was fine.

Now this was all very well in the case of a Morris, who had already given us his *Guenevere;* and it probably couldn't much dam-
age even a Cunninghame-Graham—for he was a rebel in any case, a
Highland rieve by birth, and all these isms were to him simply so
many gauntlets which he could fling in the faces of the fat fools he
despised: when he charged the ranked policemen in Trafalgar
Square on Bloody Sunday, ostensibly in the cause of Democracy, he
was really only giving expression, I am sure, to his eternal contempt
for the *canaille;* he turned socialist because he was an aristocrat. But
in the case of a youngling like Shaw, a tender emotionalist fed
hitherto wholly on the sweet-stuff of opera and still viewing the

world in terms of Shelley and Wagner, it simply amounted to ravish-ment. It mean thrusting all his soft faculties into a premature mould; it meant emphasizing and petrifying and fixing for ever on his char-acter just those quaint qualities of contemptuousness and ingenuous disdain which in the ordinary way would just have been softly erased by experience once their first task of setting him producing was performed. It means that instead of prompting him to some piece of self-vindication, some earnest proof of individual worth and power, his boyish bumptiousness began straightway to boast in its own name and make an ambition of mere self-assertiveness.

For of course he was helpless. Face to face with such a force, what could a poor romantic do? He yielded at a touch—fell like a shot sea-bird—was culled like a slender wayside flower. With the echoes of the hammer-song still hammering in his head, he saw him-self as a Sigurd among Alberics—and since everywhere about him the old obvious evils spawned and sprawled, all the generous decen-cies of youth joined with its egotisms to make him vow to have a drive at London-Fafnir. "My destiny is to educate London," he as-sured himself solemnly; and set about the job without delay. He himself has described how the final vision descended and crystal-lized all his vague cravings. Perceive him flutteringly approach the fateful Webb. He has strayed into one of the meetings of the myriad societies of that day, a body calling itself (doubtless for some per-fectly adequate reason) the Zeletical Society—and this is the stirring sight he beheld:—

> The speaker was a young man, about twenty-one, with a profile that suggested, on account of the nose and imperial, an improvement on Napoleon the Third. He had a fine forehead, a long head, eyes that were built on top of two highly developed organs of speech (according to the phrenologists) and remarkably thick, strong, dark hair. He knew all about the subject of the debate; knew more than the lecturer; had read everything that had ever been written on the subject; and remem-bered all the facts that bore on it. He used notes, read them, ticked them off one by one, threw them away, and finished with a coolness and clearness that to me, in my trembling state, seemed miraculous. This young man was the ablest man in England—Sidney Webb.

And he was exactly Shaw's own age. The butterfly was caught. He too would be a dictator, an authority, a liberator, a dogmatic and precocious oracle. This was grand opera and literature and a noble knightliness combined—De Reszke, Ruskin, and Sigurd in one. He went at once into training. Nervous—unready—hypersensitive—naïve —with subtlety of apprehension and a consuming fondness for fine-ness the very first characteristics of all his faculties—he was prepos-

terously unfitted for the part; but (and this is specially interesting)
the very susceptibility that ought to have saved him made him as
wax to the suggestion—the very imagination which he ought to have
carried far away from platforms to some place where it could work
undisturbed now flushed the dreary planks with limelight—disguised
and garlanded the prospect—deluded him into seeing the cheap and
prosy game of demagoguing as the very embodiment of romance.
"I vowed I would join Webb's society, go every week, speak every
week, and become a speaker or perish in the attempt. And I carried
out this resolution. I suffered agonies no one suspected. During the
speech of the debate I resolved to follow my heart used to beat as
painfully as a recruit's going under fire for the first time. I could not
use my notes; when I looked at the paper in my hand I could not
collect myself enough to decipher a word. And of the four or five
wretched points which were my pretext for this ghastly practice of
mine I invariably forget three—the best three." Flaubert and Pater
undergoing flagellation in the hope of being granted purity of prose
underwent far less torment than did this equally fine artist to learn
the tricks of Cockney repartee:

> I attended the Hampstead Historic Club once a fortnight, and spent
> a night in the alternative weeks at a private circle of Economists. I made
> all my acquaintances think me madder than usual by the pertinacity
> with which I attended debating societies and haunted all sorts of hole-
> and-corner debates and public meetings and made speeches at them. I
> was President of the Local Government Board at "an amateur Parlia-
> ment"

—and he even turned the very novels that might have proved his
salvation (by giving his creative energy a path of escape) into
mimic debating societies too—not only rising up in the name of each
character in turn (Connolly, Lydia Carew, Cashel, Trefusis) to
deliver a short address on some selected topic, but actually turning as
many of the characters as possible into working models, draft sketches,
of that omniscient, imperturbable Sigurd-Shelley-Wagner-Webb
which he had resolved Bernard Shaw must become. "I am thoroughly
well-satisfied with myself," says Elinor McQuinch in *The Irrational
Knot.* "At last I have come out of a scene without having forgotten the
right thing to say." Connolly, in the same book, is "concentrated and
calm, making no tentative movements of any kind (even tying a white
tie did not puzzle him into fumbling), but acting with a certainty of
air, and consequent economy of force, dreadful to the irresolute."
These, it may be said, are simply self-reflections, involuntary mim-
ings of the artist in his picture. Looking back at Connolly now, when
Shaw has grown so like him, it is natural to regard him as an uncon-

scious copy of his maker. But it is Shaw who is the consequence, Connolly the cause. These novels of G.B.S.'s nonage were indeed mirrors held up to his nature—but only in order to help him fix his make-up. "He looked at his programme and calculated how soon his time to sing would come. Then he unrolled his music and placed two copies ready to his hand upon the table. Having made these arrangements with a self-possession that quite disconcerted the clergyman, he turned to examine the rest of the company." This is the curious projection of an ideal, not unwitting self-portraiture; and "you cannot want a thing and have it too." Modelling these little mannequins—studying their gestures—perfecting their effectiveness with his pen—putting them into predicaments to learn how to behave and continually calling on them for impromptu speeches— "There, by the Grace of God," mutters our young author savagely, "will one day go George Bernard Shaw." Fate, when she began to fool him, hadn't reckoned on this solemnity. The joke was already going rather far.

IV

It went further very shortly. The result of these efforts, heroically sustained (our Sigurd being meanwhile financially supported, it is ironic but right to recall, by a radiant Mimmy in the person of that romantic young mother to whom he owed the imagination he was thwarting), the result of these pig-headed efforts, this topsy-turvy idealism, was the construction of one of the most remarkable verbal weapons ever forged by a literary craftsman. It was an instrument built expressly for cut-and-thrust platform work; and every irrelevant qualification or charm was ruthlessly threshed out of its texture. Now to get rid of these alloys and yet maintain the thing's temper meant the invention of a whole new range of prose devices; and it is the way he worked at these, the devouring adroitness he showed, the fresh formations and annealings and interlockings of language which he resourcefully invented and perfected, that really give us our first absolutely infuriating idea of the triumphs he would have brought us, the work he might have done, if only he had never been drugged and trepanned and wastefully sold into eternal slavery whilst asleep. Much has been written in praise of his work; but of his workmanship, I always feel, far too little; never yet, at any rate, have I seen any adequate acknowledgment of the extraordinary perfection and technical importance of his style. "More stiletto than style!" someone murmurs, a bit sourly—but that is only the peevishness of pedantry. Shaw's prose can be used to carve creatively as well as to kill—and in other hands than his it surely will be; whatever else Shaw has done he has hung a glittering new and needed weapon in the armoury of the arts. Conditioned absolutely by the special character of the campaign he had in view—submitting to every limitation without shuffling, and taking advantage of every licence without shame—it is the very finest example in the whole range of English letters of prose written to be uttered with physical forcibleness on the rapid levels of man-to-man speech, and yet retaining, unsuspected, all those subtle powers of balance, of rhythm and picturesqueness, whose aid must be employed before all defences can be carried and which steal triumphantly into the citadel of the mind of the hearer through insidious emotional doorways whilst the colloquialisms keep the common sense engaged. Technically, that is certainly its supreme innovation—and that will always make it an essential part of the history of the development of our English prose. The hour of oratory was over; the peroration was punctured; purple passages, instead of being banners to kindle men's hearts, had become mere red rags to rouse restiveness: for mutinous democrats and fierce vegetarian-anarchists wanted utterances that hit and looked like lumps of steel. And the problem, briefly, was therefore how to appear to be using this blunt life-preserver sort of language without really relinquishing the air of the subtler devices which had hitherto been looked on as the sole prerogative of rhetoric.

Well, Shaw found a way. His hearers wanted straight talk: so he cast periods like horizontal bars. But they were bars that worked like piston-rods: all built for thrust and drive, they displayed the splendid beauty of clean speed; and so, at the very moment when they seemed to be contemptuously discarding all merely emotional adjuncts, they were actually dizzying the audience with that supremely unusual excitement, the intoxicating ecstasy of pace. Shaw stripped all his sentences of those trailing wreaths and ropes of metaphor which Ruskin, his predecessor in these paths of sensual socialism, had elaborately wound round his message—and then he multiplied still further the effect of impetuousness thus obtained by devoting all the energy that might have gone to making garlands to the task of fitting clause into clause with such ingenious sockets that never a joint could be seen, and a long sentence really made up of many added items lay when finished as level as a spear, streaking past as though launched with one lunge. It is extraordinarily interesting to watch this process being perfected: first of all the studious assemblage of the parts, then the gradual speeding-up of the machine.

Mr. Reginald Harrington Lind, at the outset of his career, had no object in life save that of getting through it as easily as possible; and this he understood so little how to achieve that he suffered himself to be married to a Lancashire cotton-spinner's heiress. She bore him three children, and then eloped with a professor of spiritualism, who deserted her on the eve of her fourth confinement, in the course of which she caught scarlet fever and died. Her child survived, but was sent to a baby farm and starved to death in the usual manner.

That is an early effort, from *The Irrational Knot*. Already, it will be seen, the desired effect of imperturbability is there, gained by that diligent maintenance of a monotone; and the crowded middle sentence does nearly take the listener's breath away by telescoping four travails, two tragedies, and a comic professor of spiritualism into a couple of level lines. But there are still a few defects: the jolts at the commas break the pace rather badly, and the sentences, though they are still comparatively short ones, are only kept continuously making each clause cannon the next instead of plunking past like a rifle-bullet straight from stop to stop. Months of practice and experiment, on paper by day and on platforms each night, taught him how to overcome these conditions. The sentence that follows was one written for an actual speech (and written, it is interesting to note, in that last home of the old school of rhetoric, William Morris's Manor House at Kelmscott), and the reader will see how perfectly the sense of precipitancy is secured to it by the simple device of dropping its successive items into the slots of a kind of eternally expanding carrier which branches forward from a single steady verb:—

One can see that the Local Government Board of the future will be a tremendous affair; that foreign States will be deeply affected by the reaction of English progress; that international trade, always the really dominant factor in foreign policy, will have to be reconsidered from a new point of view when profit comes to be calculated in terms of net social welfare instead of individual pecuniary gain; that our present system of imperial aggression, in which, under pretext of exploration and colonization, the flag follows the filibuster and trade follows the flag, with the missionary bringing up the rear, must collapse when the control of our military forces passes from the capitalist classes to the people; that the disappearance of a variety of classes with a variety of what are now ridiculously called "public opinions" will be accompanied by the welding of society into one class with a public opinion of inconceivable weight; that this public opinion will make it for the first time possible effectively to control the population; that the economic independence of women, and the supplanting of the head of the household by the individual as the recognized unit of the State, will materially alter the status of children and the utility of the institution of the family; and that the inevitable reconstitution of the State Church on a democratic basis may, for example, open up the possibility of the election of an avowed Free-thinker like Mr. John Morley or Mr. Bradlaugh to the deanery of Westminster.

It is nothing but a series of separate statements, but they are so socketed that the result is torrential: the sentence seems positively to go whipping through its supporting semicolons much as a telegraph wire does through the posts when you watch it racing past from a swift train. And additional practice still, the months stretching into years, enabled him to eliminate even slotted frames and posts: in the paragraph that follows, written at the height of his powers, those recurrent "thats" have been replaced by absolutely imperceptible piers, so that as the reader's mind is carried over it experiences a helpless vertigo—it clutches its guide giddily, yielding him a blank subjection, like the limp obedience paid a Blondin by the fellow on his back—a far completer surrender (at any rate till we touch solid ground again) than the reverence offered to a Fors-Clavigerating Ruskin:—

Therefore do not misunderstand my plain statement of the fundamental constitution of London society as an Irishman's reproach to your nation. From the day I first set foot on this foreign soil I knew the value of the prosaic qualities of which Irishmen teach Englishmen to be ashamed as well as I knew the vanity of the poetic qualities of which Englishmen teach Irishmen to be proud. For the Irishman instinctively disparages the quality which makes the Englishman dangerous to him; and the Englishman instinctively flatters the faults that make the Irishman harmless and amusing to him. What is wrong with the prosaic Englishman is what is wrong with the prosaic men of all countries: stupidity. The vitality which places nourishment and children first, heaven and hell a somewhat remote second, and the health of society as an organic whole nowhere, may muddle successfully through the comparatively tribal stages of gregariousness; but in nineteenth-century nations and twentieth-century empires the determination of every man to be rich at all costs and of every woman to be married at all costs must without a highly scientific social organization produce a ruinous development of poverty, celibacy, prostitution, infant mortality, adult degeneracy, and everything that wise men most dread. In short, there is no future for men, however brimming with crude vitality, who are neither intelligent nor politically educated enough to be Socialists. So do not misunderstand me in the other direction either: if I appreciate the vital qualities of the bee, I do not guarantee the Englishman against being, like the bee (or the Canaanite), smoked out and unloaded of his honey by beings inferior to himself in simple acquisitiveness, combativeness, and fecundity, but superior to him in imagination and cunning.

Lightened of all adjectives, nimble with nouns, turning categories into keyboards, he is wont to ripple us a run and, avoiding vowels in order to get the snap of consonants, it rattles past at a rate that makes the best of Swift seem slow, and pelts the brain with stinging drops like driving hail. It is deliberately cold and colourless, but it produces a kind of glow, an unusual warmth that almost melts the icy argument, almost turns it into something rich and wild. For rapidity, poignancy, unanimity, promptness, an exquisite timing and adjustment of its parts, there is no prose to be compared with it in English. And just as an athlete is more beautiful than an æsthete, so it grows more sensuous the more austere it becomes, positively practising a bodily seductiveness by seeming wholly to rely on an appeal to cold-blooded intelligence. It was very interesting, very curious virtuosity; with of course a fundamental justness in its paradox. For it was really Shaw's joyous sense of picturesqueness that made him pick this sour pose of acid reasonableness and sustain it with such zest; it was a vivid, romantic imagination that enabled him to perfect it, living into the part with all his power; and so it was therefore profoundly logical that the result should be a romantic reputation— a name for remorseless common sense that had the goblin quality of legend, prevailing on men and artists to regard his gift of lightning logic with an uneasy twilight reverence and awe.

v

Then why bewail its acquisition? In face of all these merits, why pity the manufacturer of this pitiless prose and propound this dark theory about his being the dupe of a decoy? There are reasons in plenty. Hitherto we have spoken of this instrument of expression as though it were something solid and separable—as a sword, which he forged; as a flute, which he played on; a detachable piece of his equipment. That is one of the weaknesses of rhetoric. It was actually his own mind that he put on the anvil and altered; it was his own larynx that he fitted with patent stops. The sword cut both ways, carving the hand that controlled it; the flute was a magic flute that filled the mind of the player with all the tunes that flowed through it, compelling his thoughts to move in step with its piping. The parallel-bars of his prose have seemed to us thus far a firm apparatus on which he could perform acrobatically. We have now to face the fact that they were the bars of a cage, and that Shaw had shut himself and his capers inside it.

And by this self-restriction something much more malignant is meant than the mere hemming-in of his mind with wrong subjects. It is true, indeed, that the man who trains himself to speak

> without notes, of Rent, Interest, Profit, Wages, Toryism, Liberalism, Socialism, Communism, Anarchism, Trade-Unionism, Co-operation, Democracy, the Division of Society into Classes, and the suitability of Human Nature to Systems of Just Distribution

is building up his views rather badly—too hastily leaving the principal sites of his brain to a rabble of reach-me-down tenants. But if there had been nothing worse than this, Shaw would have pulled through, after a check; he had creative energy enough to make even Interest interesting, and to convert Rents into a human reality; he would have ultimately humanized these ill-conditioned aliens much as a rich soil will regenerate and civilize a top-dressing of undesirable settlers. No, the fatal thing was not the type of topic he discussed; it was the attitude he struck whilst discussing. It induced a spiritual deformity, a perpetual kink which he will carry to his grave; you might say (I, at any rate, would have no right to reprove you) that it produced a condition of permanent hump. We have seen how he slaved to acquire a tone of icy arrogance. Well, once found, it fairly froze to his tongue. The æsthetic fashion of the hour favoured contempt, tirades, antagonisms, an omniscient school-mastering of creation. Instead of wearing it a moment and then tossing it aside, this man hugged it to him till it became a second skin.

And the reason for this rueful permanence, like all the primary causes in this amazing comedy of errors, only make the result the more perverse. For it was exactly Shaw's unsuitability for the rigid part of pedagogue that made him adopt the Dotheboys demeanour so exuberantly; it was exactly because he was an artist, wholly governed and swayed by the artist's deep, controlling sense of consistency of form, that he refused to relinquish his rôle of bitterness and rancour and persisted in displays of conscious bad form. A weaker artist would have suffered less: our Cranes soon ceased their clamour, our Carpenters turned craftsmen, working happily at a bench instead of irascibly endeavouring to occupy one. All the genuine born propagandists too, on the other hand, changed their manner quite cheerily; the Salts of the earth, after acting as irritants for a time, sociably subsided later on into agreeable condiments—as Secretaries to the Humane Society, and so on.

But Shaw is utterly incapable of this carnalness. He is overwhelmingly consumed by the poet's passion for unity and symmetry. He feels forced to adhere to all the attitudes of his salad-days—down even to

their devotion to salad; he is incapable of confessing sunnily that those
early passions for rolled oats were really only another of youth's
ways of sowing wild ones. That accusation of capriciousness so often
brought against him—how heartily one wishes it were true! He lacks
the courage to abandon his Convictions. Like his own Sergius, he
"never withdraws." He may advance—that is another thing; but,
even so, he always carries his old opinions carefully with him, no
matter what the extravagant cost of carriage, ingeniously persuading himself, and us, as he does so, how absolutely essential they are
to his equipment. He somewhere reminds us that we all die once
each eight years—but in his own case the estate is strictly entailed;
he takes these intimate ancestors of his with the most tremendous
seriousness; he would sooner die than repudiate their pledges; and
many of his apparently wildest and least forgivable extravagances
have been simply due to his proud attempt to fulfil these contracts.
There is perhaps a kind of cowardice here—but what I do want us to
realize is that it is the cowardice that comes from an artist's horror
of the disgracefulness of making or drawing a false stroke. Shaw
wouldn't a bit mind giving himself away; what he cannot bear is the
thought that he has involuntarily done so. It would seem so very
careless. Taking life with the triple seriousness of Art, of Ireland,
and of Youth, the idea of having wasted a drop of it would anguish
him; and almost all his irresponsibilities have been the result of this
terrifying sense of personal responsibility. It is this, for example,
and not freakishness, that makes him dwell so disproportionately on
apparent trivialities of dress and diet—on his way of eating and
drinking, of spelling "cigarets" and not smoking them; and when
he rages so fantastically over our refusal to agree, he is in reality just
beating back desperately any private qualms as to his rightness,
frantically justifying himself to himself. It is the same boyish fear
that sets him eternally chattering explanations. He is often not so
much trying to discover the truth as to find some further proof that
he has told it. When he buttonholes us so officiously outside his
own plays—prefacing, promising, assuring—for all the world like a
Showman blarneying desperately away outside his booth before he
dares let us in—he is really not so much trying to humbug *us* with
his harangues as to reassure and satisfy himself. He uses all the
vigour of his imagination to hypnotize that vigour; his wit never displays a more wonderful nimbleness than when trying to reconcile
his own sallies. He will found a philosophy to escape admitting a
jest was idle,[1] and then write a play to prove the philosophy humanly

[1] See, for example, the solemn Note at the end of *Cæsar and Cleopatra*, where
Mr. Shaw desperately improvises a solemn theory about the Influence of Climate
Upon Character and the Comparative Unimportance of Racial Influx, in order to

true,[2] and then extend the philosophy to include clauses which declare a dramatist's characters are free and independent personalities, quite uncontrolled by the conscious will of their creator, and that he himself is a dramatist in that sense.[3] In brief, he is the kind of man who, rather than admit, even to himself, that he has got into a hole, would remorselessly chip corners off his own character till it fitted, no matter what the mutilation cost him.

And this, and even worse than this, is precisely the horrible practice we are now to see him engaged in. Worse, because his thrawn thoroughness, the artist's instinct perverted, made him mangle and carve his conception of the whole of the rest of mankind in order to make it fit into his own forced malformities. His instinct for harmony made him insist that disharmony was an essential condition of health. "In this world," he declared, "if you do not say a thing in an irritating way, you might just as well not say it at all, since nobody will trouble themselves about anything that does not trouble them." "The fact is," he said again, "there is nothing the public despises so much as an attempt to please it. Torment is its natural element: it is only the saint who has any capacity for happiness."

He actually persuaded himself that it is necessary to hurt in order heal; that the only way to encourage men is to discourage them, and that it is necessary to be thoroughly disagreeable in order to persuade them to agree. Simply to save himself from the agony of admitting to himself that his early attitude and insolences had been largely just juvenile egregiousness, he determined to agonize the rest of the world. He began a campaign of universal irritation, repeating feverishly, like a missionary muttering godless prayers, that taunts and intolerance were logically much the best of all methods of preaching and spreading the gospel of The Brotherhood of Man.

And of course it couldn't end with that absurdity. The disguise had to get deeper, his voice had to rise louder in order to deafen his own ears. Other arguments had to radiate, flung out to balance and support the first: once his creative energy got working in this acci-

[2] See *John Bull's Other Island*, where that impromptu Britannus theory about the Influence of Climate Upon, etc., is dragged out again in order to be propped up, exhumed in order to be properly animated.

[3] See Preface to *Man and Superman,* p. xvii; Preface to *John Bull's Other Island,* p vii; and other amendments innumerable.

persuade himself that the pantomime fooling with Britannus is a piece of penetrating historical portraiture and a subtle psychological study. The gravely reproduced portraits of Cæsar and General Burgoyne in the same volume and the solemn resurrection of a contemporary print of the Pharos of Alexandria are analogous devices for cunningly satisfying his conscience that he has been spending his powers on work of an adequate dignity. One sometimes feels Mr. Shaw must have less humour than levity—the latter seems so often to outrun the first.

dental twig it shot out branches till it burst into a self-supporting tree, seeking a satisfying symmetry. The first corollary that ran out, to act as stay and flying buttress, and subsequently to become a parent stem of its own (so that it now sometimes seems the central pillar of them all, the very tent-pole of his patent storm-proof creed), was the formula that all men's miseries are the result of the discrepancy between the sentimental version of life fed into most of us and life as it actually is, and that to hack away these sweetnesses and cauterize the wounds, to kill what he (wrongly) called "the romantic convention" with the cruellest acid and steel he could find, was therefore hero's work, hygienic work, a harsh but holy warfare, a completion of the surgery begun by old Cervantes. Now there *was* some of the sap of human truth in this at least—it did touch actual earth: it is a diagnosis, indeed, that we can find an instant use for, here and now, for doesn't it form the perfect definition of the source of all Shaw's own disasters? It is because he sentimentally sees himself as a satirist and harsh realist, instead of harshly realizing he is actually a romantic, that he has gone so hopelessly astray; it is because he sees himself as a Cervantes when he is really a Don Quixote (down even to his personal appearance, by the way: G.B.S. and G.K.C.—the Knight and Sancho, irresistibly; and down even to the famous misadventure with the dolls—for Shaw's chief mistake about the theatre, as we will see, is his solemn attribution to the marionettes he found there of powers they never have possessed) that he has suffered the Don's own doom. But the vitality in this principle, ironically enough, only served to sustain him while he unconsciously provided a perfect demonstration of its fatal action; and if a sudden, shivering sense of its personal aptness did ever assail his subconsciousness, it simply hurried him on with the task of planting, on the other side, as a stout protection against any lurking fatuousness, the famous pair of reciprocating twin hypotheses—the hypotheses of the Artist-Philosopher and the Superman.

The urgent necessity for these will be recognized. The theory of the Superman was essentially nothing but a defence of platform-dogmatism; to bully and brow-beat in the name of *Egalité, Fraternité* was decently impossible without some such extension of the synthesis; and to the aid of the announcement that "no one having any practical experience of Proletarian Democracy has any belief in its capacity for solving great political problems or even for doing ordinary parochial work intelligently," there came that fine suggestion of the Life-force working up and up, through speechless monsters, and stupid, stuttering minor men, seeking for a brain that could express it, till at length, through the intellect of the Artist-Philosopher (another name for Sigurd-Ruskin-De Reszke) it achieved articulation, became conscious of its own desires, and delivered its commands and warnings brusquely to the unemerged remainder of its carcase:

> The mysterious thing we call life organizes itself into all living shapes, bird, beast, beetle, and fish, rising to the human marvel in cunning dwarfs and in laborious muscular giants, capable, these last, of enduring toil, willing to buy love and life, not with suicidal curses and renunciations, but with patient manual drudgery in the service of higher powers. And these higher powers are called into existence by the same self-organization of life still more wonderfully into rare persons who may by comparison be called gods, creatures capable of thought, whose aims extend far beyond the satisfaction of their bodily appetites and personal affections, since they perceive it is only by the establishment of a social order founded on the common bonds of moral faith that the world can rise from mere savagery.[4]

"Men of genius are the men selected by Nature to carry on the work of building up an intellectual consciousness of her own instinctive purpose." "The great man incarnates the philosophic consciousness of life." "All his treatises and poems and scriptures are the struggle of Life to become divinely conscious of itself instead of stumbling blindly hither and thither in the line of least resistance." This Life-force says:

> I have done a thousand wonderful things unconsciously by merely willing to live and following the line of least resistance: now I want to know myself and my destination and choose my path; so I have made a special brain, a philosopher's brain, to grasp this knowledge for me. "And this," says the Life-force to the philosopher, "must thou strive to do for me until thou diest, when I will make another brain and another philosopher to carry on the work."[5]

So were arrogance justified and self-suspicion stilled: our infatuated Don Quixote has a Dulcinea now—this stringy, sterile German spinster of a Life-force; and rides on solemnly enchanted. No lifting his hallucination now! "Metaphysic" is only "metaphor" spelt in four syllables; never yet was there a poet could resist one. Watch, now, how his conception forthwith clings and spreads—dilating organically, expanding spontaneously, exhibiting all the signs of true vitality, as all conceptions do, even the most damnatory, if ever they get a purchase in an artist's generative consciousness, and suck at his divine but undiscriminating vigour. Dogma dovetails into dogma; pedant theories flower as plays; these scatter seeds that

[4] *The Perfect Wagnerite.*
[5] *Man and Superman.*

shoot up fresher saplings to support and screen the skinny parent crook. Thus, the Superman plainly needing some solid social backing if he were going to keep the Artist-Philosopher on his feet, there spontaneously sprang to support him the now familiar Shavian doctrine (so soon, alas, to grow sadly shop-soiled) declaring the healthiness of wealthiness and the heavenliness of worldliness and the crime of being crushed.[6] This in turn disclosing dangers (*we* know the hands it played into—the greasy souls it fed with self-approval), up rose a fresh law to protect it—the law asserting that there is a safe Saturation-point to Human Sensuousness, that self-restraint follows indulgence, and licence observes limits, and "the road of excess leads to the palace of wisdom." And when this too wavered dubiously (for what of our rakes in their muck?—and aren't there indulgences that go on without deepening—blisses that keep step with life cunningly, feeding on it craftily, careful to keep their prey in condition?—and aren't there satisfactions that dim the mind to soothe the body?)—when this, in turn, tottered, a last convulsive inspiration, the impulse of self-preservation hard at work, made it shoot out a further branch that caught and clung round a formula that made G.K. Sancho think Shaw an ascetic, that by a lucky loop led right back to the parent stem—the formula, namely, that men don't like happiness, that bliss only bores them[7]—thus perfectly completing the sinister circle by backing up the first defence of offensiveness, filially feeding into and fortifying the falsity by which it was primarily fed.

Oh yes, it was neat; and none the less because it turned its very neatness to account by declaring clear thinking the supreme effort of the Life-force. But those who know that the clearness of a system is a proof of incompleteness, that definition is only gained by blurring truth, mustn't allow their possession of that knowledge to prevent them from perceiving the passion and glow that lie beneath these cold, clipped, charmless, lucid leaves. For to do that is to miss the real cause of the coldness, and to make the miserable, fashionable, unforgivable mistake of seeing Shaw as a mere marvellous mental machine. The thing to remember is the central tap-root of this rigid tree of thought—that accursed grafted crab of studied sourness. It is that which diverts the good juices and chills them with gall, embittering the ultimate fruit; it is that initial, unnatural

---

[6] "The universal regard for money is the one hopeful fact in our civilization, the one sound spot in our social conscience." "The greatest of evils and the worst of crimes is poverty; our first duty, a duty to which every other consideration should be sacrificed, is not to be poor."

[7] "Nobody wants bliss particularly or could stand more than a very brief taste of it, if it were attainable." "The pursuit of happiness is the most miserable of human occupations."

theory of the virtue of venom (as though a serpent's wisdom were communicated by its fangs!) that has governed the whole habit of the growth. It makes its pity appear pitiless, it curdles its kindliness, it forces the chivalry to emerge as contempt. The exasperating thing about all Shaw's utterances isn't their surface savagery or cynicism; it is the sight of the sweet sap being choked and changed behind; cut through the metallic coating that covers all his leaves with that glib, repellent, acrid shine, and you get generosity, wonder, wistfulness, awe, any amount of lovableness and love. His heart is in the right place; it is only his tongue that has gone wrong; it has taken a permanent twist into his cheek. When he tries to preach gentleness, it turns the words into jeers; it makes him malevolent in the cause of mercy, quarrelsome in the name of peace; and when he strives to shout friendly advice this interpreter, tutored too well, changes the message into a cold snarl of disdain. He sits down to write a play (called *Widowers' Houses*) pleading the cause of the oppressed; and the result makes the whole world howl him down as heartless and inhuman. He writes another (*Major Barbara*) to demonstrate "the central truth of Christianity—the vanity of revenge and punishment," and his hearers shiver at the sight of its ferocity. When he tries to stop the practice of cutting up live animals he can only do so by rending the character of doctors. He believes that "every man is a temple of the Holy Ghost" and promptly calls us "shirks, duffers, malingerers, weaklings, cowards." All his announcements are denouncements; he must attack to defend, his affirmations reach our ears as denials, all his most positive utterances seem harsh strings of no's.

And observe that always, like a prisoner tightening his knots by struggling, the curbed creativeness within him increases these grimaces, the cordial energy straining and jerking at the mask till it becomes a very nightmare of menace. For the choked delight in music and gaiety, in rhapsody and heartiness, bubbling up where it can, spends itself on ecstasies of insolence, wild arias of acrimony, arpeggios of contumely and spleen. For instance:

> . . . the physician is still the credulous impostor and petulant scientific coxcomb whom Molière ridiculed; the schoolmaster remains at best a pedantic child-farmer and at worst a flagellomaniac; the philanthropist is still a parasite on misery as the doctor is on disease; the miracles of priestcraft are none the less fraudulent and mischievous because they are now called scientific experiments and conducted by professors; we shake our heads at the dirt of the Middle Ages in cities made grimy with soot and foul and disgusting with shameless tobacco-smoking; public health authorities deliberately go through incantations with burning sulphur (which they know to be useless) because the people believe in

it as devoutly as the Italian peasant believes in the liquefaction of the
blood of St. Januarius; and straight-forward public lying has reached
gigantic developments, there being nothing to choose in this respect
between the pickpocket at the police-station and the minister on the
Treasury bench, the editor in the newspaper office, the City magnate
advertising bicycle tyres that do not side-slip, the clergyman subscribing
the Thirty-nine Articles, and the vivisector who pledges his knightly
honour that no animal operated on in the physiological laboratory suffers
the slightest pain. Cowardice is universal: patriotism, public opinion,
parental duty, discipline, religion, morality, are only fine names for
intimidation, and cruelty, gluttony, and credulity keep cowardice in
countenance. We cut the throat of a calf and hang it up by the heels to
bleed to death so that our veal cutlet may be white; we nail geese to a
board and cram them with food because we like the taste of liver disease;
we tear birds to pieces to decorate women's hats; we mutilate domestic
animals for no reason at all except to follow an instinctively cruel fashion;
and we connive at the most abominable tortures in the hope of discovering some magical cure for our own diseases by them.

Some people call that courage; it is really self-indulgence. It is
poetry perverted, imagination amok, a pure love of harmony, gaiety,
sufficiency, intoxicated by the rush of recitative and simply carried
away out of joyfulness into a rising crescendo of wrath. Stifle a
virtue and you always get a vice—and outbursts like these are simply the revenges taken by his temperament for being thwarted. And,
regarded as revenges, their success is profound—for they utterly ruin
the cause for which the sacrifice was made. No doubt at all about
that. Exactly as in Ruskin's case, the piston-rod rhetoric sinks the
ship it was invented to drive; the imaginations of both these men,
turned into wrong channels, ruined the cases they were kidnapped
to plead. Shavian rhapsodies like that either produce patronizing
titters, as at the newest caper of our mountebank; or else an irritation that ends in opposition. Whilst poor humanity's humblest answer to such trouncings and tirades would after all be by far the
most crushing: "You say I am a duffer, a weakling, a coward? My
kindheartedness merely cowardice, my morals a mush, my honour a
pitiable sham? Very well. You are wiser than I am; are indeed (if I
take you aright) the very Universe become articulate and aware; I
am therefore bound to believe what you say. Only, if these are my
qualities, then they must also be your keyboard. It is upon them you
must play in order to alter and guide me. Deftly adapting your message to my stupidity and cowardice, you will tactfully teach me the
truth. Yet—you don't do this. I misunderstand you completely—you
say so yourself. But to me, in my darkness, that seems simply a proof

that—you must have misunderstood me. You say you see all my weaknesses; I appoint you my teacher; five minutes later you start flogging me like a positive Squeers for my failure to comprehend your remarks. It doesn't seem in keeping. Either there is something wrong with your voice, which you cannot possibly help; or there is something wrong with your estimate of my hearing. In either case— who is to be blamed? I feel there must be something wrong with your credentials. Perhaps your voice is not the voice of the Universe after all. Or perhaps you are not a very good judge of other people's hearing. Myself, I favour both views. I don't fancy a Universe talking falsetto; and I don't think you are a good judge, not a particularly good judge of other people. These thoughts are meant kindly to you. A blind leader of the blind will probably bring about disaster— but at least he will consider his poor companion's shortcomings. How much wickeder, wastefuller, more shameful and ludicrous, would be the case of the clear-sighted leader who broke his client's neck because he couldn't be bothered to remember his afflictions. Good-day, Mr. Shaw. Here's your fee. We part friends." So, in his humble way, says Everyman.

And his complaint brings up naturally to the culminating scene in our Comedy. We are now going to contemplate Mr. Shaw being compelled to proclaim and believe himself a dramatist, and, at the same time, by the self-same power and process, being carefully un-fitted for the rôle.

PART II

I

The first half of this epitome, the way Shaw's early pose of rebel insolence placed him on a track which propelled him implacably toward play-writing, is easily traced by simply jotting down some dates. Recapitulate rapidly the early facts of his life in a straight-forward string, and you see chronology creeping up to this crisis. In 1876, twenty years old, he crosses from Ireland to London, knowing more and thinking more of pictures and music than of anything else in the world. A couple years later, entirely by accident, he hears a certain young Sidney Webb (exactly his own age) laying down the laws of life to an audience of awe-stricken adults; and resolves to become a platform speaker too. In pursuit of this fell purpose he permeates all the societies for scolding Society which were a feature of the London of that time, and by 1882 he has so out-woven Webb, has caught the trick of all-around truculence so perfectly, that even the most hardened and ferocious food-reformer, dress-reformer, land-reformer, reformer-reformer, *et hoc genus omne,* will blench at

the mention of his name. And in 1885, at the age of twenty-nine
(perhaps feeling that this fearless independence had depended on
his mother long enough), he is looking out for some settled job in
journalism.

Now, what would you expect to happen? Naturally, he was made
a musical critic. "I have never had a programme," he once said, "I
simply took the job that was given me and did it the best way I
could"; but in those days of alert editors a man who knew more
about pictures and music than anything else in the world, and who
had learned to express himself imperiously, was journalistically a
dedicated soul. He became art critic to *The World* in 1885, musical
critic to the *Star* in 1888, and in 1895, following the course of nature,
he was unhitched from the *Star* by Mr. Frank Harris and installed as
dramatic critic to *The Saturday*.

The inevitability of all that is as evident as $2 \times 2 = 4$. What happens next has the same infernal neatness. It was a perfect repetition
of his earlier innocent display among the societies and Socialists. He
had taken rebelliousness more seriously than the rebels themselves,
and played the part with an overpowering completeness. He now
idolized the theatre in the same impulsive way, and was once more
taken in by his own eloquence. For Shaw's besetting weakness is a
certain stubborn pride of soul which cannot permit him to admit,
even in a whisper to himself, that the cause he is engaged in is not
crucial; and he now reacted exactly as such a character could be
counted on to react, with results distinctly startling to the stage. For
no sooner had Mr. Harris seen him settled in his stall than he sprang
up declaring it a choir-stall in a cathedral. "The theatre," said he, "is
a place where two or three are gathered together, with an apostolic
succession as serious and as continuously inspired as that younger
institution, the apostolic succession of the Christian Church." "The
theatre," he said, "is as important as the Church was in the Middle
Ages, and much more important than the Church in London now."
It is "a factory of thought, a prompter of conscience, an elucidator
of conduct, an armoury against despair and dullness, and a temple
of the Ascent of Man." Its plays were "identical with a church service as a combination of artistic ritual, profession of faith and sermon"; and its players, to their own immense embarrassment, were
hailed as "hierophants of a cult as eternal and sacred as any professed religion in the world." Our Don Quixote, dear romantic, was
discomfiting the marionettes by taking them with unintended seriousness.

The completion of the operation will be plain. Mr. Shaw may
never persuade us that the theatre exerts a power equal to that
which established Inquisitions, and curdled Europe into Crusades,

and shot the great frozen fountains of Chartres and Rouen into mid-sky; but he quickly persuaded himself. Just as his first infatuation made his pride produce a theory which put the case for contentious-ness so confoundedly convincingly that it enthusiastically endeared to him an attitude it was only intended to excuse, so now his heated declarations of the supreme importance of the drama burgeoned out into corollaries so credible that he had to believe in them himself. He became convinced that Drama was the thing best worth doing. It was therefore the work worthiest of his powers. He was already middle-aged—but no matter. In 1898 he stole away from his mere stall. Before the end of the year he was known to the world as the author of *Plays Pleasant and Unpleasant.*

II

Nothing, then, could be clearer than that Mr. Shaw became a dramatist—not as a result of predilection—but simply because he was propelled into the part by circumstances. Once one realizes that, one also sees the huge unlikelihood of him turning out the born dram-atist he claimed to be; and, indeed, it could easily be shown that even his power "of conjuring up imaginary people in imaginary places and finding pretexts for theatrical scenes between them" (on which he plumes himself in the Preface to *Plays Pleasant*) is much more the novelist's dramatic knack than the playwright's, that his mere sense of the physically dramatic, taking that alone, is far from being the true sense of the theatre. But these initial, native deficien-cies wouldn't have mattered so much if it hadn't been for that other element; the grim fact that the very circumstances which had made him dramatist had simultaneously robbed him of his best right to be one. Be one, that is to say, in his own high sense of it—a maker of works of art depicting the daily life of the world, phials filled with essence of actuality. A man of his wit and force couldn't, of course, fail to contrive stage-pieces with a good deal more pith and picturesqueness about them than the majority of plays turned out by the class of brains the stage deserves; but anything bigger, any-thing adequate to his own definition, he had already forfeited the faculty to produce. He was trebly disqualified—and the first of these three handicaps stares out at us so brazenly from the record of his life that the wonder is it never warned him off; so plain is it indeed that it has visibly stamped itself into the framework of his house, making an ominous writing on the walls of his home. *"They say. What say they? Let them say."* These are the words (his biographer tells us) that Mr. Shaw has had carved above the fire-place in his study. They are sufficiently significant. Admirable enough as the motto of a callow rebel, the old contemptuous Border battle-cry amounts to a surrender of his sword when heard on the lips of a dramatist. For, being interpreted, it really means that "I, the under-seated, owner of this hygienic hearth, boast a deliberate lack of that imaginative sympathy which is the chief credential of the interpreter of character." And by sympathy, in this sense, one does not mean a slobbering pity; for pity can be as partial as contempt. By imagina-tive sympathy one simply means the jolly power of watching, with a chuckling absorption and delight, the doings of every sort and size of people; and of this happy gift, if ever he had it, Shaw by now had been wholly dispossessed. Sympathy is something hardly to be discerned in a man who has deliberately made disdain a working principle; who has learned to study human nature in the spirit of an opponent; and whose idea of "a generous passion" has become a "passion of hatred" for all the "accursed middle-class institutions that have starved, thwarted, misled and corrupted us from our cradles." *Tout comprendre, c'est tout pardonner:* you cannot cut your enemy and know him too. That is a sort of vivisection that *is* fruitless. And Shaw really admitted his own incapacity for play-writing when he affirmed that the average audience was a set of soapy stupids, "part of them nine-tenths chapelgoers by tempera-ment, and the remainder ten-tenths blackguards." For the stage at its best is only a mirror held up before the face of the watching house. The big play is composed of little players; it must compre-hend them even when they don't comprehend it.

That, then, is the first of Mr. Shaw's three acquired deficiencies; his socialism has made him unsociable: his confirmed habit of wiping somebody out, which he formed among the Fabians because it was so effective there, becomes here a disastrous obliteration of his model; he is like an archer (not William, though!) who has set up a target with care and then discovered it has used up all the wood meant for arrows. And now, on the top of it, driving it in further, comes acquired defect number two—one that limits still further his already narrowed range of subjects, and one that is all the more mischievous because it is masked by a quality that may have done much at the outset to convince him that drama was his line. All Shaw's early efforts as a writer were given, as we have seen, to the task of forming a medium of expression apt for physical utterance— a type of diction he could debate with and dictate with dog-matically, dealing it out from his hustings or stabbing it into his so-cieties in successive sentences as pat and purposeful as neatly planted blows. Now, that meant good dialogue; and so, long before he had ever dreamt of turning dramatist, he had perfectly acquired the great trick which so many playwrights never do learn: the art of making all his words fit live lips and leap alertly off the tongue, as slick and natural as slang, fresh with the colours of actual intercourse. But whilst his platform-work thus taught him the acoustics of the stage and how to make his characters talk like human beings, it also confirmed him in a foible which reacted on those characters to make them human beings of one particular kind. For the essence of his own speeches had been their slitting, pelting salience: it had been his work to resolve the old vague rumblings of oratory into a rattle of definite drops—and nothing, he found, sped a period so well as a core of cute meaning, self-contained. With the result that a crisp statement soon became essential to his sentences: he could no more begin to write one without an assertion to maintain it than a cabby could go a drive without a fare.

But though this confirmed inability to ask a question, or to suggest, or appeal, or submit, or discriminate, or qualify, or use art as a means of evocation, summoning a wisdom deeper than the artist knew he controlled—although this limitation was an immense asset on a platform, it obviously became a fatal barrier to completeness when the habitual asserter set to work to write a play. For it meant that the stage-door of his theatre had to be shut in the faces of a throng of very necessary characters; all the dim folk and foggy folk, the puzzled and perturbed, the groping, hoping, helpless, humble, unassertive humans, who act by instinct instead of by reason and whose deeds speak so much more clearly than their words —all these he was compelled to turn away. He couldn't employ them, for he couldn't equip them with a part. His sympathies, we have seen, were already limited——but even if he were filled with a positive affection for such characters he couldn't take them on—no, not even to take them off; for although he understood them they did not understand themselves; and for people who don't know their own minds and can't communicate the knowledge clearly, Shaw has no form of speech that will do. He can write none but definite dialogue; and definite dialogue entails definite minds; and the result is that all the members of his cast seem members of one exclusive caste. *A specimen of the sensible, highly educated young Englishwoman; prompt, strong, confident, self-possessed. . . . A man of cool temperament and low but clear and keen intelligence, with the imperturbability of the accurate calculator who has no illusions. . . . A vigorous, genial, popular man of forty with a sound voice which he uses with the clean athletic articulation of the practised orator. . . . A dignified man, a born chairman of directors. . . . A strong man, with a watchful face. . . .* Pass them in parade, from Vivie Warren to Andrew Undershaft, and you find they have all had to be endowed

with this rare faculty—a power of quick, precise, and ruthless calculation and self-confidence, the necessary adjunct to the way they'll
have to speak. Each has a ready point of view, bright and finished
as a rapier; and the drama has to resolve itself into the ring and
rattle of these weapons, the multiplex duel we get when they all
unsheathe their points and prettily proceed to cross opinions. What
fun it is, how exciting it can be, we all, to our happiness, well know.
But we have to admit that the mirror misses much. It is odd to reflect that his democracy is the cause of this exclusiveness.

III

Yet if these are serious handicaps I fear the third is even heavier.
It was bad enough to be compelled to insist on his *dramatis personæ* all coming clearly provided with opinions; but what was
worse was the fact that the exigencies of platform work had compelled him to add a pack of neat opinions to his own equipment,
and that his haste and his innocence and the highly peculiar circle
of his friends made the pack in many ways a faked one. *"To be set
too early,"* says Meredith, somewhere, *"is to take the work out of
the hands of the Sculptor who fashions men. A character that does
not wait for circumstances to shape it is of less worth in the race that
must be run."* Well, Shaw set too soon. The pressure of those early
days of gleeful mutiny, the need for being dogmatic, precipitated
his young ideas in a premature philosophy, to which ever since he
has clung; and at the same time the material out of which he had to
get his ideas, the personal experience he turned into opinions, were
quite unfairly lopsided, incomplete, artificial. The idiosyncrasy of
his troupe he might to some extent have counterbalanced by picking
their points of view with care and then arranging these so that they
partly reproduced the pattern and poise of reality; but such ingenuity availed nothing whatever against the bias of his own point
of view. He might (and he did) arrange his rapiers like spokes to
look like a mimic Wheel of Life; but to no purpose, for the hub was
out of truth. And it was out of truth because, quite literally, what
he had taken as his centre was really eccentric, and what he had accepted in his innocence as a genuine axle was actually only a crank.

For remember, once more, where he was when he formed his
views: remember the New Woman and *The Woman Who Did,* and
the Ibsen Society and rational dress, and the general dank, indoor,
stuffy, insincere atmosphere of devotees and defiance in which he
formed his first impressions and made one. It was suburban in the
worst sense—under the Town, shut in and overshadowed by its mass.

"I am a typical Irishman," he once said, "my family came from York-shire." Actually, he is a typical Cockney: he came from the country before he had learned that Middlesex wasn't the middle; and what he ought to have said was: "I am a true Metropolitan: my views are so very provincial." Shut up in one pigeon-hole, he felt he was sur-veying the whole room; he took it for granted that the highly spe-cialized existence he shared was a fair sample of reality: he got his ideas of human society from the members of his societies; and in-nocently accepted the New Woman as woman. He knew nothing of the working North, nothing of pastoral England, nothing even of the genuine suburbs or the actual provinces, or the places where life does expand with some serenity, repeating its comeliest delights. Morris had had Kelmscott to use as a base, his grey manor with its immemorial beauties was his hub; and when he looked out from it he realized that Shaw's little London was a mere dirty splash on one of the spokes. But though Shaw took a Hertfordshire house many years later, and though a healthy Hibernian longing for the open has no doubt always been mixed with his motives, yet he never let that longing take him to his true kingdom; and his work has been far more a product of indoor dilettantism than that of Mr. Henry James. For Mr. James has travelled tirelessly, shedding old shib-boleths and learning the non-existence of horizons; whereas Shaw has always remained complacently satisfied that his early contact with life was remarkably complete. He is constantly pluming himself on the breadth of his experience: "Like a greengrocer and unlike a minor poet, I have lived instead of dreaming and feeding myself with artistic confectionery." "Three times every week I could escape from artistic and literary stuff and talk seriously on serious subjects with serious people. *For this reason—because I persisted in Socialist propaganda—I never once lost touch with the real world.*" So does he point proudly to the bars of his prison and boast of how they keep reality before him. He honestly believed that a brisk debate with Mr. Belfort Bax brought him very near to the simple heart of human nature. He felt that he understood the democracy because he knew so many democrats.

It was as a Fabian meeting multiplied, then, that Shaw first be-held the race of man; and his views of life were largely formed to fit this fascinating vision. Let me give one example of the way he gen-eralized, of the way he accepted a suburban experience as a sym-bolical episode and framed a law on the strength of it which he promptly applied to the rest of creation. Let it be his theory of the relation of the sexes—of woman as the huntress and man as the prey. It reappears constantly, for it is one of the several steelyard rules which he can handle easier than golden ones; but its first appearance is in *The Philanderer*. Now we have the assurance of Mr. Shaw's biographer that *The Philanderer* exhibits an attitude towards women induced in Shaw by "unpleasant personal relations with women prior to the time at which the play was written. . . . The first act is a more or less accurate replica of a scene in Mr. Shaw's own life." There you have it! The core of *Man and Superman* is simply a twisted point of view manufactured out of the shoddy and unreliable material circumstances brought him when he had to take what he got to make opinions. Not all the adroitness in Ireland could overcome that initial drawback. He may declare that "Ann is Everywoman" as loudly as he will, and swear that her demonstration, that the initiative in sex transactions remains with women, is a piece of pure impartial drama, the result of "a creative process over which I have no control." We know better. Falsified from the commencement, the piece had to be a fantasy. It is one of the most delightful variety entertainments ever witnessed on the stage, but it holds no mirror up to life. What it reflects is an impatient youth of genius being impeded by a pack of spinsters who can't spin, the female intellectuals peculiar to a little patch of London (and a patch which has by now been ploughed and broken), and deciding that his predicament must be typical of Everyman's, that he has discovered a Universal Law which nobody before him has had the honesty to announce. . . .

IV

Then his plays are an imposture? Pardon me, I never said so: what I say indeed is that he has acted with perfect sincerity, that all the errors in the result must be attributed to our time. It is because they are not a fair indictment that they do become a grave one. But then, on the other hand, it is when we realize their vices that we discover his true virtues. For the fine thing is this—and this the only use of critics' efforts—that once the limitations of the plays are realized they cease to possess any; once you see that Shaw has done the best he could for us under the circumstances, then his effort is seen in relation to those circumstances and its errors instinctively allowed for. Recognize that a passion for purity, gentleness, truth, justice, and beauty is the force at the base of all his teaching, and you will find his message one of the most tonic of our time. Realize further how he has limited himself by the philosophy he has expounded, and you will escape all danger of being hurt by its deficiencies. And instead of the irritation, the bewilderment, or (what was worse) the priggish complacency with which you regarded them, you find yourself turning to them with sympathy, with comradeship and eager friendliness, able to use all their strong medicine without being embittered by the taste. It is only when you regard them, in short (and this is the summary of the whole irony), it is only when you regard them with the very sympathy they doggedly deride that you receive the help which they hunger to offer.

PHILIP LITTELL

1917

The Bondage of Shaw

Just as Synge makes the ordinary run of contemporary plays sound poor in speech, as Chekhov makes them look too tidily arranged, as Hauptmann shows up their author's failure to compose them with anything deeper than ingenuity, so Shaw makes them appear unintelligent, the work of specialists in theatricals, of men without ideas.

At the theatre, watching a farce, one often guesses that its point of departure was found by answering a question like this: In precisely what circumstances would an almost normal person refrain from telling something which even an idiot, were the circumstances ever so little different, would have stopped the play by telling at once?

Mr. Shaw needs none of these doctored situations to start his farces with. They get under way as simply as his comedies, move at the same pace, and pursue the same end. You cannot, in fact, divide his plays into comedy and farce. All of them, one with a thicker and another with a thinner veil over its serious purpose, seek to destroy illusion.

Of course all comedies try more or less to do this, and the better they succeed the better they satisfy the classic idea of comedy. But the scope of comedy is so wide that the illusions may be anything you please. In Miss Austen, for example, they are Emma's illusions as to the feeling of one individual towards another. The mistakes corrected by Molière are graver, more anti-social, matter more to the community. Yet Molière keeps always a faith in the old wisdom of the world. The self-deceptions he exposes are tried before judges assumed to be competent, before a society whose general good sense is taken for granted. Mr. Shaw denies the existence of any such common sense. He is forever telling contemporary society the bad news

Reprinted from *The New Republic,* April 21, 1917.

that illusion is part of its structure. The self-deceiver he assaults and
exposes is society itself.

No wonder such a radical fighter puzzled us all at first. His appearance in our meaningless theatre was more surprising than the
first appearance, about eighteen-eighty-something, of grapefruit on
our tables, many sizes larger than our familiar breakfast dishes, and
how much more pungent. Nowadays all grapefruit tastes alike. So
with Mr. Shaw's plays. They are as pungent as ever, they are larger
than of old, but they are no longer new. His late plays are not newer
than his earliest. His originality is not a plant of slow growth. Seldom has an artist-philosopher, coming so early into his fortune of
convictions, reached the age of sixty with fewer losses of conviction,
fewer gains, so little change in the nature of his investments. He believes what he believed and feels what he felt. Hence his uniformity.
None of his plays differs from another in tone so widely as *The
Master Builder* differs from *An Enemy of Society*, or in doctrine so
widely as *Une Visite de Noces* differs from *La Femme de Claude*.
Shaw's is the work of a witty and pugnacious demonstrator, never
depressed by the brutality and injustice all about him, always impatient of the lying done in their defense, enjoying mightily his
attacks on these lies.

Dumas fils had an even greater talent than Mr. Shaw's for preaching from the stage, but his propaganda was immensely less important. In *Une Visite de Noces*, and everywhere else, his attention is
fixed upon some variety of love. Mr. Shaw looks further afield, knows
ever so much more, thinks ever so much more, pays attention to
more parts of life. He has examined war, property, education, marriage, home life, romantic love, as they exist in the British world,
and he sees that they are bad. His method of proceeding against
them is not to turn a full stream of anger directly upon these institutions themselves. His weapon is not anger against things and facts.
It is impatience with the romantic idealism which keeps evil alive
by seeing things and facts as they are not and by telling lies about
them. War, for example, is hateful to Mr. Shaw, but his way of
getting rid of it is by exposing and ridiculing the stuff and nonsense
talked about military glory. So strong is his preference for talking
this way that sometimes one suspects him of detesting conventional
notions of military glory more cordially than he detests the realities
of war.

Pestilent archaic institutions are the objects of his attack, but its
method is such that he seems to be giving most of his attention to the
flattering reflection of these institutions in the conventional idealiz-
ing mind. He is much less a realistic describer and exhibitor than a
preacher of the realistic habit. Learn to see things realistically, great

things and small, and the future will be better than the present. Once the tribe of romantic liars has been exterminated there will be no war in the world, no profiteering, no parasites living in idleness. Home life will be better and there will be less of it.

Shaw the propagandist, the physician to an ailing society, is so effectively in earnest that everybody who can take his medicine at all comes sooner or later to take it seriously. Most of us pass through several stages. At first we are puzzled and amused by these plays, in which the speeches glitter like razors after a cakewalk, and the *mots d'auteur* are brilliant as poppies in the wheat. Then it disconcerts us to discover that this paradoxist means bodily harm to the existing order. Next we are exhilarated and stimulated and compelled almost to think for ourselves by his doctrine, so lucid and emphatic and cocksure. It is at a later stage, when we are trying to escape from the prison of Mr. Shaw's common sense, that we take him most seriously.

It is all very well, we say at this stage, to talk against illusions, but are not some illusions necessary? George Meredith has shown us

Yonder midnight ocean's force,
Thundering like ramping hosts of warrior horse,
To throw that faint thin line upon the shore!

If the warrior horse were realists, if they foresaw the inevitable faintness and thinness of any line they could rationally hope to throw, with all their ramping, wouldn't they ramp less, and the line on the shore be even thinner and fainter? Illusions do harm, we admit, yet it is by illusion's help that the world does its work. Would not the sanest ambitions dwindle, and the highest hopes fail, if the extent of their future satisfaction could be accurately known?

That way of escaping Mr. Shaw's influence is possible, no doubt, but not for a convert whose mind he has ever thoroughly won. For Mr. Shaw believes the world can get along without any man's best if he be such a weakling that he cannot do his best without telling himself lies. One of these days the world will be manned by a tough-minded realistic crew, whose labor will be none the less diligent because they direct it to strictly attainable ends. And even after illusion has gone instinct and impulse will remain. At present married life is made worse than it need be by the romantic idealism of men and women who expect to find it better than it can be. But a more rational expectation, a clear foresight, will not weaken the instinct which brings men and women together. Expecting less happiness in marriage than they now foolishly expect, they will gain a solider happiness than they can have now. The artistic impulse, again, is so inextinguishable that artists will keep pegging away after they have

scrapped all their illusions. A painter can stick to his work though he
has no hope of beating Velasquez. He paints to make his picture
represent what he has seen as he has seen it. So with "the instinct
of workmanship" wherever found, and it will be found in abundance.

But if we yield the point, if we grant the truth of all that Mr.
Shaw teaches us about illusions, if we concede that all are harmful,
that none is necessary, are we condemned never to loosen his grip
upon us? At least we can try. To see mankind as divisible into realists
and romantic idealists, we may say, is only one way of seeing the
world. Turn from Mr. Shaw, for whom it is the only way of seeing
things as they are, to whatever life we happen to know. No attempt
to separate people into realists and romantic idealists can long survive contact with miscellaneous experience. Most of the men and
women one sees do not spend most of their time in realizing Mr.
Shaw's ideals of realism or romantic idealism. They are quite as sig-
nificantly classifiable upon other systems. They are not easily classifiable upon any. If we keep his classification in mind long enough,
until it looks as strange as a familiar word repeated over and over,
it will at last appear arbitrary. Imagine a sculptor who should begin
each of his portrait busts with a determination to have the look of
it tell us whether the sitter did or did not believe that land ought to
be taxed to its full rental value. An exaggeration? Of course. But
what of? Of just the impression left on me when I try to remember
Mr. Shaw's plays as a whole.

A self-conscious passion for seeing things realistically, or as they
are, is a blood relation of its caricature, the passion for seeing things
as other people don't. And this, again, is no distant relative of the
passion for denying what other people see, even when they see truly.
Take physical courage, for example, which Mr. Shaw dislikes and
denies because it is, after all, the one best bet of the romantic idealists who have invented the myth of military glory. This dislike appears again in his fondness for putting fear, physical fear, upon the
stage. Take for another example love, the spring in which rivers of
romantic lies have their source. Except as pure life-force, Mr. Shaw
has a poor opinion of love. He would resent the behavior of Sir
Samuel Romilly, whose wife's death drove him to suicide at the age
of sixty-one, because such doings are evidence of a kind not, I admit,
very abundant, but still evidence, that passionate love may survive
twenty years of marriage. Friendship, too, with its irrational loyal-
ties and its odor of good old times, has been the occasion of the Lord
knows how much romantic idealism. Hence, in all Mr. Shaw's plays,
so far as I can remember, no representation of friendship on the best
terms, between equals. Together with human relations at their in-
tensest and most disinterested, as in friendship and love, he excludes

human beings at the full tide of their energy. So much lying has been done about great men that he is impatient of greatness. Julius Caesar is not greater than John Tanner or Andrew Undershaft. Vivie Warren seems almost as great a man as Napoleon.

This denial of the exceptional, this dislike and distrust of it, what are they in Mr. Shaw, but the other side of affirmation that society must be turned into a happier place for average men and women? He is at his most modern in his effort to overthrow all those institutions which keep the poor dependent upon the idle or the active rich, and in his warfare against the romantic lies which sicken and divide all selves except the callous and the blind. His concern for mankind, for a world exempt from tyranny, brutality, unearned leisure, intimidation, for a world in which no man's will is the slave of another man's, and which is filled with men and women who had rather forfeit their respectability than their self-respect, who are neither afraid without cause nor afraid, when there is cause, of being afraid—all this progeny of aspirations is the issue of Mr. Shaw's modern democratic passion.

A modern passion he does not feel is the passion for observing and representing the greatest possible amount of human nature, just because it is human nature. He is almost a stranger to that omnivorous curiosity, so widespread nowadays among novelists, historians and psychologists, which is eager to contradict or verify what our fathers have told us about man, to make discoveries, to treat nothing as negligible if it be human. Such a disinterested curiosity would perhaps be an encumbrance to an artist as bent on changing our minds as Mr. Shaw is. Accordingly we find his gift of sharp observation used for the most part upon men and women when they are in contact with romantic idealism, either as its destroyers or its victims, and especially at the moment of their conversion to realism. He has some observation to spare for them at other moments, but unless you remember his purpose, his central drive, you cannot help wondering why he has not more.

"Philosophy serves culture," said Pater, "not by the fancied gift of abstract or transcendental knowledge but by suggesting questions which help one to detect the passion, and strangeness and dramatic contrasts of life." This is not the kind of philosophy people have in mind when they excuse Mr. Shaw's narrowed gaze by calling him an artist-philosopher. Artist-reformer would be nearer the truth, and the distinction between him and the mere artist would remain. The mere artist, whom you may call either a convictionless or a disinterested artist, just as you please, is known by his eagerness to look again and again at the world with fresh eyes. He values life more for its variety and its capability of surprising him than for its conformity with his previous reports upon it. The artist is known by what he omits, the artist-philosopher by what he omits to observe. His subconscious tells him either that his philosophy would be different if he observed more, or else that he would have no end of trouble trying to squeeze his new material into his old system. In this his subconscious does the artist-philosopher a good turn. We forgive Mr. Shaw the hardness and fastness of his conclusions because we know he has observed nothing, literally nothing, that is inconsistent with them. We should never forgive him if he saw all life, and saw it merely as all raw premise for his finished conclusion-product.

It is by never forgetting Mr. Shaw is an artist-philosopher that we escape from his bondage. An artist-philosopher is a system-maker, and no system can be true. But even when we are equipped with this knowledge escape from him is not easy. His hold upon us is tenacious. He relaxes our will to get away. As a mere artist his power is not easy to resist. One of the greatest masters of clear statement that have ever lived, a humorist of the first rank, one of the great wits of the world, he knows how to use his wit and humor and clearness to serve his own will, the will to make us disbelieve. A while ago I spoke of his *mots d'auteur*, but really all his plays are *mots d'auteur*, spoken with a practical object. Will the next century read and see his plays? I have not the slightest idea. No words of mine, gentle reader, and a fortiori no words of yours, can tell how little we know about the tastes of our successors. But I am willing to bet, if they do read him, that they will find singularly little to skip.

Mr. Shaw's destiny is an odd one. All his articulate life he has been telling what he took to be subversive and unpleasant truths. His reward has been money, a reputation for brilliancy, few converts. Then the war came. He did as he had always done, said what he had always said, and with the same fresh wit and energy. This time, at last, he roused thousands and thousands to fury. So his chance has come for showing, now that he is about sixty years old, the courage he would have shown all along, if he had had the chance.

LUDWIG LEWISOHN

1922

Shaw Among the Mystics*

Bernard Shaw is sixty-five and in despair. The mad peace finished
what the mad war had begun. We still live in a state of "boyish,
cinema-fed romanticism"; we are governed by grown-up children
and defectives. Strongly and naturally the doubt arises "whether the
human animal, as he exists at present, is capable of solving the social
problems raised by his own aggregation." So the human animal must
be changed; we must transform the biological process from a process to a weapon and a tool. We must harness the Life Force, the *élan
vital,* to our chariots and drive into a city of God which we ourselves
have built. It is sheer mysticism; and that Shaw, like the aged
Comte, has become a mystic is something like a tragic disaster. He
accepts the full position of the mystic and glories in it. "When a man
tells you that you are a product of Circumstantial Selection solely,
you cannot finally disprove it. You can only tell him out of the depth
of your inner consciousness that he is a fool and a liar." Alas, that
sort of inner consciousness has borne witness to a flat earth and a
wheeling sun, to virgin births and to transubstantiation, to the special creation of species, to the righteousness of human slavery and
war and persecution. It is our old friend faith, the evidence of things
unseen. It is beautiful and pathetic. But it has been the source of un-
told errors and miseries when not strictly limited to the forever
unseeable. If the Neo-Darwinians are right, Shaw exclaims, "only
fools and rascals could bear to live." That is what the bishops told
Huxley; it is the cry of every timid sentimentalist whose world will
not conform to his vision of what it should be. And this from Bernard Shaw!

Reprinted from *The Drama and the Stage* by Ludwig Lewisohn. Copyright 1922
by Harcourt, Brace and Company. Used by permission of the publishers.
* *Back to Methuselah. A Metabiological Pentateuch.* By Bernard Shaw.

He builds his mystical structure upon a basis of apparently scientific reasoning. According to the modern followers of Lamarck, "organisms changed because they wanted to," and the chief factor in the transmutation of species was use and disuse. According to the followers of Darwin, the same process is accounted for by natural selection, that is, by the propagation of a species through those individuals which are best adapted to survive in a given environment. Shaw identifies the use and disuse of the Neo-Lamarckians with Schopenhauer's Will, with his own Life Force, with Bergson's *élan vital,* with the Holy Ghost. He plays ducks and drakes with the distinction between inherited and acquired biological characters and declares that creative evolution, "the genuinely scientific religion," means literally that we can shape the evolutionary process to our liking as we go along. The human animal will change when it wills to change.

How should it will to change? First in the direction of longevity. We die before experience has ripened into wisdom. We do not attain vision and so muddle intolerably the affairs of the world. If we lived three hundred years we would, at least, transcend the lower delusions of mortality. What these delusions include no close student of Shaw can doubt. That magnificent intellect has always been a little disembodied. His asceticism is icy and his fastidiousness not quite human. He regards sex as a nuisance and art as a bauble. He is offended not only by disorder and dirt; he is offended by the processes of procreation and metabolism. In a word, he hates the body. If he is something of a superman in clarity and fire of mental vision, he is also a super-Puritan in his anxiety to burn away the world and the flesh in the flames of that visionary fire. The three-hundred-year-old sages are not his goal. They are still born of woman and nourished by the fruits of the earth. Nor do the eerie, sleepless Ancients of the three-hundredth century satisfy him except through their ultimate aspirations. "But the day will come when there will be no people, only thought." On that day the goal will be reached—"the goal of redemption from the flesh to the vortex freed from matter to the whirlpool in pure intelligence." There is no variableness nor shadow of turning in Bernard Shaw. Relentlessly he follows the logic of his own nature. It takes him to the "vast edges drear and naked shingles of the world." But he does not stop. He has no eyes for the green earth or its poor, passionate, struggling inhabitants. He whirs his iron wings and sets out on his lonely quest into the intense inane.

The five dramatic books of the revelation of the new vitalist religion are less brilliant than Shaw's earlier works, less humanly sagacious in detail, and, despite several bravura passages, less eloquent.

But they have all his old energy and rapidity of intellectual movement and the last two, *The Tragedy of an Elderly Gentleman* and
As Far as Thought Can Reach, are matchless exercises of a cold
imaginative vigor building its structures out into the void. Yet so
divorced from essential human feeling are these stupendous para-
bles and legends that Shaw never suspects, for instance, the true
character of his Ancients. He means them to inspire awe; they
arouse pity and disgust like the Struldbrugs of Swift. Did he, by any
chance, remember his great predecessor and draw the parallel?
Swift, having castigated the follies and the crimes of mankind, holds
up as a saving ideal the simplest goodness, gentleness, and innocence of soul. Shaw, suaver in gesture but in reality more terrible,
finds no hope in any quality of human nature. It must be transcended; it must be obliterated; it must be remembered with loathing
and contempt. Man must return "to the whirlpool in pure force"
whence the world arose. Form itself has become an ache to Shaw.
He thirsts for nothingness. He destroys the cosmos not like Faust
with an imprecation, but with an argument. In no sense will mankind take his bleak parable to heart. It is the monument of a great
despair. But men do not despair. They are sustained by the very
things that Shaw holds to be negligible if not noxious—by love and
art, food and wine, and even by a little warmth when, after darkness, the goodly sun returns.

GEORGE JEAN NATHAN

1931

Mr. Shaw and the Ogre

Observes H. G. Wells in *The Way the World Is Going:* "He (George Bernard Shaw) has made free use of the phrase, the Life Force, but what meaning he attaches to these magic words is unknown. . . . He has an aversion from sex . . . which may be either Butler or temperamental, and he seems to want mankind to try laying parthenogenetic eggs, and coming out of them fully whiskered."

The notion thus somewhat facetiously expressed by the acute Wells restimulates a similar notion that for some time has been impertinently agitating my encephalon. That Shaw, as Wells says, appears not only to have an aversion to sex but also what amounts almost to a fear of it has not been lost upon those who have carefully pondered his writings. The reason for the peculiar aversion and for what seems to be even fear is difficult to make out, but the antipathy and distrust nevertheless remain clearly visible and often emphatic. Shaw's canon plainly betrays his dislike of sex and his evasion of it. In all his work from beginning to end I know of no instance where he has not deftly avoided self-commitment on the subject or has not indulged in equivoque of one sort or another in his treatment of it.

It is impossible, within the limits of the present essay, to go fully into Shaw's writings and draw from them a comprehensive catalogue of illustrations. But one may suggest the color of his intrinsic and general attitude by skimming through them and extracting a few sufficiently pointed and revelatory examples. That, when he laid hold of the incalescent Cleopatra, he chose to contemplate her at the age of sixteen and, in spite of the fact that sixteen was maturity in that gala era, insisted upon comfortably regarding her as a species of pre-Mary Pickford flapper, that he presented the Caesar who had a baby by her as an historical Crocker Harrington, and that he once achieved the remarkable feat of writing sexlessly about the madam of a bordello, are phenomena familiar to everyone. That, also, in the series of interviews gathered by Archibald Henderson into "Table Talk of G. B. S.," he orally betrayed an indifference, even antipathy, to sex is as readily recalled. I quote a few passages: (*a*) "It is admitted that alleged rejuvenations (*vide* Steinach) do not prolong life. And it is longevity which interests me and not the ghastly prospect of seeing all the moribund people bustling about and pretending to be gay young dogs"; (*b*) "There is never any real sex in romance. What is more, there is very little, and that of a very crude kind, in ninety-nine hundredths of our married life"; (*c*) "One man's poetry is another man's pruriency"; (*d*) "The novel which says no more about sex than may be said in a lecture on the facts to a class of school-girls of fifteen can be enormously more entertaining than a novel wholly preoccupied with sexual symptoms"; (*e*) "I could not write the words Mr. Joyce uses: my prudish hand would refuse to form the letters"; and (*f*) "Is any treatment of sex in the interest of public morals?" And where the interviewer shot embarrassingly direct questions on sex to the interviewed, the latter is remembered as having cleverly avoided direct answers in such circumlocutions as "A playwright has no patience with novels," or in disquisitions on economics, capitalism and what not.

Let us glance haphazardly through Shaw's work. Having presented us with a virginal Cleopatra and a Caesar whose amatory exercises are confined to lifting her upon his knee and playing horsie, he presents us with the inflammable Great Catherine as one of the Four Marx Brothers, and not Harpo either. He gives us a Pygmalion who will have none of his perfected Galatea and who, to use Shaw's own words, excuses his indifference to young women on the ground that they have an irresistible rival in his mother. "If an imaginative boy has a . . . mother who has intelligence, personal grace, dignity of character without harshness, and a cultivated sense of the best art, . . . she sets a standard for him against which very few women can struggle, besides effecting for him a disengagement of his affections, his sense of beauty and his idealism from specifically sexual impulses. This makes him a standing puzzle to the huge number of uncultivated people . . . to whom literature, painting, sculpture, music and affectionate personal relations come as modes of sex if they come at all." He gives us even a Don Juan who moralistically announces, "I tell you that as long as I can conceive something better than myself, I cannot be easy unless I am striving to bring it into existence or clearing the way for it. That is the law of my life!" His Larry, in *John Bull's Other Island,* prefers his friend Tom to the woman who implores his love. "I wish I could find a country to live in where the facts were not brutal and the dreams not unreal," is the character's oblique anatomical lament. His Dick Dudgeon, in *The Devil's Disciple,* pronounces the word *love,* "with true Puritan scorn." His Lady Britomart, in *Major Barbara,* "really cannot bear an immoral man." And his Eugene, in *Candida,* romanticizes his emotions out of sex.

"Moral passion is the only real passion," announces Tanner, in *Man and Superman.* "All the other passions were in me before; but they were idle and aimless—mere childish greediness and cruelties, curiosities and fancies, habits and superstitions, grotesque and ridiculous to the mature intelligence. When they suddenly began to shine like newly lit flames it was by no light of their own, but by the radiance of the dawning moral passion. That passion dignified them, gave them conscience and meaning, found them a mob of appetites and organized them into an army of purposes and principles." "Virtue," Shaw notes in *The Revolutionist's Handbook,* "consists not in abstaining from vice but in not desiring it." Charteris, in *The Philanderer,* accused of philandering, states that he is not guilty of any such low thing. "I hate it; it bores me to distraction!" Praed observes to Crofts of Mrs. Warren, apropos of a hint of sexual intimacy, "Your delicacy will tell you that a handsome woman needs some friends who are not—well, not on that footing with her." And Mrs. Warren repentantly thus: "Do you think I was brought up like you—able to pick and choose my own way of life? Do you think I did what I did because I liked it, or *thought it right,* or *wouldn't rather have gone to college* and been a lady if I'd had the chance?"

Speaking of the marriage contract in one of his prefaces, Shaw alludes to sex stimulation as "the most violent, most insane, most delusive and most transient of passions," expresses his disbelief that married people as a rule really live together, and says that "a man as intimate with his own wife as a magistrate is with his clerk . . . is a man in ten thousand." In response to the General's timid "But there are calls of nature—," in *Getting Married,* Shaw makes Lesbia reply, "Don't be ridiculous." And when the General is so much as allowed to venture on another occasion the word *assignation,* the Shavian get-out is accomplished thus: "Oh yes; she began the correspondence by making a very curious but very natural assignation. She wants me to meet her in Heaven"—the while Mrs. Bridgenorth comments on the "everyday vulgarities of earthly love." "I sinned in intention," says Juno in *Overruled.* "I'm as guilty as if I had actually sinned." Lina, in *Misalliance,* takes out her surplus energy on a flying trapeze and recommends the same diet to her adoring Tarleton. And in *Arms and the Man,* we find the Shavian protagonist not too proud for sexual dalliance, but too tired.

The point is not that Shaw's imaginative writing is sexless—that is a fact too well known to call for repetition; the point is that the body of his work as a whole reveals a man to whom sex, in the sense that the word is commonly used, is at once unpleasant, deplorable and disgusting. There are times, true enough, when he seems to advance the opposite point of view, but it will be found that, when he does so, he does so only subsequently to refute and demolish it. Nor is his argument of the other point of view even momentarily persuasive; it hasn't the ring of sincerity; it is a dummy set up merely for tackling purposes. Among conspicuous modern English men of letters and English critics of life, he alone is indefatigable in waving the white banner of biological asceticism. One of the cleverest dialecticians of our time, he is sometimes successful in concealing his true attitude for a moment, in masking his ferocious personal convictions and in giving a bland performance in the rôle of a hell of a fellow, but it fools no one. Chesterton once observed that it is the weak man who always, when taking a walk, most vigorously thwacks the bushes along the roadside with his cane. A mistrust of his own philosophical attitude toward sex may similarly account for Shaw's disputatious thwacking of it.

After reading *Cashel Byron's Profession,* Stevenson wrote to William Archer: "If Mr. Shaw is below five-and-twenty, let him go his path; if he is thirty, he had best be told that he is a romantic, and pursue romance with his eyes open. Perhaps he knows it." Shaw is still the romantic that he was when a boy. And his romanticism is no more clearly to be detected than in his animadversions on sex. He declines to see it for what it is; he cannot bring himself to regard it save in terms of sentiment, love, the Indian policy, Marxian socialism or the League of Nations. And all the fine irony and rich humor which he occasionally has visited upon the subject cannot conceal the romanticist hiding behind them and seeking to protect himself through them from the charge of romanticism. Shaw has always set up smoke-screens or avoidances of the issue to protect himself from himself. The hero of his early novel, *The Irrational Knot,* in answer to the query as to what he is going to do about his wife's elopement with a former lover, says, "Eat my supper. I am as hungry as a bear." His charming Szczymplica, in *Love Among the Artists,* is in her potentially most romantic moments restrained by the "soul commercial" that Shaw, with a cannily masked apprehensiveness, injects into her. Lydia Carew, whose "body is frail and brain morbidly active," is made to think coldly of the splendid Cashel Byron in terms of eugenical science. In *An Unsocial Socialist,* Shaw smears his inborn convictions with grease-paint and tries to make us believe that he believes the seven deadly sins, as Prof. Henderson notes them, are respectability, conventional virtue, filial affection, modesty, sentiment, devotion to women, and romance.

We have Shaw speaking of the wickedness and abandonedness of Offenbach's music and of the morals of Händel's. We find him waxing impatient with "the female figure free from the defect known to photographers as under-exposure" that he encounters on the statues and fountains in Paris. He writes, "What Hofmannsthal and Strauss have done is to take Clytemnestra and Ægistheus and by identifying them with everything that is evil . . . with the murderous rage in which the lust for a lifetime of orgiastic pleasure turns on its slaves in the torture of its disappointment and the sleepless horror and misery of its neurasthenia, to so rouse in us an overwhelming flood of wrath against it . . . that Elektra's vengeance becomes holy to us . . ." "In our sexual natures," he states in the preface to *Androcles and the Lion,* "we are torn by an irresistible attraction and an overwhelming repugnance and disgust." Again, "Marriage turns vagabonds into steady citizens; men and women will . . . practice virtues that unattached individuals are incapable of." In the preface to *Overruled,* thus: "That jealousy is independent of sex is shown by its intensity in children." Again, "Adultery is the dullest of themes on the stage, and from Francesca and Paolo down to the latest guilty couple . . . the romantic adulterers have been bores." Yet again, "It is ridiculous to say . . . that art has nothing to do with morality."

"If a young woman, in a mood of strong reaction . . . were to tell Mr. Herbert Spencer that she was determined not to murder her own instincts and throw away her life in obedience to a mouthful of empty phrases," he once said, "I suspect he would recommend the *Data of Ethics* to her as a trustworthy and conclusive guide to conduct. Under similar circumstances I should unhesitatingly say to the young woman: 'By all means do as you propose. Try how wicked you can be. . . . At worst, you will only find out the sort of person you really are. At best, you will find that your passions, if you really and honestly let them all loose impartially, will discipline you with a severity your conventional friends . . . could not stand for a day.'" In the preface to *Getting Married,* we come upon this: "The assumption that the specific relation which marriage authorizes between the parties is the most intimate and personal of human relations . . . is violently untrue." In *The Apple Cart,* we engage the anatomically paradoxical spectacle of a King's platonic mistress. And, by way of a climax, we have a Garden of Eden in *Back to Methuselah* in which, when Shaw's Eve learns the secret of sex, "an expression of overwhelming repugnance" crosses her features and she "buries her face in her hands"!

JOSEPH WOOD KRUTCH

1935

The Shavian Dilemma

I have previously suggested that a number of the plays written in America during the last ten or twelve years were not without a certain literary significance, even though they might seem to lack the definite socio-political implications characteristic of both the older "problem play" and the newer "revolutionary drama." It seems obvious enough that much less can be said in favor of the Victorian theater against which Bernard Shaw conducted his relentless campaign. Notoriously it depended upon adaptations from the French for even semi-serious plays, and the literary as well as the sociological significance of the native drama was very nearly nil. There have been, as a matter of fact, only two or three periods during which the history of the English drama became a part of the history of English literature and this was decidedly not one of them.

Broadly speaking it may be said that between Sheridan and Oscar Wilde no successful writer for the English stage deserves to be ranked as a man of letters. It is true that the names of a few plays— *Richelieu* and *The Lady of Lyons, The Two Orphans* and *The Bells* —are dimly remembered. It is also true of course that Byron and Shelley and Tennyson and Browning wrote sometimes in the dramatic form. But their plays either were not intended for the stage or were unsuccessful when acted, and one may safely make a sweeping generalization: during most of the nineteenth century in England the men of letters were not successful playwrights and the successful playwrights were not men of letters.

Of all the literary forms the acting drama is undoubtedly the one which seems to have the greatest difficulty in maintaining a connec-

Reprinted from *The Nation*, September 11, 1935.

tion with serious literature, and the lamentable unsuccess of the few eminent Victorians who attempted to reestablish the connection merely indicates how completely it has been broken.

In a sense, the theater flourished. It boasted actors who were reputed to be great and who with apparent insouciance alternated their interpretations of Shakespeare with declamations of the most dreadful drivel. It was also popular as a peculiar sort of diversion apparently relished by people who took for granted that they would not find in it any pretense at the intelligence or integrity which they expected in poetry or the novel. Through the Victorian novel runs the current of the best thought and the most acute sensibility of the time. But the age which produced and enjoyed Dickens, George Eliot, Thackeray, and Meredith seemed ready to assume that no attempt to reach a comparable level was to be expected in the theater.

The only explanation of both the barrenness of the Victorian theater and the complacency with which it was accepted seems to be that the drama had been completely given up as a form of serious expression. Though Tennyson, like Henry James somewhat later, happened to be taken with an odd ambition to write plays, the general feeling seems to have been that the acting drama was lost to literature and that it could no longer be used by the serious literary artist.

From this situation it could be rescued only by a kind of revolution, and that revolution—astonishingly successful in the end—was, of course, the one inspired by Ibsen and, in England, generated by Shaw. The revolution was, moreover, carried out by the boldest of possible methods, since it proposed to emphasize in dramatic writing the very virtues which had been the most completely nonexistent in the current tradition, namely, the intellectual. The Victorian drama was unusually bad from almost every standpoint except, perhaps, that of pure mechanics. It made little effort in the direction of either any valid representation of character or the utilization of any except a distinctly sub-literary style. But in no respect was its lag more conspicuous than in the staleness of its moral and social ideas, which were not merely vulgar but also vulgar in a fashion distinctly behind the time. Yet "the new drama" as championed —and, as he himself admitted, to some extent merely imagined—by Shaw, was to be primarily intellectual. The drama was not merely to catch up with the best of current thought; it was to be ahead of it, and from having constituted a stagnant backwater it was to become a roaring torrent in which the most advanced and vertiginous ideas were to sweep onward.

To an amazing degree these ambitions were actually realized. Shaw himself might contemptuously announce that there was nothing original in his plays. His startled readers need not go even so far afield as Ibsen and Nietzsche. They could find it all in their own neglected genius, Samuel Butler. And yet, though there is a good deal of truth in this, the fact remains that it was largely through the "new drama" that these "modern" and "advanced" ideas were actually popularized, that the premises of an Ibsen or a Shaw ceased to be the esoteric possession of a few and gradually came to constitute the general background of early twentieth-century thought.

It is true of course that the drama had no exclusive right to them; they passed either from the drama or from other original sources into general literature. It is also true that the drama as reading exercised far more influence than could have been exercised by the relatively infrequent performances of the best of the new plays. On the whole, moreover, printed volumes of Shaw and Ibsen and Strindberg and Hauptmann and the rest were read for the most part less because their audience was interested in the theater than because it was interested in ideas. The importance of the plays was only secondarily their importance as dramatic literature, and to that extent the intention to intellectualize the drama may be said to have overstepped itself. But however one may think of Ibsen and Shaw, the fact remains that their plays present in compact and vivid form the convictions and attitudes which were revolutionizing the intellectual background against which the literature of the whole of one generation was to be written. The drama had come back with a vengeance.

The peculiar, almost unique character of the plays consists in the fact that, to a degree nearly unprecedented in dramatic literature, their authors were fighting their audience. Shaw's central criticism of Shakespeare—that his point of view was merely that of the Elizabethan man in the street—is based upon an accurate observation. But, speaking broadly, much the same thing might be said of Sophocles or of Molière. That directness and simplicity which marks all the great works of literature and which gives them the air which is vaguely called "classic" is possible only when the author can take for granted the whole substratum of knowledge and belief, the whole system of values, by reference to which the story achieves its meaning. Such works are, in other words, the final flowers of an established and flourishing culture. Even when, as in the case of Molière, they included important critical elements, the criticism is rather corrective than revolutionary. It involves no fundamental readjustment of standards, and the determination to "transvaluate values" is so completely alien to the classic spirit that it is incompatible with the creation of a classic work.[1]

Much of the awkwardness, as well as much of the characteristic quality, of the drama stemming from Ibsen arises out of the fact that its authors were trying to tell stories the intended significance of which could not emerge unless the auditor could be made to revolutionize his moral and intellectual equipment. Ibsen, being somewhat more of an artist and somewhat less of a teacher than most of the rest, was content to leave in his plays a certain ambiguity inevitable in a story whose premises remained not wholly comprehended. Shaw, being the most voluble as well as, in certain respects, the most prosy of the lot, tried to get around the difficulty by the long prefatory sermons whose purpose was to implant in the mind of the prospective reader those ideas necessary for the correct comprehension of the play. But neither Ibsen's willingness to remain provocatively puzzling nor Shaw's interminable preliminary discourses relieved either of the necessity of a great deal of explanation and argumentation as he went along.

Ghosts, to take a familiar example, is in its most "classic" aspect a tragedy of ineluctable fate taking the form of hereditary disease. On a different level it is also a story whose theme is the evil wrought by hypocrisy and concealment. But that is not all. When Molière wrote *Tartuffe* he could safely assume that his audience would recognize the hypocrisy of the central character as precisely that. Ibsen on the other hand knew that, to at least many in his audience, the hypocrisy of Parson Manders would appear not as hypocrisy at all but only as a form of decency which shrank from mentioning the unmentionable. He knew also that the parson's refusal to tell Oswald the truth about his disreputable father was based upon the conviction that children should be encouraged to follow the Biblical injunction, "Honor thy father and thy mother." On the whole, the audience would tend to agree rather with Parson Manders than with Ibsen, and it was accordingly necessary to introduce various debates upon this and other subjects, which debates—and this is the important point—were relevant not to the action but to the premises in terms of which the action could become meaningful.

One result of all this is that even such a play as *Ghosts*, certainly one of the best of the school, must always have seemed slightly awkward. It could not move forward with the swift decisiveness of the popular melodrama, which takes for granted everything except

[1] I am not, of course, forgetting that *Tartuffe* was the occasion of a scandal, but the scandal was not the result of any revolutionary definition of morality. It was due solely to the fact that the villain was a priest.

the particular action itself, or of, say, a tragedy by Shakespeare, who could at least take for granted that his purely intellectual premises were near enough those of the Elizabethan man in the street to require no defense. Another result is that for us, some half a century later, most of the arguments have become mere boresome excrescences, for the simple reason that the issues with which they deal are no longer living.

Thus both Ibsen and Shaw have suffered from the fact that they argued too well. Their paradoxes have turned into platitudes, and it does little good to remind ourselves that it was they who made them platitudinous. Parson Manders asks Mrs. Alving if she feels any better for having read certain shocking books on her table, and when Mrs. Alving replies that she feels not better but "safer," she sounds uncomfortably like Mr. Marquis's Hermione, because Hermione is exactly a person who goes on repeating "advanced ideas" which are no longer advanced.

At its flattest—for example, in the plays of Brieux—"the new drama" was no more than a pamphlet in dialogue form upon some very limited and concrete topic. At its best—say, in *Hedda Gabler*— it very nearly transcends its own limitations. The problem there is a problem of character and cannot become platitudinous for the reason that a platitude must necessarily be statable as a simple proposition. In general, the most lasting work of the best "new dramatists" is that which is least specific, and plays like *A Doll's House* and *Widowers' Houses* are almost completely dead, while *The Wild Duck* and *Man and Superman* are still interesting, precisely because the two first prove a point which can be equally well argued in abstract intellectual terms.

To say this is by no means to say that these dramatists should have written otherwise. The only culture or "ideology" which they could have taken for granted was one whose vitality was already exhausted, and their choice was probably limited to a choice between mere conventionality and the sort of pioneering work which they chose to do. The time was out of joint; but, as an artist, any one of them might have been forgiven for exclaiming, "Oh, cursed spite, that ever I was born to set it right." It was the necessity for doing just that which made it necessary for even Ibsen, surely the greatest of the group, to spend much of his time either in the effort to establish his premises or in the composition of works bound to lose their interest as soon as they should have accomplished their purpose.

Though he never, as far as I know, made any public profession of the fact, it is evident that Shaw came to realize at last that his pioneering work had been finished. However backward society may have continued to be, and however superficial the acceptance of "advanced ideas" may have remained, audiences were, nevertheless, ready to accept plays written from the Shavian point of view. The next step was obviously to abandon the effort to propagandize these ideas and actually to write the plays which their acceptance made possible. To Shaw's credit it must be said that from *Saint Joan* on that is exactly what he attempted to do. Perhaps most of the later plays were not very good. Perhaps they were conspicuously less successful in achieving their purpose than the early ones had been in achieving a different purpose. But the intention was admirable. The premises of a newer drama had been established and, logically, the next task of the dramatist was to create that drama.

EDMUND WILSON

1938

Bernard Shaw at Eighty

Time has shifted our point of view on Bernard Shaw, yet he is still worth our contemplation. Let us cast a look back over his career.

George Bernard Shaw was born in Dublin, July 26, 1856, the son of shabby-genteel parents who had connections with the Irish nobility. The elder Shaw became an alcoholic, and the boy had to go to work as a clerk at the age of fifteen. Mrs. Shaw finally left her husband and went to London, where she made a living by teaching music. Her son came to live with her when he was twenty and wrote novels which he was unable to sell and picked up through journalism such money as he could. He remained with his mother till he was forty-two.

In the fall of 1882 he happened to attend a lecture on land nationalization delivered by Henry George in London. The result was a revelation: "It flashed on me," he writes, "that 'the conflict between religion and science' . . . the overthrow of the Bible, the higher education of women, Mill on Liberty and all the rest of the storm that raged around Darwin, Tyndall, Huxley, Spencer and the rest, on which I had brought myself up intellectually, was a mere middle-class business. . . The importance of the economic basis dawned on me." He read George's *Progress and Poverty*—then someone told him to read *Das Kapital*. "Karl Marx," he once said, "made a man of me."

The result of the depression of the eighties was a revival of socialist agitation. Bernard Shaw became a socialist and spoke in halls, on street corners, in Hyde Park. The "insurrectionism" of the period reached a climax in the "Bloody Sunday" of November 1887, when the socialists, at the head of a working-class demonstration, invaded Trafalgar Square and were routed by the police. After this, business revived and took up the slack of unemployment, and the agitation quieted down.

In the meantime, Shaw had attached himself to the socialist statistician, Sidney Webb, and with others they had founded the Fabian Society, which had "agreed to give up the delightful ease of revolutionary heroics and take to the hard work of practical reform on ordinary parliamentary lines." Webb was a civil servant with a post in the colonial office and later a member of the London County Council; Shaw became a vestryman, then a borough councilor. The Fabians continued to treat Marx with respect, but the polite and reasonable criticism to which they subjected him was designed to discredit some of his main assumptions. Marx had asserted that the value of commodities was derived from the labor which had gone to produce them; and the Fabians, by elaborating a counter-theory that made value depend on demand, shifted the emphasis from the working class to the "consumer." They also repudiated the class war, showed that it would never occur. Socialist nationalization was to be accomplished by a corps of experts who should "permeate" government and business, quietly invading Whitehall and setting up state departments which, unassisted by the action of the masses, should put socialist ideas into effect. Shaw boasted that the Fabians had made socialism respectable.

This variation of Marxism in England was natural to the place and time. A period of prosperity during the seventies had deflated the Chartist agitation (I am indebted to Mr. Mark Starr for a Marxist analysis of Fabian Marxism); and it was not until the eighties, when British commercial domination was being challenged by the United States and Germany, that the dangers of the capitalist system began to become generally plain. But now attention was principally directed toward the evils of competition. The development of large-scale industry was eliminating competition and making municipal ownership seem desirable, not only to the lower layers of the middle class, but even to private enterprise itself, which benefited from good housing and cheap tram-lines. The professional middle class were in a position to see the value of nationalization, and the working class had not yet discovered that for them there was not very much difference between being exploited by a private employer and being exploited by a government that was controlled by the propertied classes. The Fabians looked no further than their reforms.

In Bernard Shaw's case, this compromise Marxism played in with the elements of his character and influenced its subsequent development. Coming to London, as he has recently told us, with a conviction of his own superiority and a snobbish family tradition, but with no money and no social experience, Shaw was himself one of the dispossessed, and the socialist criticism of the class system based on property strongly recommended itself to him. Yet at the same time that in all good faith he was working to destroy that system, there is apparent in his career a tendency in the inverse direction to this. At the same time that he was spurred by a moral need to work for a future society consistent with his sense of justice, he was spurred, also, by a social need to vindicate his rightful position in the society in which he lived. He has told us that his father's bad habits had caused his family to be dropped socially in Dublin and that when he first came to London he was so shy that he would not accept dinner invitations and would "sometimes walk up and down the Embankment for twenty minutes or more before venturing to knock at the door" of a house to which he had been asked. He goes on to say, "The house and its artistic atmosphere were most congenial to me; and I liked all the Lawsons; but I had not mastered the art of society at that time and could not bear making an inartistic exhibition of myself; so I soon ceased to plague them." There has always been thus in Shaw a certain amount of social snobbery mixed up with his intellectual snobbery.

The confusion produced in his thought by these two conflicting tendencies is curiously illustrated in a passage from his autobiographical preface to the collected edition of his works: "Finding one's place may be made very puzzling," he writes, "by the fact that there is no place in ordinary society for extraordinary individuals. For the worldly wiseman, with common ambitions, the matter is simple enough: money, title, precedence, a seat in parliament, a portfolio in the cabinet, will mean success both to him and to his circle. But what about people like St. Francis and St. Clare? Of what use to them are the means to live the life of the country house and the West End mansion? They have literally no business in them, and must necessarily cut an unhappy and ridiculous figure there. They have to make a society of Franciscans and Poor Clares for themselves before they can work or live socially. It is true that those who are called saints are not saintly all the time and in everything. In eating and drinking, lodging and sleeping, chatting and playing: in short, in everything but working out their destiny as saints, what is good enough for a plowman is good enough for a poet, a philosopher, a saint or a higher mathematician. But Hodge's work is not good enough for Newton, nor Falstaff's conversation holy enough for Shelley. Christ adapted himself so amicably to the fashionable life of his time in his leisure that he was reproached for being a gluttonous man and a winebibber, and for frequenting frivolous and worthless sets. But he did not work where he feasted, nor flatter the

Pharisees, nor ask the Romans to buy him with a sinecure. He knew when he was being entertained, well treated, lionized: not an unpleasant adventure for once in a way; and he did not quarrel with the people who were so nice to him. Besides, to sample society is part of a prophet's business: he must sample the governing class above all, because his inborn knowledge of human nature will not explain the anomalies produced in it by Capitalism and Sacerdotalism. But he can never feel at home in it."

But which is true: that the St. Francis or the St. Clare can't "live socially" till they have "made a society of Franciscans and Poor Clares" or that "in eating and drinking, lodging and sleeping, chatting and playing," "what is good enough for a plowman is good enough for a saint?" And as for Shaw's description of Christ, it evokes an incongruous picture: what one sees is the preacher of the Sermon on the Mount very much pleased with himself on the beach at the Riviera or playing Santa Claus at Lady Astor's Christmas party.

And other influences, from his early education, came to deflect the straight line of his socialism.

The escapades of the romantic hero, from Childe Harold through Don César de Bazan, with his "Tant pis! C'est moi!," to Siegfried, had been a protest against the meanness and dullness of the commercial bourgeois world; but this revolt was itself merely a further phase of the tradition of individual assertion which, deriving from the Protestant conscience, had produced the anarchic individualism of the competitive commercial system. The romantic, like the old-fashioned capitalist, proclaimed the power of the personal will in defiance of society and God.

William Archer tells us that the first time he ever saw Shaw, the latter was sitting in the British Museum studying alternately the French translation of *Das Kapital* and the score of *Tristan und Isolde*. When Shaw first came before the public, he fell instinctively into dramatizing himself as a semi-romantic character—and this in spite of the fact that he was managing to figure at the same time as the arch-enemy and blasphemer of romanticism. The impulse to satirize romanticism implies, as in the case of Flaubert, a strong predisposition toward it; and the exploded romantic, Captain Brassbound, is offset by the Devil's Disciple. It is true that Shaw's conscious intention was to ridicule and shame his audience out of exclusive preoccupation with the emotions of their personal lives—especially, with romantic love—and to interest them in the problems of society. Here is the fine and well-known passage from *Man and Superman*, in which he defends what he calls the "artist-philosophers" against the "mere artist": "This is the true joy in life, the being used for a purpose recognized by yourself as a mighty one; the being thoroughly worn out before you are thrown on the scrap heap; the being a force of Nature instead of a feverish selfish little clod of ailments and grievances complaining that the world will not devote itself to making you happy." Yet is this not, too, a kind of romanticism—romanticism *par excellence?* The ego has now, to be sure, identified itself with a force of Nature, but this simply makes the ego seem godlike. There is nothing to guarantee that it will respect either the feelings or the interests of others. The ideal artist-philosopher of Bernard Shaw has always a strong social conscience, and his heroes are likely to be philosopher-statesmen or social prophets or saviors of society; but there is nothing to guarantee that they shall be, in the socialist sense, genuine popular leaders, deriving their power from, as well as guiding, the dispossessed: they may be simply despot-heroes—as Shaw's Julius Caesar actually is— acting in the right of their own superiority and giving people what they know to be good for them.

And finally, of course, Bernard Shaw was not only a political prophet struggling for socialist ideas, but an artist trying to realize himself through art. There was a poet in Shaw, still partly suppressed, or at any rate terribly overtaxed, by the round of political meetings, the functions of vestryman and borough councilor, and the years of theatergoing and weekly article-writing about the theater, which he had come to judge almost exclusively in terms of the sort of thing that he wanted to do himself. His own plays he had been writing in note-books while traveling on the tops of buses between one engagement and another. Now in 1898, when he was forty-two, he had what seems to have been a general collapse as the result of a bad fall and a serious injury to his foot. When he recovered, he married an Irish lady, well-to-do but belonging like Shaw to the general "advanced" movement, who gave him for apparently the first time in his life a comfortable place to live and took the most excellent care of him. Thereafter, he was able to give up the journalism on which he had depended for a living and to devote all his best energies to his plays. He remained a public man, but he spoke no more at dockers' strikes.

By 1905 he was writing *Major Barbara*, in which the type of Christian sainthood, an aristocratic Salvation Army worker, is confronted with a self-made munitions manufacturer, the type of successful capitalism; and ending the play with an alliance between them. In his preface, he made out a ringing case for the man who recognizes poverty as the worst of all the evils and consequently the worst of all the sins, and who saves himself from it at any cost. *Major Barbara* contains one of the best expositions of the capitalist

point of view ever written. Bernard Shaw, like his hero, Andrew
Undershaft, had come by that time to know what it was to make
one's way in capitalist society and to occupy a position of power.
He had himself become the type of the critic, who, by scolding the
bourgeoisie, makes good with it and becomes one of its idols. He
was gradually, for all the scandal of his début, turning into a de-
pendable member of the British propertied classes; and he was to
end as an esteemed public figure in a country where an aristocratic
governing class was still able to contribute to public life a certain
distinction and glamor.

II

The real Shaw has thus never been the single-minded crusader
that people at one time used to think him. Except for a limited
period during the eighties and early nineties—when he wrote his
only straight socialist plays, *Widowers' Houses* and *Mrs. Warren's
Profession*—he has never really been a practicing socialist. And I
am inclined to believe that the future will exactly reverse the opinion which his contemporaries have usually had of him. It used always to be said of Shaw that he was primarily not an artist, but a
promulgator of certain ideas. The truth is, I think, that he is a considerable artist, but that his ideas—that is, his social philosophy
proper—have always been confused and uncertain. As he has grown
older and as the world has been shaken out of the pattern to which
he had adapted his attitudes, the inadequacy of those attitudes has
been exposed.

One is struck, as one goes through the volumes of the collected
edition of Shaw, which includes a good deal of his journalism, by
the fact that, though his writing on musical and theatrical and literary subjects remains remarkably fresh, the pieces on public affairs
and on social questions in general prove very much less satisfactory
than one had remembered their seeming when they first came out.
There are passages of admirable exposition and passages of wonderful eloquence—some of which, such as the peroration to *The
Intelligent Woman's Guide to Socialism and Capitalism*, will probably always stand among the classics of socialist literature. But the
political writing of Shaw does not drive you into taking up a position as the greatest socialist writing does: indeed, before he has
finished—and he is likely to go on talking too long—he has often
seemed to compromise the·points which you had imagined he was
trying to make, and has produced, with much earnestness and emphasis, an impression rather blurred by rhetoric. Both his intelligence and his sense of justice have prevented him from assailing the

capitalist system with such intolerant resentment and unscrupulous methods as Voltaire trained on the Church. With Voltaire, it *is* the crusader that counts; with Shaw, it is the dramatic poet.

The volume which covers the wartime exposes Bernard Shaw's contradictions in a particularly striking manner. Though he was perfectly familiar with the Marxist theory of capitalist expansion and aggression, and had expounded it on many occasions, he had always been liable to fits of admiration for the exploits of the British Empire. Irishman though he was, he had never been an Irish patriot; and, critical though he was of the English, he had in *John Bull's Other Island*—which was written for but declined by the Abbey Theater—backed them against the Irish on account of what he regarded as their superior enterprise and practicality. And though he denounced the Denshawai massacre in Egypt, he supported the British against the Boers at the time of the South African war, because the Boers represented for him a backward civilization and the British a progressive one. When the civilizing forces of the various nations had finally collided in 1914, it was Lenin, the revolutionary exile, not Shaw, the successful British citizen, who wrote *Imperialism: The Last Stage of Capitalism.*

What Bernard Shaw did write was *Common Sense about the War,* which, although it raised a terrible outcry in the fall of 1914 on the part of certain elements of the British public who thought that Shaw ought to be put in the Tower, seems today rather a double-facing document. Shaw, to be sure, makes a certain amount of effort still to keep before the minds of his readers the socialist interpretation of the War. "Will you," he writes, "now at last believe, O stupid British, German and French patriots, what the Socialists have been telling you for so many years: that your Union Jacks and tricolors and Imperial Eagles ('where the carcase is, there will be eagles be gathered') are only toys to keep you amused, and that there are only two real flags in the world henceforth: the red flag of Democratic Socialism and the black flag of Capitalism, the flag of God and the flag of Mammon? What earthly or heavenly good is done when Tom Fool shoots Hans Narr? The plain fact is that if we leave our capital to be dealt with according to the selfishness of the private man he will send it where wages are low and workers enslaved and docile: that is, as many thousand miles as possible from the Trade Unions and Trade Union rates and parliamentary Labour parties of civilization; and Germany, at his sordid behest, will plunge the world into war for the sake of disgracing herself with a few rubber plantations, poetically described by her orators and journalists as 'a place in the sun.' When you do what the Socialists tell you by keeping your capital jealously under national control and reserving your shrapnel for the wasters who not only shirk their share of the industrial service of their country, but intend that their children and children's children shall be idle wasters like themselves, you will find that not a farthing of our capital will go abroad as long as there is a British slum to be cleared and rebuilt or a hungry, ragged and ignorant British child to be fed, clothed and educated."

This sounds spirited enough by itself, yet the burden of *Common Sense about the War* is that the war must be supported and vigorously prosecuted. Shaw afterwards visited and wrote about the front at the invitation of Sir Douglas Haig and even did some work for the propaganda department of the government. In his discussion of compulsory military service in *Common Sense about the War*, he defends his position as follows: "In my own case, the question of conscientious objection did not arise: I was past military age. I did not counsel others to object, and should not have objected myself if I had been liable to serve: for intensely as I loathed the war, and free as I was from any illusion as to its character, and from the patriotic urge (patriotism in my native country taking the form of an implacable hostility to England), I knew that when war is once let loose, and it becomes a question of kill or be killed, there is no stopping to argue about it: one must just stand by one's neighbors and take a hand with the rest. If England had adopted me, as some of my critics alleged in their attempts to convict me of gross ingratitude, I could have pleaded that she must take the consequences without claiming any return; but as I had practically adopted England by thrusting myself and my opinions on her in the face of every possible rebuff, it was for me to take the consequences, which certainly included an obligation to help my reluctant ward in her extremity as far as my means allowed."

Frank Harris, in his book about Shaw, reproached him for supporting the war; and Shaw retorted in a postscript that Harris "could not stop to ask himself the first question . . . of the intellectually honest judicious critic, 'What else could I have done had it been my own case?'" Yet surely there were other courses open to a man of Shaw's opinions. He could have expressed his disapproval and shut up, as John Morley and others did. But it is impossible for Shaw to shut up, and he went on talking incessantly through the whole four years of slaughter. Much of what he had to say was intelligent, and it required some courage to say it. Compared with most of the British writers, he seemed at the time to an American remarkably cool and sagacious. The atmosphere was feverish with panic and stupefying with the fumes of propaganda, and Shaw did do something to clear the air for a discussion of the origin and aims of the war. But when we reread what he wrote today, he looks a little foolish. The old socialist has gone down into the mêlée and sacrificed something of his moral dignity: we hear him remonstrating, scolding, exhorting, making fun of the politicians and at the same time lending a hand to the government, pleading for the conscientious objectors and at the same time "joy-riding at the front"—and doing everything with equal cocksureness.

Before the Peace Conference, he had great hopes of Wilson. Before the Washington Disarmament Conference, he was cynical. Later, he spoke a kind word for the League of Nations. And in the meantime the Russian Revolution had set him off on a different tack. He would alternately lecture Lenin and Trotsky on the futility of what they were trying to do and applaud them for succeeding in doing it: he was alternately a middle-class socialist using Fabianism against the Marxists and a Marxist using Lenin and Trotsky against the British governing class. (It is interesting to note that Lenin characterized him as "a good man fallen among Fabians," and that Trotsky, of whom Shaw wrote enthusiastically as "the Prince of Pamphleteers," expressed the wish, apropos of his own exclusion from England, that "the Fabian fluid that ran in [Bernard Shaw's] veins" might have "been strengthened by even so much as five per cent of the blood of Jonathan Swift." It is amusing to see Trotsky's indignation in his *Where Is Britain Going?* over Shaw's cavalier suggestion that Marx had been superseded by H. G. Wells's *Outline of History*: Trotsky had gone to the trouble of procuring and looking into Wells.)

In his political utterances since the war, it is hardly too much to say that Bernard Shaw has behaved like a jackass. In the autumn of 1927, he was staying in Italy on the Lago Maggiore and throwing bouquets at Mussolini. It was his old admiration for the romantic hero, his old idealization—which was as likely to be set off by an imperialist as a Marxist theme—of the practical Caesarean statesman who makes people stand around. Mussolini had, according to Shaw, "achieved a dictatorship in a great modern state without a single advantage, social, official or academic, to assist him, after marching to Rome with a force of Black Shirts which a single disciplined regiment backed by a competent government could have routed at any moment. . . After the war the government of Italy" had been "so feeble that silly Syndicalists were seizing factories, and fanatical devotees of that curious attempt at a new Catholic church called the Third International were preaching a *coup d'état* and a Crusade in all directions, and imagining that this sort of thing was Socialism and Communism. Mussolini, without any of Napoleon's prestige, has done for Italy what Napoleon did for France, except that for the Duc d'Enghien you must read Matteotti." When Gaetano Salvemini reminded Shaw that, so far from being "without a single advantage," Mussolini had had behind him "the money of the banks, the big industrialists and the landowners," and that his Black Shirts had been "equipped with rifles, bombs, machine-guns, and motor-lorries by the military authorities, and assured of impunity by the police and the magistracy, while their adversaries were disarmed and severely punished if they attempted resistance," Shaw's rebuttal was almost unbelievable: Why, he demanded, had Mussolini been able to command the support of the army officers and capitalists "instead of Signors Salvemini, Giolitti, Turati, Matteotti and their friends, in spite of the fact that he was farther to the Left in his political opinions than any of them? The answer, as it seems to me, is that he combined with extreme opinions the knowledge that the first duty of any Government, no matter what its opinions are, is to carry on, and make its citizens carry on, liberty or no liberty, democracy or no democracy, socialism or no socialism, capitalism or no capitalism. Until Salvemini and his friends convince Italy that they understand this necessity as well as Mussolini does they will never shake his hold on the situation. To rail at him as Shelley railed at Castlereagh and Eldon, Marx at Napoleon III and Thiers, Kautsky at Lenin, is to play the amusing but inglorious part of Thersites." Now a dramatist in his capacity of dramatist may make out a very interesting case for a Castlereagh or a Napoleon III; but why should Shaw in his capacity as a political writer take the part of such politicians against their philosophical opponents? He is himself of the company of Shelley and Marx—the company of the poets and prophets; and railing at the Castlereaghs and Napoleons—of which Shaw himself has done plenty on occasion—is by no means the least valuable of their functions. The analogy between these other cases and Kautsky complaining of Lenin is certainly a silly and dishonest one.

That spring he had finished a long treatise—*The Intelligent Woman's Guide*—in which he had made a more comprehensive effort than he had ever done in his socialist days in the eighties to analyze capitalist society and to argue the case for socialism. Perhaps the book should have been written in the eighties. Ramsay Macdonald and Sidney Webb had come to power with the Labour Government in 1924, and Macdonald had not yet definitely sold out; and the whole story is repeated in general in the familiar Fabian terms—to which Shaw, without Fabian sanction, had added equality of income as a prime item of his socialist program. Through many pages of swift exposition, perhaps Shaw's most precise and limpid writing, which, together with the magnificent close, give the book an enduring value, he makes his way to conclusions that perplex us in proportion as the reasoning becomes more fine-spun and that do not seem

finally to land us in any very realistic relation to the England of
after the war. "A series of properly prepared nationalizations may
not only be understood and voted for by people who would be quite
shocked if they were called Socialists, but would fit in perfectly with
the habits of the masses who take their bread as it comes and never
think about anything of a public nature." And in the meantime the
road to socialism remains for a good part of the way—through
"nationalizations, expropriative taxation and all the constructive
political machinery"—identical with the road to state capitalism. So
that Lenin, says Shaw, had been quite in the wrong when he had
denounced the methods of the Fabians as state capitalism.

But Lenin had been aware of the psychological pitfalls in the approach of the Fabians toward socialism—pitfalls which no amount
of lucid explanation was able to get them over and which Shaw
continued to stumble into himself. From the moment that you propose to benefit people from the point of view of imposing upon them
what is best for them rather than of showing them the way to what
they ought to have and awaiting the moment when they will know
that they must have it, what is to prevent your slipping—the post-
Lenin period in Russia has proved it as much as the Ramsay Macdonald Labour Government—into imposing upon the people something which will benefit you yourself?

I shall not here pursue the story of the subsequent career of the
Fabians, as I want to show further on how it was reflected in Bernard Shaw's later plays. But I will note here that in 1931 he visited
Soviet Russia in company with the Tory Lady Astor and with the
liberal Marquess of Lothian, had an audience with Stalin, at which,
as he said, they treated Stalin like "a friendly emperor," and, on his
return, began loudly endorsing Russia and especially scolding the
United States for not following the Soviet example. Later, in his
Preface on Bosses in his volume of plays of 1936, he was back praising Mussolini again and even throwing a few kind words to Hitler,
whom he described as "not a stupid German" (did Bernard Shaw
prefer a crazy Austrian?) and whose persecution of the Jews he characterized considerately as "a craze, a complex, a bee in his bonnet, a
hole in his armour, a hitch in his statesmanship, one of those lesions
which sometimes prove fatal." Of the systematic persecution by the
Nazis of Communists, Socialists and Pacifists, of everybody—including critics and artists—who belonged to Bernard Shaw's own camp,
he had nothing whatever to say save to mention it and minimize it
in passing as "plundering raids and *coups d'état* against inconvenient
Liberals or Marxists." At the time of the Ethiopian War, he came out
strongly for Mussolini on the same grounds on which he had
formerly defended the behavior of the British in South Africa, and

insisted that the League of Nations, on behalf of which in 1928 he had written a Fabian pamphlet, should never have tried to interfere.

Thus in this period of disastrous dictatorships, when it was very important for a socialist to keep clear in the eyes of the public the difference between the backing and aims of Lenin and the backing and aims of Mussolini, Bernard Shaw has done a good deal to confuse them and, parliamentary socialist though he claims to be, to exalt the ideal of the dictator. When the socialist dictatorship of Lenin gave way to the despotism of Stalin, Shaw did not seem to know the difference, but applauded the suppression of the old Leninists, on the ground that most professional revolutionists ought to be shot the morning after the revolution, and, on the principle that the socially harmful had to be got out of the way, gave his blessing to the Russian concentration camps, with their millions of political prisoners.

All this he has handled, of course, with his marvelous cleverness and style. Analyzing everybody perpetually, he is a great master of the smoke-screen against criticism. It is done partly by sheer personal hypnotism and Irish gift of gab. Before you arrive at any book of Bernard Shaw's—from *What I Really Wrote About the War* to his correspondence with Ellen Terry—you have almost invariably been told what to think of it in a preface by which Shaw has protected himself against your possible perception of his weakness. If you submit to his spell, you will allow him to manipulate the lights in such a way that, by the time the curtain goes up, you find Shaw looking noble in the center of the stage with everything else left in semi-obscurity, and yourself with your discriminatory powers in a temporary state of suspension, under the illusion that you must either accept or reject him. (Of late the exhibitionistic vanity which seemed dashing in his early days when he was assailing the philistines with such spirit has come to be tiresome and even repellent—as, for example, when his comment on the death of one of his distinguished contemporaries takes the form of the irrelevant reflection, "I'll be dead very soon myself!")

But there has been also an odd kind of trickery involved in the whole of Bernard Shaw's career. It depends on a technique which he has mastered of functioning on three distinct planes and of shifting from one to another. His air of certainty, his moralist's tone, his well-drilled sentences, his regular emphasis, all go to create an impression of straightforwardness. But actually the mind of Shaw is always fluctuating between various emotions which give rise to various points of view.

The mechanics seem to be somewhat as follows: At the bottom of Shaw is a commonsense sphere of practical considerations; above this is a plane of socialism, of the anticipated reorganization of society in the interest of ideal values; and above this, a poet-philosopher's ether from which he commands a longer view of life *sub specie aeternitatis* and where the poet allows himself many doubts which neither the socialist nor the bourgeois citizen can admit. Shaw has never really taken up his residence for any great length of time on any one of these three planes of thinking. The socialist, for example, denounces war; but when England actually goes to war, the respectable householder backs her. The moralist denounces marriage; but the conventional married man always advises young people to get married. The socialist takes sword in hand to battle for a sounder society based on a redistribution of income; and the long-view philosopher-poet comes to sap the socialist's faith with misgivings as to the capacity for intellect and virtue of the material of common humanity as contrasted with philosopher-poets. The poet gets a good way above the earth in the ecstasy of imaginative vision; but the socialist reminds him that it is the duty of art to teach a useful social lesson, and the householder damps the fires of both by admonishing them that the young people in the audience oughtn't to be told anything that will get them into trouble. The result is that reading Shaw is like looking through a pair of field glasses of which the focus is always equally sharp and clear but the range may be changed without warning.

So adroit are Shaw's transitions that we are usually unaware of what has happened; and when we have come to be conscious of them, we wonder how much Shaw is aware. It is curious to go back over his work and see him juggling with his various impersonations: the socialist, the fascist, the saint, the shrewd businessman, the world genius, the human being, the clever journalist who knows how to be politic, the popular speaker who knows how to be tactful. It is quite as if they were the characters in a comedy, each of whom he can pick up where he has dropped him and have him go on with his part.

III

But comedies are best presented in the theater; and in the theater Shaw's conflicts of impulse, his intellectual flexibility and his genius for legerdemain—all the qualities that have had the effect of weakening his work as a publicist—have contributed to his success as an artist.

One of the prime errors of recent radical criticism has been the assumption that great novels and plays must necessarily be written by people who have everything clear in their minds. People who

have everything clear in their minds, who are not capable of identifying themselves imaginatively with, who do not actually embody
in themselves, contrary emotions and points of view, do not write
novels or plays at all—do not, at any rate, write good ones. And—
given genius—the more violent the contraries, the greater the works
of art.

Let us consider Shaw as an artist.

Bernard Shaw's great role in the theater has been to exploit the
full possibilities of a type of English comedy which had first been
given its characteristic form during the seventies of the nineteenth
century in the comedies of W. S. Gilbert. The comedy of the Restoration, which had culminated in Congreve, had been the product
of an aristocratic society, which depended for its ironic effects on
the contrast between artificial social conventions and natural animal instincts, between fine manners and fine intelligence, on the one
hand, and the crudest carnal appetites, on the other. The comedy of
the nineteenth century—setting aside Oscar Wilde—depended on the
contrast between the respectable conventions of a pious middle-class
society and the mean practical realities behind them, between the
pretension to high moral principles and the cold complacency which
underlay it. As with the dramatists of the Restoration, it was always
the pursuit of pleasure that emerged from behind the formalities, so,
in the comedies of Gilbert which preceded his Savoy operas and
of which the most famous and successful was *Engaged* (1877), it is
always the greed for money that extrudes from behind the screen of
noble words and discreet behavior. "Dear papa," says the Victorian
young lady in one of the scenes of *Engaged,* when she has just heard
of the failure of a bank in which the fortune of her fiancé was invested, "I am very sorry to disappoint you, but unless your tom-tit
is very much mistaken, the Indestructible was registered under the
Joint Stock Companies Act of '62 and in that case the stockholders
are jointly and severally liable to the whole extent of their available
capital. Poor little Minnie don't pretend to have a business head; but
she is not quite such a little donkey as that, dear papa!" The characters of Gilbert's comedies, who talk the language of Victorian
fiction, are never for a moment betrayed by emotion into allowing
themselves to be diverted from the main chance; and the young men
are perfectly ready, not from appetite but from sheer indifference, to
make equally passionate professions to any number of young ladies
at the same time. It is not far from the Symperson family and
Cheviot Hill of *Engaged* to Shaw's *The Philanderer* and *Widowers'
Houses.*

But neither Gilbert nor Dickens nor Samuel Butler—those two
other great satirists of the money-minded English, to whom, also,

Shaw is indebted—could teach him to analyze society in terms of economic motivation or to understand and criticize the profit system. This he learned to do from Karl Marx, whose work during his English residence, the period when *Das Kapital* was written, was itself of course a product of and an ironical protest against English nineteenth-century civilization. Bernard Shaw thus brought something quite new into English imaginative literature. His study of economics had served him, as he said, for his plays as the study of anatomy had served Michael Angelo. And with economic insight and training he joined literary qualities of a kind that had never yet appeared in combination with them—qualities, in fact, that, since the century before, had been absent from English literature entirely.

The Irish of Bernard Shaw's period enjoyed, in the field of literature, certain special advantages over the English, due to the fact that, since Irish society was still mainly in the pre-industrial stage, they were closer to eighteenth-century standards. If we compare Shaw, Yeats and Joyce to, say, Galsworthy, Wells and Bennett, we are struck at once by the extent to which these latter writers have suffered from their submergence in the commercial world. In their worst phases of sentimentality and philistinism, there is almost nothing to choose between them and the frankly trashy popular novelist; whereas the Irish have preserved for English literature classical qualities of hardness and elegance.

Bernard Shaw has had the further advantage of a musical education. "Do not suppose for a moment," he writes, "that I learnt my art from English men of letters. True, they showed me how to handle English words; but if I had known no more than that, my works would never have crossed the Channel. My masters were the masters of a universal language; they were, to go from summit to summit, Bach, Handel, Haydn, Mozart, Beethoven and Wagner. . . For their sakes, Germany stands consecrated as the Holy Land of the capitalistic age." Einstein has said that Shaw's plays remind him of Mozart's music: every word has its place in the development. And if we allow for some nineteenth-century prolixity, we can see in Shaw's dramatic work a logic and grace, a formal precision, like that of the eighteenth-century composers.

Take *The Apple Cart,* for example. The fact that Shaw is here working exclusively with economic and political materials has caused its art to be insufficiently appreciated. If it had been a sentimental comedy by Molnar, the critics would have applauded its deftness; yet Shaw is a finer artist than any of the Molnars or Schnitzlers. The first act of *The Apple Cart* is an exercise in the scoring for small orchestra at which Shaw is particularly skillful. After what he has himself called the overture before the curtain of the conversation between the two secretaries, in which the music of King Magnus is foreshadowed, the urbane and intelligent King and the "bull-roarer Boanerges" play a duet against one another. Then the King plays a single instrument against the whole nine of the cabinet. The themes emerge: the King's disinterestedness and the labor government's sordid self-interest. The development is lively: the music is tossed from one instrument to another, with, to use the old cliché, a combination of inevitableness and surprise. Finally, the King's theme gets a full and splendid statement in the long speech in which he declares his principles: "I stand for the great abstractions: for conscience and virtue; for the eternal against the expedient; for the evolutionary appetite against the day's gluttony," etc. This silver voice of the King lifts the movement to a poignant climax; and now a dramatic reversal carries the climax further and rounds out and balances the harmony. Unexpectedly, one of the brasses of the ministry takes up the theme of the King and repeats it more passionately and loudly: "Just so! . . . Listen to me, sir," bursts out the Powermistress, "and judge whether I have not reason to feel everything you have just said to the very marrow of my bones. Here am I, the Powermistress Royal. I have to organize and administer all the motor power in the country for the good of the country. I have to harness the winds and the tides, the oils and the coal seams." And she launches into an extraordinary tirade in which the idea of political disinterestedness is taken out of the realm of elegant abstraction in which it has hitherto remained with the King and reiterated in terms of engineering: "every little sewing machine in the Hebrides, every dentist's drill in Shetland, every carpet sweeper in Margate," etc. This ends on crashing chords, but immediately the music of the cabinet snarlingly reasserts itself. The act ends on the light note of the secretaries.

This music is a music of ideas—or rather, perhaps, it is a music of moralities. Bernard Shaw is a writer of the same kind as Plato. There are not many such writers in literature—the *Drames philosophiques* of Renan would supply another example—and they are likely to puzzle the critics. Shaw, like Plato, repudiates as a dangerous form of drunkenness the indulgence in literature for its own sake; but, like Plato, he then proceeds, not simply to expound a useful morality, but himself to indulge in an art in which moralities are used as the motifs. It is partly on this account, certainly, that Bernard Shaw has been underrated as an artist. Whether people admire or dislike him, whether they find his plays didactically boring or morally stimulating, they fail to take account of the fact that it is the enchantment of a highly accomplished art which has brought them to and kept them in the playhouse. It is an art that has even had the power to preserve such pieces as *Getting Married,* of which the 1908 heresies already seemed out of date twenty or thirty years later but of which the symphonic development still remains brilliant and fresh. So far from being relentlessly didactic, Shaw's mind has reflected in all its complexity the intellectual life of his time; and his great achievement is to have reflected it with remarkable fidelity. He has *not* imposed a cogent system, but he has worked out a vivid picture. It is, to be sure, not a passive picture, like that of Santayana or Proust: it is a picture in which action plays a prominent part. But it does not play a consistent part: the dynamic principle in Shaw is made to animate a variety of forces.

Let us see what these forces are and to what purpose they interact.

IV

What are the real themes of Bernard Shaw's plays?

He has not been a socialist dramatist in the sense that, say, Upton Sinclair has been a socialist novelist. His economics have served him, it is true, as anatomy served Michael Angelo; but to say that is to give as little idea of what kind of characters he creates and what his plays are about as it would of the figures of the sculptor to say that they were produced by an artist who understood the skeleton and the muscles. It is quite wrong to assume, as has sometimes been done, that the possession of the social-economic intelligence must imply that the writer who has it writes tracts for social reform.

Shaw is himself partly responsible for this assumption. In his early days, when he *was* a social reformer, he wrote books about Wagner and Ibsen which introduced them to the English-speaking public as primarily social reformers, too. There is of course a social revolutionist, a man of 1848, in Wagner, and a critic of bourgeois institutions in Ibsen. But Bernard Shaw, in his brilliant little books, by emphasizing these aspects of their work at the expense of everything else, seriously misrepresents them. He appreciates Siegfried and Brunhilde in their heroic and rebellious phases; but Wagner's tragedies of love he pooh-poohs; and it is sometimes just when Ibsen is at his strongest—as in *Brand* or *Rosmersholm*—that Bernard Shaw is least satisfactory on him, because the tragic spirit of Ibsen does not fit into Shaw's preconception. In Ibsen's case, Shaw is particularly misleading, because Ibsen disclaimed again and again any social-reforming intentions. His great theme, characteristic though it is of nineteenth-century society, is not a doctrine of social salvation: it is the conflict between one's duty to society as a unit in the social organism and the individual's duty to himself. Ibsen treats this theme over and over but in a number of different ways, sometimes emphasizing the validity of social claims as opposed to the will of the individual (*Little Eyolf*), sometimes showing them as unjustified and oppressive (*Ghosts*); sometimes showing the individual undone by self-indulgence or perverse self-assertion (*Peer Gynt* and *Brand*), sometimes showing him as noble and sympathetic (the hero and heroine of *Rosmersholm*); sometimes dramatizing the two poles of conduct in the career of a single individual, like Dr. Stockman in *An Enemy of the People*, who begins by trying to save society but who later, when society turns against him, is driven back into an individualistic vindication of the social conscience itself with the realization that "the strongest man is he who stands most alone." But the conflict is always serious; and it usually ends in disaster. Rarely—*A Doll's House* is the principal example—does it result in a liberation. Ibsen is hardly ever a social philosopher: he goes no further than the conflict itself.

Now is there any such basic theme in Bernard Shaw? Has he been creating a false impression not only about Ibsen but also about himself? Certainly the prefaces he prefixes to his plays do not really explain them any more than *The Quintessence of Ibsenism* really explains Ibsen.

The principal pattern which recurs in Bernard Shaw—aside from the duel between male and female, which seems to me of much less importance—is the polar opposition between the type of the saint and the type of the successful practical man. This conflict, when it is present in his other writing, has a blurring, a demoralizing effect, as in the passage on Saint Francis *et al.* which I quoted at the beginning of this essay; but it is the principle of life of his plays. We find it in its clearest presentation in the opposition between Father Keegan and Tom Broadbent in *John Bull's Other Island* and be-between Major Barbara and Undershaft—where the moral scales are pretty evenly weighted and where the actual predominance of the practical man, far from carrying ominous implications, produces a certain effect of reassurance: this was apparently the period—when Bernard Shaw had outgrown his early battles and struggles and before the war had come to disturb him—of his most comfortable and self-confident exercise of powers which had fully matured. But these opposites have also a tendency to dissociate themselves from one another and to feature themselves sometimes, not correlatively, but alternatively in successive plays. In *The Devil's Disciple* and *The Shewing-up of Blanco Posnet*, the heroes are dashing fellows who have melodramatic flashes of saintliness; their opponents are made comic or base. *Caesar and Cleopatra* is a play that glorifies the practical man; *Androcles and the Lion* is a play that glorifies the saint. So is *Saint Joan,* with the difference that here the worldly antagonists of the saint are presented as intelligent and effective.

Certainly it is this theme of the saint and the world which has inspired those scenes of Shaw's plays which are most moving and most real on the stage—which are able to shock us for the moment, as even the "Life Force" passages hardly 'do, out of the amiable and objective attention which has been induced by the bright play of the intelligence. It is the moment when Major Barbara, brought at last to the realization of the power of the capitalist's money and of her own weakness when she hasn't it to back her, is left alone on the stage with the unregenerate bums whose souls she has been trying to save; the moment when Androcles is sent into the arena with the lion; the moment in the emptied courtroom when Joan has been taken out to be burned and the Bishop and the Earl of Warwick are trying each to pin the responsibility on the other. It is the scene in *Heartbreak House* between Captain Shotover and Hector, when they give voice to their common antagonism toward the forces that seem to have them at their mercy: "We must win powers of life and death over them. . . There is enmity between our seed and their seed. They know it and act on it, strangling our souls. They believe in themselves. When we believe in ourselves, we shall kill them. . . We kill the better half of ourselves every day to propitiate them." It is the scene in *Back to Methuselah* when the Elderly Gentleman declares to the Oracle: "They have gone back to lie about your answer [the political delegation with whom he has come]. I cannot go with them. I cannot live among people to whom nothing is real!"—and when she shows him her face and strikes him dead.

But now let us note—for the light they throw on Bernard Shaw in his various phases—the upshots of these several situations. In *Major Barbara,* the Christian saint, the man of learning, and the industrial superman form an alliance from which much is to be hoped. In *Androcles and the Lion,* written in 1913, in Shaw's amusing but least earnest middle period, just before the war, Androcles and the lion form an alliance, too, of which something is also to be hoped, but go out arm in arm after a harlequinade on the level of a Christmas pantomime. In *Heartbreak House,* which was begun in 1913 and not finished till 1916, the declaration of war by the unworldlings takes place in the midst of confusion and does not lead to any action on their part.

In *Back to Methuselah,* of the postwar period, the Elderly Gentleman is blasted by the Oracle in a strange scene the implications of which we must stop to examine a moment. The fate of the Elderly Gentleman is evidently intended by Shaw to have some sort of application to himself: though a member of a backward community in which people have not yet achieved the Methuselah-span of life, he differs from his fellows at least in this: that he finds he cannot bear any longer to live among people to whom nothing is real. So the Oracle shrivels him up with her glance.

But what is this supposed to mean? What *is* this higher wisdom which the Elderly Gentleman cannot contemplate and live? So far as the reader is concerned, the relevation of the Oracle is a blank. The old system of Bernard Shaw, which was plausible enough to pass before the war, has just taken a terrible blow, and its grotesque and gruesome efforts to pull itself together and function give the effect of an umbrella, wrecked in a storm, which, when the owner tries to open it up, shows several long ribs of steel sticking out. The Life Force of the man and woman in *Man and Superman* no longer leads either to human procreation or to social-revolutionary activity. The Life Force has been finally detached from socialism altogether. In the *Intelligent Woman's Guide,* Shaw will reject the Marxist dialectic as a false religion of social salvation; but the Life Force is also a religious idea, which we have always supposed in the past to be directed toward social betterment, and now, in *Back to Methuselah,* we find that it has misfired with socialism. Socialism has come and gone; the planet has been laid waste by wars; the ordinary people have all perished, and there is nobody left on earth but a race of selected supermen. And now the race of superior human beings, which was invoked in *Man and Superman* as the prime indispensable condition for any kind of progess whatever but which was regarded by Shaw at that time as producible through eugenic breeding, has taken here a most unearthly turn. It has always been through the superman idea that Shaw has found it possible to escape from the implications of his socialism; and he now no longer even imagines that the superior being can be created by human idealism through human science. The superior beings of *Back to Methuselah* are people who live forever; but they have achieved this superiority through an unconscious act of the will. When they have achieved it, what the Life Force turns out to have had in store for them is the mastery of abstruse branches of knowledge and the extra-uterine development of embryos. Beyond this, there is still to be attained the liberation of the spirit from the flesh, existence as a "whirlpool in pure force." "And for what may be beyond, the eyesight of Lilith is too short. It is enough that there is a beyond."

Humanity, in *Back to Methuselah,* has dropped out for the moment altogether. The long-livers of the period of progress contemporary with the Elderly Gentleman are not the more "complete" human beings, with lives richer and better rounded, which Marx and Engels and Lenin imagined for the "classless society": they are

Shavian super-prigs who say the cutting and dampening things
which the people have always said in Shaw's plays but who have
been abstracted here from the well-observed social setting in which
Shaw has always hitherto presented them. And the beings of the
later epoch are young people playing in an Arcadia and ancients
immersed in cogitations, alike—both cogitations and Arcadia—of the
bleakest and most desolating description. There is in *Back to
Methuselah* nothing burning or touching, and there is nothing genuinely thrilling except the cry of the Elderly Gentleman; and that,
for all the pretense of revelation, is answered by a simple extinction.
In the *Tragedy of an Elderly Gentleman*, the Elderly Gentleman
is frightened, but his tragedy is not a real tragedy. *Saint Joan*
(1924) is an even more frightened play, and, softened though it is by
the historical perspective into which Shaw manages to throw it
through his epilogue, it was the first genuine tragedy that Shaw had
written. The horror of *Back to Methuselah* is a lunar horror; the
horror of *Saint Joan* is human. The saint is suppressed by the practical man; and even when she comes back to earth, though all those
who exploited or destroyed her are now obliged to acknowledge
her holiness, none wants her to remain among them: each would do
the same thing again. Only the soldier who had handed her the cross
at the stake is willing to accept her now, but he is only a poor helpless clown condemned to the dungeon of the flesh.

v

Back to Methuselah is a flight into the future; *Saint Joan* is a flight
into the past. But with *Heartbreak House* Bernard Shaw had already begun a series of plays in which he was to deal with the postwar world and his own relation to it in terms of contemporary
England—a section of his work which, it seems to me, has had too
little appreciation or comprehension.

Heartbreak House has the same sort of setting and more or less
the same form as such Shavian conversations as *Getting Married*
and *Misalliance;* but it is really something new for Shaw. There is
no diagram of social relations, no tying-up of threads at the end.
Heartbreak House, Shaw says in his preface, is "cultured leisured
Europe before the War"; but the play, he told Archibald Henderson,
"began with an atmosphere and does not contain a word that was
foreseen before it was written," and it is the only one of his plays
which he has persistently refused to explain. "How should *I* know?"
he replied, when he was asked by his actors what it meant. "I am
only the author." Heartbreak House, built like a ship, with its old
drunken and half-crazy master, the retired adventurer Captain Shot-

over, is cultured and leisured England; but the characters are no longer pinned down and examined as social specimens: in an atmosphere heavily charged, through a progression of contacts and collisions, they give out thunder and lightning like storm-clouds. Brooding frustrations and disillusions, child-like hurts and furious resentments, which have dropped the old Shavian masks, rush suddenly into an utterance which for the moment has burst out of the old rationalistic wit. For once, where Bernard Shaw has so often reduced historical myths to the sharp focus of contemporary satire, he now raises contemporary figures to the heroic proportions of myth.—An air-raid brings down the final curtain: Heartbreak House has at last been split wide. The capitalist Mangan gets killed, and there is a suggestion that they may all be the better for it.

But in 1924 the Labour Party came to power, with Ramsay Macdonald as Prime Minister. Macdonald had been a member of the Executive Committee of the Fabian Society, and he brought with him two other Fabians, Sidney Webb and Sydney Olivier, who took the portfolios of Minister of Labour and Secretary of State for India. When Macdonald was re-elected in 1929, he was accompanied by no less than twenty Fabians, of whom eight were cabinet members. The Fabians had now achieved the aim which was to have been the condition for the success of their ideas: they had "interpenetrated" the government. But in the meantime the competition of the British Empire with the German had culminated in a four years' war; and in England of after the war, with the top manhood of her society slaughtered and the lower classes laid off from their wartime jobs, and with English commercial domination further damaged by the United States, the influence of the Fabians could do little to bridge over the abyss which had been blasted between the extremes of the British class society. The best measures of the Labour Government were able to accomplish no more than just to keep the unemployed alive; and when the capitalists began to feel the pinch, they openly took over control. Ramsay Macdonald, in 1931, became Prime Minister in a Nationalist government and cleared his socialists out of office.

At the moment of the second accession of the Labour Party to power, Shaw had written *The Apple Cart,* in which Macdonald is caricatured as Proteus, the Prime Minister of a labor government. This government is represented as really controlled by Breakages, Limited, a great monopoly which opposes industrial progress for the reason that it has an interest in perpetuating the inferior and less durable machinery that requires more frequent repairs. But one finds in *The Apple Cart* no comment on the Fabianism, which, after all, has been partly responsible for Proteus: the blame is laid at the door, not of that socialism by interpenetration which has ended by itself being interpenetrated, but of something which Shaw calls "democracy"; and what is opposed to the corrupt socialism of Proteus is not socialism of a more thoroughgoing kind, but the super-constitutional-monarch, King Magnus. Again, Shaw has given the slip to his problems through recourse to the cult of the superior person.

Yet in 1931, after the final collapse of the Labour Government, Bernard Shaw visited Russia and, by applauding the Soviet system, incurred unpopularity in England for the first time since the war. In the same year, he wrote *Too True to Be Good,* a curious "political extravaganza," in which he turns back upon and criticizes his own career. Here the theme of the bourgeois radical of the eighties, disillusioned with himself under stress of the disasters of the twentieth century, is treated in the same vein, with the same kind of idealist poetry, now grown frankly elegiac and despairing, which Shaw had opened in *Heartbreak House* and which had made the real beauty of *The Apple Cart.*

A rich young English girl of the upper middle class is languishing with an imaginary illness in a gloomy Victorian chamber, fussed over by a Victorian mother. Into this sickroom erupt two rebels: a young preacher and a former chambermaid, who is an illegitimate child of the aristocracy. The chambermaid has been masquerading as the heiress's trained nurse, and she and the preacher have a plot to steal the heiress's pearl necklace. The girl comes to from her megrims and puts up an unexpected struggle. The preacher becomes interested in his victim and says that he has always wondered why she does not steal the necklace herself. Why doesn't she take it and go and do what she pleases, instead of staying home with her mother, moping and fancying herself sick? Why doesn't she let him and his accomplice sell the necklace for her, taking 25 per cent of the price apiece and giving her the other 50? The girl enthusiastically agrees, and while she is getting dressed to go with them, the preacher jumps up on the bed and delivers one of those live-your-own-life sermons with which Shaw, in the nineties, made his first success. Then he is off—in the excitement of his rhetoric, at first forgetting the necklace, which the heiress has to remind him they need.

All three sail away together to an imaginary Balkan country reminiscent of *Arms and the Man,* where they are able to do whatever they like but where their revolt turns out to lead to nothing and eventually to bore them to death. Shaw has evidently put into *Too True to Be Good* a sort of recapitulation of his earlier themes, the shams of bourgeois society: the capitalistic doctor of *The Doctor's Dilemma* is as much a fraud as ever; the pompous British military officer, though retaining an air of authority, has practically ceased even to pretend to be anything other than a fraud and is quite willing to leave the command to a private (drawn from Lawrence of Arabia), if he can only be left in peace with his water-colors; the old-fashioned materialist-atheist who is also the most rigorous of moralists, of the type of Roebuck Ramsden in *Man and Superman,* has lived through into a world where his morality has no power to prevent his son's turning thief, etc. Finally everyone except the preacher sets out for the "Union of Sensible Republics."

The preacher is left alone on the shore, abandoned between two worlds. He had come too late for the old and too early for the new. He had had the courage once to steal a necklace but he hadn't carried through his idea. He had given it back to the owner and they had made common cause together: the liberated bourgeois girl had gotten 50 per cent of the price, the radicals only 25 apiece. In this last scene, the darkness comes, the clouds gather; the morale of the preacher breaks down. He can only go on explaining and exhorting, whether or not he has anything to say. A keen wind is blowing in, and it may be the breath of life, but it is too fierce for him to bear.

This, Shaw tells us, is a political fable; and now he is to return to politics proper. In *On the Rocks* (1933), he appears to drive himself into a corner as he has never before done and then comes out with a political position which still manages to be somewhat equivocal.

The first act shows a liberal Prime Minister, hard beset during a period of depression. Pall Mall and Trafalgar Square are full of excited crowds. The Prime Minister, on the verge of a breakdown, can think of nothing to do except to call out the police against them, but he is dissuaded by the Police Commissioner himself and finally induced to go away for a rest. He has just been visited by a labor delegation who have impressed him with the importance of Marxism, and he takes volumes of Marx and Lenin away with him.

When the curtain goes up on the second act, the Prime Minister has read Marx and Lenin; but the effect upon him is unexpected. He has gained an insight into economic motivation, an understanding of the technique of making use of it; but he has not been converted to socialism: he has worked out, on the contrary, an exceedingly clever scheme for preserving the capitalist state through a program, essentially fascist, of partial nationalization and taxation of unearned incomes. He will conciliate the various social groups which would normally be antagonistic by promising a concession to each. The plan seems bidding fair to succeed when it runs aground on Sir Dexter Rightside, the Liberal Prime Minister's Tory colleague in a coalition National Government. Sir Dexter represents the blind conservatism which sticks to the *status quo* through sheer obstinacy and inability to imagine anything else: he threatens to put colored shirts on "fifty thousand patriotic young Londoners" and to call them into the streets against the proposed program of the government. The Prime Minister has to give up his attempt, but he is now forced to face his situation: "Do you think I didn't know," he confesses to his wife, "in the days of my great speeches and my roaring popularity, that I was only whitewashing the slums? I couldn't help knowing as well as any of those damned Socialists that though the West End of London was chockful of money and nice people all calling one another by their Christian names, the lives of the millions of people whose labor was keeping the whole show going were not worth living; but I was able to put it out of my mind because I thought it couldn't be helped and I was doing the best that could be done. I know better now! I know that it can be helped, and how it can be helped. And rather than go back to the old whitewashing job, I'd seize you tight around the waist and make a hole in the river with you. . . Why don't I lead the revolt against it all? Because I'm not the man for the job, darling. . . And I shall hate the man who will carry it through for his cruelty and the desolation he will bring on us and our like."

The shouting of the crowd and the crash of glass is suddenly heard outside. The people have broken into Downing Street. The police begin to club them and ride them down. The people sing, "England, arise!"

Sir Arthur Chavender's more or less liberal fascism has been defeated by the reactionary fascism of his Tory colleague in the National Government, with whom he is indissolubly united. (There is no question any longer of the superior man: King Magnus has disappeared from the scene.) There is a third point of view, opposed to both, but this, also, sounds rather fascist. Old Hipney, the disillusioned labor veteran, who speaks for the dissatisfied classes, seems to be looking for a Man on Horseback, too: "Adult suffrage: that was what was to save us all. My God! It delivered us into the hands of our spoilers and oppressors, bound hand and foot by our own folly and igorance. It took the heart out of old Hipney; and now I'm for any Napoleon or Mussolini or Lenin or Chavender that has the stuff in him to take both the people and the spoilers and oppressors by the scruffs of their silly necks and just sling them into the way they should go with as many kicks as may be needful to make a thorough job of it." But Chavender declines the job; and the people begin throwing bricks.

The conclusion we are apparently to draw is that parliamentary fascism must fail; and that we may then get either a Lenin or a Mussolini. Is this also a final confession of the failure of Fabianism, which depended on parliament, too?

In any case, at the end of this play, we have come in a sense to the end of Shaw. With the eruption of the uprising, we should be plunged into a situation which could no longer be appropriately handled by the characteristic methods of his comedy. He is still splendid when he is showing the bewilderment of the liberal governing-class prime minister: it is suprising how he is still able to summon his old flickering and piercing wit, his old skill at juggling points of view, to illuminate a new social situation—how quick and skillful he is at describing a new social type: the communist viscount, with his brutal language, which shocks his proletarian allies. But with the shouts and the broken glass, we are made to take account of the fact that Shaw's comedy, for all its greater freedom in dealing with social conditions, is almost as much dependent on a cultivated and stable society as the comedy of Molière, who had his place in the royal dining-room and depended on Louis's favor for the permission to produce his plays. Shaw, as much as Molière, must speak the same language as his audience; he must observe the same conventions of manners. And further than *On the Rocks*—in depicting the realities of the present—we feel that he cannot go.

Then we realize that, after a detour of the better part of half a century, of almost the whole of his artistic career, Shaw has only returned to that Bloody Sunday of 1887 when the Socialists had headed a demonstration and been driven away by the police; and we remember, apropos of Molière, that the most celebrated of British dramatists for a long time found it impossible to get a theater in London for *On the Rocks*.

Shaw's most recent pieces are weaker. *The Simpleton of the Unexpected Isles* (1934) is the only play of the author's which has ever struck me as silly. In it, the Day of Judgment comes to the British Empire, and the privilege of surviving on earth is made to depend upon social utility. But, by setting up a purely theocratic tribunal, Shaw deprives this scene of social point: the principle of selection is so general that it might be applied by the fascists as readily as by the socialists, at the same time that the policy of wholesale extinction seems inspired by an admiration for the repressive tactics of both. The play ends with a salute to the unknown future, which, like the vision of infinity of *Back to Methuselah*, seems perfectly directionless. *The Millionairess* (1936) makes a farce out of the notion that a natural boss, deprived of adventitious authority, will inevitably gravitate again to a position where he can bully and control people, and sounds as if it had been suggested by the later phases of Stalin.

Here it cannot be denied that Bernard Shaw begins to show signs of old age. As the pace of his mind slackens and the texture of his work grows looser, the contradictory impulses and principles which have hitherto provided him with drama begin to show gaping rifts. In his *Preface on Bosses* to *The Millionairess*, he talks about "beginning a Reformation well to the left of Russia," but composes the panegyric on Mussolini, with the respectful compliments to Hitler, to which I have already referred.

Yet the openings—the prologue to *The Simpleton*, with its skit on the decay of the British Empire and the knockabout domestic agonies of the first act or two of *The Millionairess*—still explode their comic situations with something of the old energy and wit; and the one-acter, *The Six of Calais*, though it does not crackle quite with the old spark, is not so very far inferior to such an earlier trifle as *How He Lied to Her Husband*. It is interesting to note— what bears out the idea that Shaw is at his best as an artist—that the last thing he is to lose, apparently, is his gift for pure comic invention, which has survived, not much dimmed, though we may tire of it, since the days of *You Never Can Tell*.

And he has also maintained his integrity as a reporter of the processes at work in his time—in regard to which his point of view has never been doctrinaire but always based on observation and feeling. He has not acted a straight role as a socialist; a lot of his writing on public affairs has been nonsense. But his plays down to the very end have been a truthful and continually developing chronicle of a soul in relation to society. Professionally as well as physically—he has just turned eighty-one as I write—he is outliving all the rest of his generation.

Nor can it be said that the confusions of his politics have invalidated his social criticism. Of his educative and stimulative influence it is not necessary today to speak. The very methods we use to check him have partly been learned in his school.

W. H. AUDEN

1942

The Fabian Figaro

If biographies of writers are justifiable—and there is much to be said for the view that their own works contain all that is relevant—it is because, in their case, the ways in which they accept and revolt against their immediate situation are peculiarly easy to watch, and the acceptance of and revolt against the immediate is the central human problem of free will.

The sin of the popular writer is an accidie that accepts the social values of his day as absolute; the sin of most good modern writers is a pride that perceives their imperfections in these values and revolts against them, but in so doing, adopts as final values which are opposite but also partial, the mirror image of what it attacks. A writer is great—there are no perfect writers—in the degree to which he transcends both simple acceptance and simple revolt, so that later generations are conscious in reading him less of his relevance to his age and more of his relevance to themselves. In the speech of the Inquisitor in *Saint Joan,* for example, Shaw is a great writer; in *As Far as Thought Can Reach* he is only an interesting example of liberal thought at the beginning of the twentieth century. In both cases he is concerned with religion and politics, which he has declared to be the two proper concerns for an adult (his deliberate omission of love makes his adult religion and politics a little strange), and his success in the one and his failure in the other may serve as a starting point from which to consider his life and work.

If we do not know it already, Mr. Hesketh Pearson's account[*] of his childhood would make it very clear that what was presented to Shaw as the Christian faith was not Christian but unitarian, the eternal religion of this world. The greater the social prestige and

Reprinted from *The Commonweal*, October 23, 1942.
[*] G. B. S., *A Full Length Portrait.* Hesketh Pearson.

153

political and economic power of the Church, the greater must always be her temptation to "confound the Persons and divide the Substance," i.e., to make God the purely transcendent First Cause of the Greek philosophers, the absentee landlord of the universe, and herself His bailiff. The Word made Flesh must then be either safely imprisoned, like the Emperor of Japan, within the ecclesiastical organization—the danger for Catholicism—or safely "humanized" and turned into a good boy scout—the danger for Protestantism. In either case the Christian *faith* has been abandoned for a political *religion,* more agreeable to the bourgeois Haves in society. Unfortunately, in attacking this heresy, the bohemian Have-nots are tempted to make God purely immanent, in a Great Man, a race, or a class, to deny the Father in the name of the Son.

But this too is a political religion and, moreover, only tenable so long as one is the opposition and therefore without positive political responsibility for human suffering, so long as one is not in a position to make good one's promise of creating a heaven on and out of earth.

As the leader of the English opposition from a time when Darwin was still shocking until Hitler's Blitzkrieg over London, Shaw as a man and as a writer, his highly personal formulation of the Have-not religion, his quirks and biases, his insights and blind spots, deserve the closest consideration.

The Fairy Godmother never bestows her favors singly but always in contrasted pairs: if she gives a power, she also gives a weakness; if she provides a source of happiness, she never fails to add a source of suffering. This has led some psychologists to diagnose the weakness as the cause, and the power as its neurotic effect. This, of course, is rubbish. Suffering is not the cause of genius but its guardian angel, the means by which its possessor is compelled to make the use of his talent a serious matter, the limits which make his freedom a reality.

The fact that Shaw's father was a poor, conscience-stricken drunk and that his genteel mother showed him little affection did not make him imaginative, but they certainly helped to turn his imagination into a moral passion. On the other hand the same situation might have driven a child with a different hereditary make-up in quite other directions. The young Shaw was lucky enough to have the inclination to make the family skeleton dance and not in despair to seek all his life for someone to care for him. Yet the very intense vitality, intellectual curiosity and freedom from the common temptations of sex, money and a Good Time, which have been his greatest strength, have at the same time been his greatest danger. They almost prevented him from seeing that if he was right in regarding, like Plato, carnal passion as a limitation upon intellectual contemplation which could and should be removed, then, if one were, not Shaw, but only *un homme moyen sensuel,* one's only road to salvation must lie in practicing that morbid "Crosstianity" which he attacked in the preface to *Androcles and the Lion.* They almost turned him into one of those stoics who, as Pascal says, "conclude that what has been done once can be done always, and that since the desire of glory imparts some power to those whom it possesses, others can do likewise . . . that all those who are not at the high degree of wisdom are equally foolish and vicious, as those who are two inches under water."

And they almost turned him into an apologist for fascism. His criticism of a Darwinism and a behaviorism which allow no free-will to anyone but History and make evil the necessary present ground for future good—God moves in a malicious way—is brilliant and acute, but his own Lamarckism, which in theory sets no limits to human free-will and makes evil an accidental product of ignorance—my boy, you can be good if you only try sensibly—is in fact quite as pessimistic. For the worship of Universal Necessity, it substitutes the worship of Individual Virtue, the Hero, Hercules-Prometheus who defies the evolutionary Zeus on the grounds that he knows the Creator's mind better than he does himself.

But where did the hero obtain his virtue if not from a Zeus of Necessity who supervised the exceptional mutation of germ-plasm which made him what he is, or from a Zeus of Chance who allotted him a social and economic position in which he was less limited than the churlish mass of mankind? (It is noteworthy that Shaw's English predecessor, Samuel Butler, declared a private income to be a *sine qua non* for the Good Life.) Moreover, if great men are the only hope of the Evolutionary Process, they are morally bound to rule the masses for their own good—we are all here on earth to help others: what on earth the others are here for, I don't know—and the masses have no right whatsoever to resist them. The logical consequence of both the Darwinian and the Lamarckian premise is dictatorship as Hobbes and Plato respectively perceived.

Yes, his gifts almost deceived Shaw; but not quite. For he really is a great man, too intelligent not to know what conclusions would follow, but also too good-hearted and too humble to accept them. Hence, perhaps, the famous Shavian humor, for at the bottom of everything comic lies a contradiction.

He cannot, thank God, be serious for very long: the more logical his argument, the more certain he is to accompany it with a wink. Indeed his only insufferable characters are his good people (using "good" in the Shavian sense); like Candida who is a dreadful woman or Joan who talks like a lady novelist, and his most lovable characters are rogues like Candida's father.

For the same reason, perhaps, while no playwright has ever equalled Shaw in his insight into the effect of occupation upon character—he is the only writer who has read Karl Marx with real profit and most of his plays might be called studies in occupational diseases—yet the occupational type which he cannot draw is his own, the artist: Marchbanks and Dubedat are the mustiest of theatrical props. His most first-hand, realistically unheroic observation is of the political hero, the stoic in a high position. (More Shavian than Shaw, Mr. Hesketh Pearson calls this "the religious temperament!")

Reading this biography, one is shown over and over again how Shaw's instinct has consistently prevented him from becoming what for one of his extraordinary gifts was always tempting and easy, a great man of this world, a politician, and insisted upon his remaining an artist, the one worldly calling which by its nature can force its help on no one, for whatever pleasure and profit one derives from a work of art depends upon what one brings to it.

Is he in danger of becoming successful in business, something makes him walk out; is he in danger of becoming an M.P., something makes him deliver speeches which are bound to infuriate all the voters; is he in danger of leading a crusade, something makes him politely decline the honor by being too funny.

For this, both he and we may be very grateful. His plays are a joy to watch, not because they purport to be concerned with serious problems, but because they are such wonderful displays of conspicuous waste, because the energy shown by any of his characters is so wildly in excess of what their situation practically requires that if it were to be devoted to anything "worthwhile," they would wreck the world in five minutes.

All his life Shaw has been devoted to music (he was probably the best music critic who ever lived) and, as he tells us, it was from Mozart's *Don Giovanni* that he learned "how to write seriously without being dull"; and this devotion is, perhaps, the clue to his work. For all his theater about propaganda, his writing has an effect nearer to that of music than the work of any of the so-called pure writers.

The Mozart of English Letters he is not—the music of the Marble Statue is beyond him—the Rossini, yes. He has all the brio, the humor, the tunes, the clarity, and the virtuosity of that great master of Opera Bouffe.

And this is a very great deal. If now we see errors in his doctrines, the credit must go to Hitler, not to our own acumen; and the present generation, if it is honest, will have to admit that in comparison with its own spokesmen, the "vulgar old buffer" not only had nicer manners, a kinder heart, and a more courageous will, but also wrote a lot better.

JACQUES BARZUN

1943

Bernard Shaw in Twilight

Not long ago, I was part of a gathering at which someone, seeing Hesketh Pearson's recent biography on a table, turned the general conversation to the subject of Shaw.* "Does anybody," he asked, "know what Shaw's doing?"

"He's taking liver extract for his anemia," answered the doctor with malicious pleasure. "For a vegetarian," he explained, "it is a fitting end."

Before I could remark that his facts were out of date, the others took up in a sort of chorus the refrain of current opinion concerning Shaw. Shaw was virtually a fascist, said one; he never spoke a responsible word, said another. A third proved he was no artist and thought that his reputation was but a bubble blown on the breath of postwar cynicism. Only a spinster with a long memory had the courage to declare that she would not take back an ounce of her gratitude to Shaw for many evenings of high entertainment twenty years ago at the Theatre Guild. But she was promptly faced with the badness of the later plays; the doctor broke in again to say that Shaw's modes of thought were hopelessly unscientific; and talk petered out on the note that Pearson's biography was an anachronism, a superfluous and boring book.

Though unfair to a very workmanlike effort, this last note has a shadow of justification. Even when he is not quoting, Mr. Pearson relies heavily on Shaw's own words, and these now seem to lack freshness and authority. They strike up as echoes, but they are far from ringing impressively down the corridors of Time. The fact is that though Shaw is alive, he no longer has a living reputation. He is not even a deified and decrepit Grand Old Man of English

Reprinted from *The Kenyon Review*, Summer, 1943.
* *G.B.S. A Full Length Portrait.* Hesketh Pearson.

Letters. There seems to be no name for his position, which, never-theless, he is not the first to occupy. Meanwhile, he eludes our grasp and measure like a man in a fog.

He is wrapped in darkness in an even more direct sense. As al-ways happens with men who are famous while alive, what Shaw stands for, or rather a pot-pourri of his supposed opinions, has ended by obscuring the character of his thought. His interpreters and critics have succeeded too well. They have made him accessible, whether in attractive or repulsive guise, and he has been played up and played down to the point of being played out. It is perhaps significant that the last two books on Shaw are by onetime actors of his works, who conceived their task in much the same spirit. In "The Real Bernard Shaw," Mr. Maurice Colbourne told us that Shaw's invaluable doctrine being spread over four million words, it needed boiling down. In the present "portrait," Mr. Pearson tells us that Shaw is the greatest English dramatist since Shakespeare, but that apart from inventing the modern breezy historical play, Shaw's few objective creations merely reproduce on the stage his own temperament, that of the religious leader.

Clearly there is a gap between the claims made on Shaw's behalf by his attorneys and the need of critical charity in which they make him stand. What is a non-objective dramatist and how can his limited competence deserve pairing with Shakespeare's? What kind of literary master mind is he whose doctrine uses too many words and improves with reduction? Do the attorneys themselves lack faith in their client, or are they insensitive to self-contradiction? They remind us, at any rate, of certain reviewers of Mr. Pearson who, while complaining that Shaw's secret was still unrevealed, intimated that its discovery would not repay the racking of one's wits.

II

By the secret of a man's life, I suppose we mean simply an ex-planation of his motives. This may take the form of matching his intimate ways with his public acts, but a secret in the vulgar sense of hidden and hideous facts seldom means as much as a titillated public thinks. Anyhow, Shaw's mature life has been too public to hide secrets, and knowing our modern biographers' pruriency, he forestalled us with the information that his father was a drunkard. We also learned from him how in his early London years he lived on his mother and wrote five unsalable novels, when by common standards of decency he should have helped to support her. The letters to Ellen Terry, the love affairs, the strife of sixty years have all been aired. So we need not expect any sudden light from an unknown past. Even the cousin from Australia has turned up and told us nothing but jokes and irrelevancies.* The facts are all before us, they are abundant, and all the interpreting they need suggests itself the moment one goes beyond first impressions.

Strangers who have seen Shaw face to face are wont to report their surprise at his gentleness and consideration, his willingness to listen and his complete lack of pose. Clearly what irritates and baffles the anti-Shavian is that Shaw writes about himself in the same tone and with the same passionate interest as he writes about socialism or evolution. "He is an intolerable egotist." The complaint really means that Shaw does not divide himself into man, author, wit, politician and playwright, striking an appropriate attitude for each. He does not manifest himself in institutional forms, but appears rather as a one-man Ministry of All the Talents, a superior organism with more feelers, limbs, and senses than normal manhood affords.

It is in this Supermanner and not in any assignable vice or virtue, that we can discover the fairly open secret of Shaw's personality. His distinguishing trait is to be at once self-aware and facing outwards. Shaw knows at any moment, on any subject, what he thinks, what you will think, what others have thought, what all this thinking entails; and he takes the most elaborate pains to bring these thoughts to light in a form which is by turns abstract and familiar, conciliatory and aggressive, obvious and inferential, comic and puzzling. In a word, Shaw is perhaps the most consciously conscious mind that has ever thought—certainly the most conscious since Rousseau; which may be why both of them often create the same impression of insincerity amounting to charlatanism.

Yet it is by excess of honesty that Shaw has himself lent color to his representation as an inconsequential buffoon bent on monopolizing the spotlight. The very precise intent of his "Better than Shakespeare," his care in discrediting his own newspaper *boutades*, his insistence on the exact limits of his knowledge, his signalizing his own artistic decline, have all been taken by the public as disingenuous fictions, clever publicity stunts. In the beginning, when Shaw's simple shamelessness was new, it compelled an irritated and incredulous attention. Having become an expected stimulant, and sometimes a feeble formula (witness the letter certifying Hesketh Pearson as a biographer) Shaw's self-acceptance now breeds only a protective apathy.

This being in brief the history of Shaw's popularity and present neglect, the profound misunderstanding of his thought and art

* *Bernard's Brethren.* By C. M. Shaw. Henry Holt.

follows necessarily. It is not that we have ceased to care and understand, but that we never did care or understand. We were shocked, tickled, stunned; we were too amused. But in a more settled mood we can see that for the uses of the common reader, Shaw always supplied an overdose. It is not the number of his words but the load they carry that is staggering. If a normally well-trained mind had as many perceptions instantly radiating towards him from a single core as Shaw requires of him, he would be dazzled and paralyzed by the illumination. Hence such a person cannot see—least of all in the playhouse—what Shaw is getting at. The one impression he does get is that the man is showing off again. Between him and Shaw the barrier is not profundity or obscurity, but intensity and extent of thought. Let any doubter reread the 80-page Preface to *Blanco Posnet* on the Censorship of Plays and simply *count the subjects*. There has been no tour de force like it since Macaulay's Parliamentary speeches, where thirty historical allusions flash in a paragraph. Yet there is this difference, that Shaw does not merely decorate a proposition, but makes his way from point to point through new and difficult territory.

This explains why Shaw must either be taken whole or left alone. He must be disassembled and put together again with nothing left out, under pain of incomprehension; for his politics, his art, and his religion—to say nothing of the shape of his sentences—are unique expressions of this enormously enlarged and yet concentrated consciousness.

How he came by it is not entirely a mystery. First of all, Shaw reached intellectual maturity in the late seventies, when political democracy, industry, the new imperialism and the new journalism were furnishing to open-eyed youth direct evidence that the world was a cacophonous whole. It was no longer a world projecting its main events in succession on the screen of time and local intelligence, but a simultaneous world—so to speak—with groups, parties, classes, peoples, empires, and religions in unceasing orchestral chaos. The universal relevance of anything to all other things, which had always been theoretically recognized, was now grossly palpable, not indeed to the routine mind or the academically brilliant one, but to the naive and imaginative observer.

Because of his somewhat unusual family history, Shaw was just such an observer. As a child, he tells us, he lived largely in a world of vivid imaginings stimulated by books and music; his schooling was meager, and therefore harmless; his relatives were eccentric and his social life was non-existent. No better circumstances could be found for developing a dramatic and un-institutionalized mind. The head of the family being incompetent and rather disgraceful, and the mutual affection of its members being taken for granted, Shaw became in due course an abnormally shy, sensitive, untutored youth, belonging to no class, lacking gumption, though intelligent enough to know that nothing but his own will and wits could extricate him from his discomfort. Even the one pretense he had been brought up to—that of "the Shaws'" abstract eminence—he could both share and see through, since it emanated from his amiable father and was contradicted by his mother's enforced drudging.

To the boy who could make up endless stories resembling those in novels and operas, all the world was undoubtedly a stage, but to the cruelly miserable adolescent without any footing or skill, there was no possibility of self-forgetfulness as a mere spectator. He must act, and he must first learn how by taking thought. As need or curiosity prompted, Shaw taught himself shorthand and book-keeping, penmanship and public speaking, economics and etiquette, score-reading and dialogue writing—most of it solitary work spurred on by a kind of otherworldly ambition. For like Rousseau, whom he resembles even more than he resembles Voltaire, Shaw never gave social form to his assertiveness, never desired to arrive and assimilate himself, or wield authority as of right. In this respect, he is the antithesis of H. G. Wells, who rose with the tide of scientism, prospered with the new press, and always found himself at the head of the "advanced people" as the expounder of their changing ideas. Shaw never had disciples, and, after his first emancipation, never budged. He added to his information or shifted his batteries, but his faith has been the same since its first stilted expression in the five novels.

Seeing clearly within himself and always able to dodge around the ends of any position, including his own, Shaw assumed from the start the dual role of prophet and gadfly. To his contemporaries it appeared frivolous and contradictory to perform as both super-man and socialist, sceptic and believer, legalist and heretic, high-brow and mob-orator. But feeling the duty to teach as well as to mirror mankind, Shaw did not accept himself as a contradictory being. His reproach to Shakespeare is precisely this acceptance, which leads to pessimism. Instead, Shaw prepared himself, with more facts and more experience, to transcend the contradictions and repel the world's inevitable counter-attacks.

These attacks never came, of course, except in the form of commonplace insults and denials, which left Shaw building out of his enormous insecurity impregnable bastions of knowledge, logic, and wit. Critics with a psychoanalytic turn of mind will be ready to say that the natural craving for affection, denied in Shaw's infancy, is at the root of this Titanic effort. Assign what cause you will, the results are so far out of proportion with ordinary causes that it is best to go on describing effects. And as William James pointed out, the genius does not lie in the emotional abnormality but in the caliber of the mind which the dammed-up emotion propels toward its chosen goal.

Shaw's emotional development was one with his intellectual strength. His path led him into the thick of the scrimmage, where more spontaneous natures defend themselves with the usual weapons of malice, humility, bad temper or conceit. But Shaw used the death ray of imperturbability. His feelings were never hurt, his envy was never aroused, his conceit was a transparent fiction, he never quarreled. There is something Christlike about his innumerable acts of generosity and unassuming forgiveness. He would secretly obtain a knighthood for a rival playwright who openly detested him, he would patiently dissolve the rancor of plotting opponents; he would warmly praise others' work behind their backs. If we except Sir Henry Irving as his one failure, Shaw deliberately and successfully held up his friends and associates to their highest level of performance and good behavior. This is what Chesterton meant when he said after twenty years of combat with Shaw on "the most sacred and delicate essentials of existence . . . I never read a reply by Bernard Shaw that did not leave me in a better and not a worse temper or frame of mind; which did not seem to come out of inexhaustible fountains of fairmindedness and intellectual geniality; which did not savor somehow of that native largeness which the philosophers attributed to the Magnanimous Man."

Nor was this achievement the result of Socratic moderation. Everywhere, in politics, the theater, and private life, Shaw lectured and bossed those around him to within an inch of their sanity, inditing inspired diatribes which make much better reading for us than they can have made for their recipients. Yet the effect was magical. Those who laughed were won over; those who resisted or hit back were treated as if nothing had happened. Shaw's personal criticism violated all the rules of good taste in general, no doubt because he was always criticizing somebody in particular. But through it shone a loyalty and friendliness, a combination of righteous wrath and superior tact, as if a highly effectual angel were beating his wings at once to chastise and to cool the air.

The angelic strain may explain Shaw's fondness for Shelley, which seems to rest on something more than a common love of reform and vegetable diet. It implies a temperamental kinship, a disembodied quality in both men, which leads certain critics to find their art equally thin and bloodless. Aptly enough, the epithet that recurs most often in Pearson's biography is "fastidious," which connotes passion without sensuality. Remembering Byron's dictum that compared to Shelley every other man was a beast, we are not surprised to find Beatrice Webb in the early Fabian years nicknaming her friend Shaw, "the Sprite."

III

Those who dispute Shaw's claim to the title of artist, discredit equally his technique and substance. "He never created a character," says the critic; "his plays are formless conversations." "All head and no heart," echoes the man in row F, outraged by a sermon on socialism in the midst of comedy.

The technical complaint is fairly easily disposed of. Indeed, three or four lines of defense are possible. The first is that leaving aside the plays, there is such a thing as Shavian prose, which as a distinct creation assures its creator an immortality coterminous with the English tongue. The first critic to assess it justly was Dixon Scott, who died at Gallipoli twenty-eight years ago. He showed how the Shavian sentence, by obliterating connectives, becomes a sort of lash made up of fused ideas, written for ear and mind, and barbed to suit the occasion. Here is a sample taken at random, which makes it clear, incidentally, that the "lash" metaphor refers to form and not to punitive intent:

> In all emergencies the neighborly man must be before all things helpful; and to be in the thick of the mess and yet behave as if one were safe in a philosophic heaven out of range of the aircraft guns seemed to me not only sublimely selfish (which is not fundamentally an objection to it when its exponents are persons of genuinely exalted character) but liable at any moment to be reduced to absurdity by the crashing of a bomb through one's study roof. So I kept on the ground and appealed to every morality in turn to carry my points.

Like all good prose this is not identical with the spoken word— those who heard Shaw speak in New York may recall the difference —but it gives the impression of speech. It is in fact made for delivery, as Shaw's actors found out as soon as they opened their mouths instead of measuring the length of the sentence with the eye.

Mr. Herbert Read truly says that in the undecorated English style, Shaw's prose ranks next to Swift's: it is limpid, passionate and tireless, never falling much below its own standard of perfection. The Shavian matter may be dull, the medium is invariably a polished work of art. Perhaps some day a detailed study of Shaw's diction will be made, which will include a guess at its lineal ancestors. It has affinities with Dickens at his best, exhibiting the same rapid variation of purpose and device, from colloquialism to a high abstraction which by some miracle makes itself concrete as it goes; and the same humor of words, which is something else than wit. The lashing effect owes something to Ruskin and the simpler mood to the Book of Common Prayer, but the pace and pointedness are Shaw's own, and happily inimitable.

Such an achievement is quite enough to stamp a man as an artist, whether he uses it to draft resolutions or write letters to his house-keeper. But Shaw, we must remember, made his reputation as a critic. Had he died at forty, we should know him today merely as one of the great judges of the drama with Hazlitt, Lamb, and Coleridge, and as the only critic of music to put beside Berlioz.

Whether a critic is an artist is a matter of definition. Those who say so have in mind the fact that criticism has a distinct form and speech, which not everyone masters at will, despite editors' neces-sary assumption to the contrary. Shaw was obviously fitted to be-come a critic of the first rank, for in addition to the indispensable gift of awareness, he had conscience. He could separate what he felt from what he ought to feel, what was actually given from what he might expect or like to be given. More than that, he was inde-fatigable in acquiring information, knowing that to compare justly, the critic must know everything that has been said, composed or painted since the beginning of time. Lastly comes the ability to convey all this and develop its meaning. Shaw's music criticism, still instructive and enjoyable after 50 years, is a measure not only of his critical genius, but of the difference between the art of criticism and the trade of reviewing—who now reads Chorley or Dr. Franz Hueffer?

What we value in Shaw's work is his power to extract principles from the most unlikely materials, and to light up the confusion of intent and execution which affects particularly the arts of music and drama. He has, besides, a knack for touching off people, situations, sensations, merits and faults; a readiness in illustration, a sensitivity to talents of all kinds—was he not the only London critic to praise Henry James's unlucky *Guy Domville* and to see that Wilde's plays were not pure *jeux d'esprit?*—above all, he has an incorruptible equity and courage; all of which taken together make him the critical intelligence personified.

His failures merely prove that though his consciousness was ex-tended it was not infinite. But if anyone thinks that Shaw plumped too hard for Ibsen and Wagner,* let him read the critic's actual

* Mr. Pearson gives no inkling of Shaw's increasing preference, of late years, for the music of Rossini and his contemporaries as against that of Wagner. See Slonimsky, *Music Since* 1900.

words once again. True, he had a prejudice against Gilbert's comic operas; he railed at the Elizabethans and excoriated Marlowe; he had an unfortunate way of abusing "romanticism" while exemplifying it or praising its representative figures; but in none of this is it hard to find the ulterior tactical purpose, personal but principled, that animated him. The man had, after all, a stake in his own ideas, a creative bias, which kept him from being a flawless instrument. Even so, in the long-drawn-out Shakespeare controversy, Shaw turned out to know the plays better than their professed devotees, insisted on their performance in full, and strove harder than anyone to found a national theater for the Shakespeare repertory.

This brings us at last to Shaw as playwright. We have so often been told that Shavian comedy lacks form and is unlifelike, that any description of its special merits almost seems like conceding the faults and offering compensation. But if we begin by asking, What is *the* form of the comic play? tradition gives no single answer. Shaw himself does not use one unvarying pattern: he has written farces, high comedies, tragi-comedies, melodramatic comedies, comedies of manners, of situation, and of ideas. The fact that we can distinguish them argues at least a sense of tone in their maker. True, he teased his critics by calling his plays Discussions, Conversations, and the like, but when it came to the test of production under existing theatrical rules, the lines spoke well, the business could be set, and all quibbles disappeared in the great fact that the audience stayed and laughed. Molière himself desired no higher success.

Consider now the possibility of grouping Shaw's plays, not according to ideal form, but according to easily recognizable design—length, plot, climax, distribution of parts, balance of interest, and so on. This done, who can doubt that Shaw has again and again proved his ability to work within accepted late nineteenth century formulas, that he has, indeed, repeatedly worked them for all they were worth? I need only mention *You Never Can Tell, Pygmalion, The Philanderer, Widowers' Houses, Arms and the Man, Village Wooing, Fanny's First Play, Passion, Poison and Petrifaction, Overruled, Augustus Does His Bit* and a half-dozen other titles. Empty out the Shavian vocabulary and attitudes and you will have receptacles in 1, 2, 3, or 4 acts fit for any kind of romantic comedy or thesis drama you may like.

Let us then have no more of the irritating commonplace that *Candida* shows its author could have written "real plays" had he wanted to. *Candida* appeals to the anti-Shavian not because its form is more playlike, but because its subject is more like that of other plays: the woman choosing between two men. For a kindred reason *Saint Joan* has earned general approval, again not in virtue of superior form, but because of common familiarity with a story and a haircut.

Moreover when we say that *Candida* is more like other plays, we mean only more like other contemporary plays. If we extend the range of comparison and take in Aristophanes and Molière, we see at once that their subjects and technique no more resemble George Kaufman's or Noel Coward's than Shaw's do, and we find by the same token that Shaw is often closer to his great forerunners than he is even to his imitators Molnar and Behrman. One of the principal features of Aristophanic comedy is the *parabasis,* an address to the audience conveying the author's sentiments upon his theme. This device, though Greek, is not necessarily sublime; but it is respectable and convenient and Shaw should be congratulated rather than abused for reviving it in the form of the long didactic speech. Nothing then, could be more classical than the Frenchman's tirade in *Fanny's First Play,* the final monologue in *Too True to Be Good* and the epiloguing in *Saint Joan.*

Sometimes we get double measure, in a second or third harangue by the same or other characters. This is chorus work, and I shall take up in a moment its good or bad effect on characterization. Meanwhile it is certain that the whole tradition of great modern drama is behind Shaw in this usage. Molière in *Tartuffe* and the *Misanthrope,* in the two *Schools,* in the *Learned Ladies,* and in the *Bourgeois Gentilhomme;* Shakespeare in the soliloquies scattered through his plays; Racine in the great *tirades,* which the French romantic drama maintained and even extended—all of them substitute for the chorus of the ancients one or more interpolated monologues which stall the action but ballast the play. The enthusiastic actress who called Shaw's work "Italian Opera" did not know how accurately she was linking him to the continuous tradition of lyric drama.

In ancient comedy, furthermore, and in Molière to a marked extent, the abstract form is never allowed to choke off a good opportunity for laughter or propaganda, for horseplay, music or dancing. There are limits to the advisable distension of any framework, but each case must be judged on its merits. In plays like *Getting Married, Misalliance,* and *Heartbreak House,* which seem formless, the virtuosity with which Shaw digresses while maintaining the classic unities should have earned him medals from all the academies in the universe instead of the ignorant scorn of playgoing critics of the school of Mr. Curdle.

What is true of his dexterity with form applies equally to his action. Assuming that dramatic action is not physical motion, but psychological conflict which may occasionally turn into violence,

Shaw is lavish in both kinds: people slap each other, pull guns, raise pokers, hurl slippers, throw down vases in their rage, roll on the floor, besides doing the usual amount of direct namecalling. But what really counts for both action and comedy is that each speech shall amount to a twisting and turning over of the previous one—a rebuke or contradiction or misunderstanding of the interlocutor—with a view to building up in a few minutes a recognizable human situation. Every step must be swift, unforced, and in itself worth hearing. Now at this sort of skill, Shaw has no rivals but Shakespeare and Molière. An excellent test is to open a Shaw play at random and feel the tenseness generated as you read. No need to remember the story or the background of the characters. Each person is fighting all the time, making drama as he goes: only recall the crowd under the rain at the opening of *Pygmalion* or the man buying apples at the grocery in Act II of *Village Wooing*.

The question now arises whether in sustaining this tension, Shaw is "objective" and displays human feelings in their fullness and variety. Does he, in short, create characters? Mr. Pearson virtually denies it and the majority are with him when they describe a performance as "twenty people spouting Shaw." Without entering the labyrinth of distinctions between characters and types, reality and lifelikeness, individuals and ideas, I must point out that our modern views of the subject apply to a very narrow range of literature. In the sense of detailed psychological studies there are no characters whatsoever in ancient drama, in epic poetry, or in such fictions as Cervantes', Swift's, or Rabelais'. And when we come down to modern times, no two people agree on whether Scott, Dickens or Zola depict "real" characters.

The only way to settle the debate is to admit that the truth of a character does not depend on any particular substance or mode of presentation, but on his fitting the purpose and the environment provided by his creator. If you take an interest, *any* interest, in Lysistrata or Gulliver, they are real to that extent and for that purpose. Panurge is real in Rabelais and would be false in Meredith, and the converse is true about a Meredithian figure. As for "real life," it is impossible to say whether it furnishes Meredithian or Rabelaisian or Shavian characters in the raw. Fictional life is so much harder to live than actual life that most people would wither away in the rich atmosphere of Hamlet or Mr. Pickwick.

This suggests one reason why it has been fashionable to impugn Shaw's dramatis personae: they are highly articulate and self-conscious. Another is that they talk about high matters. A third, as we have seen before, is that they occasionally take on the function of a chorus speaking for the author. Listening to Shaw thus calls for constant interpretation; his dialogue may branch out in three directions. This is equally true of Shakespeare or Molière, but the passage of time has made us think that whatever they do is perfectly natural; that Alceste would of course know himself as thoroughly as Molière knows him; that a Scotch ruffian like Macbeth would examine his motives and generalize about murder; that a cowardly buffoon like Falstaff would be a wit and a poet in prose. As I say, time has helped, as well as the King-and-Queen tradition, but a time will come when the well-known spiritual eminence of the twentieth century will make it seem equally natural for a Shaw personage to combine recognizable traits with self-knowledge and philosophic reflectiveness.

This is not to say that all Shaw's creations are equally successful, but that testing their worth is not simply a matter of comparing them with our friends. In any fiction not exclusively devoted to psychology, character comes in touches. These must be abundant, fresh, and in the key of the subject. From this point of view, the persons in *The Devil's Disciple* are far inferior to the several doctors in *The Doctor's Dilemma;* yet most critics will think the former a better play and will call the second act of the latter a characterless conversation, merely because the action of *The Devil's Disciple* is more physical and exciting. As a matter of fact, in Shaw at large the scenes of pure talk are triumphs of dramatic characterization: everybody, to use Hebbel's test of real drama, "is in the right." Think of the Cabinet meeting in *The Apple Cart,* the visit in *Pygmalion,* the deputation in *On the Rocks,* the tea-party in *Fanny's First Play* and that feat of dramatized idleness, *Heartbreak House.*

But peopling the stage and keeping things going is not enough. A character has the right, in fact he has the duty, to become self-aware if it will create comedy. Likelihood may be violated when Mr. Juno in *Overruled* says to the wife who condones his flirtation:

Pardon me. I may be doing wrong: but I'm doing it in a proper and customary manner. You may be doing all right: but you're doing it in an unusual and questionable manner. I am not prepared to put up with that. I can stand being badly treated: I'm no baby, and can take care of myself with anybody. And of course I can stand being well treated. But the thing I can't stand is being unexpectedly treated.

Yet just as we treasure M. Jourdain's comments on his education we would not miss Juno's words for any likelihood in the world.

Lastly a character is privileged to spout Shaw (or Molière or Shakespeare) when the observations refer to someone else or to the general situation—flashes of insight struck off by the dramatic conflict itself. A good example is Boxer, the General, in *Getting*

Married, whose words and by-play in relation to the frigid Lesbia are perfectly within his limitations. He oversteps them only in anger or indignation at the public state of affairs, and his periodic awakenings add to the fun while establishing a result.

The objection remains that all this is brainwork. "Shaw is heartless and intellectualizes all he sees." At the risk of paradox, one must reverse the proposition and say that Shaw is passionate and makes emotion out of all he conceives. What is usually called "heart" is simply the accepted sentiments of the age. Mother love, demon rum, guilty passion, honest poverty, the equality of man, secret remorse—these things have been, still are, or may again be the objects of strong feeling for stage portrayal. But this does not mean that fears and hopes attached to other ideas do not also belong to the heart. Everyone understands Saint Joan's patriotism and her horror at the sentence passed upon her, but why suppose that in Sir Jafna's speech in *On the Rocks* we only hear Shaw lecturing? The outburst is in fact India's grievance against Britain and the white man; it is political passion personalized. What keeps us from recognizing this as legitimate emotion, and its dramatizer as a man with a heart fully as large as his mind, can only be the fact that Sir Jafna's motives are unusual, contemporary, and stripped of official façade. In this and other Shavian scenes, we should prefer more pomp and greater use of clearly labeled attitudes. We would then say "What a realist! How well he knows human beings!" for in stage dealings with history, ideas, or religion, we have come to want only the ritual hallowed by a thousand mediocre representations. We want sham Shakespeare or genuine Bulwer-Lytton.*

This preference incidentally explains why going to the theater becomes intolerable to many people after the first novelty and excitement have worn off, and why the world's great dramatic literature soon becomes unplayable. Most productions of Shakespeare, the traditional Molière at the Comédie, and the Greeks in purple-edged nightgowns are unbearable travesties, because "the stage" at any time reduces them to its own limits by a set of taboos destructive of all meaning and pleasure. Acting is no doubt a great art which adds to the written word, but it is only when a Shakespeare or a Molière or a Shaw is at work producing parts and plays for chosen performers under his own eye, that we have any sense of what the theater can do. It is while using and stretching the con-

---

* Shaw's creation of the informal historical play was a breaking through to liveliness comparable to Shakespeare's "anachronisms" in dealing with the old Romans. But just as Shakespeare's example led to a false archaic convention, so Shaw has already led to routine imitation, in which fun is made simply by having historical personages use nicknames and slang phrases, in a perfect void of dramatic or historical thinking.

ventions—as Shaw successfully did for nearly half a century—that drama takes its place with the other arts. The rest of the time we may be seeing chromos or caricatures based on great portrayals of action, but we are hardly seeing the masterpieces themselves, and perhaps only pretending to enjoy them.

Shaw's position in the history of drama is therefore traditional in the very act of flouting the limited canons of the current stage. He is in the great tradition, not in the little routine. Using everything in the theatrical shop, past and present, and holding in solution all that was stirring in the wide world of the author's mind, Shaw's plays constitute a dramatic legacy of the first magnitude. Approval of its characteristic tone and intellectual tendencies belongs to another order of consideration.

IV

Ideally, the wide world in the artist's mind is not to be inventoried, even when the mind is a far narrower one than Shaw's. The best record of it is in the author's own hand, and there we may leave it. But in view of Shaw's blurred reputation, a word or two are needed about his doctrines and public life.

As a moralist, Shaw is known for championing Ibsen, and as a socialist, for preaching Marx. More recently he has been suspected of sympathy with fascism. Plotting Shaw's course along the line joining these three points has led hasty observers to conclude that Shaw was once a rationalist who has since thrown over his early beliefs. To correct this error, it is only necessary to remember the global reach of Shaw's mind, which made him first a critic, then a dramatist, and which has inevitably conditioned his politics and religion. This is only another way of saying that his point of view has never been simple. He has never been a party-man, neither a Marxist nor a fascist, an Ibsenite nor a Wagnerite. Though he has used these isms to drive certain points home, he has never had the single-mindedness which makes the good disciple or the founder of a new religion.

Unoriginal in a sense, his rôle has been to sharpen, revivify, and reorganize the leading ideas of the first half of the nineteenth century and fill them with the contents of his own limited epoch. The best proof of this lies in the fact that his amazing awareness is in the highest degree an awareness of history. No one has ever used historical examples, near or remote, with the detail, precision, and directness to be found on every page of Shaw. From Edward the Fourth's taste in women to Rousseau's opinion on miracles, from Fielding's theatrical ventures to Marshal de Saxe's military career, he has the

telling instance at his fingertips—a dozen, if need be, for the routing
of incredulity. Nor does he simply illustrate or argue from history;
he assimilates it and thinks always under the corrective of historical relativity. In this regard, Shaw is a match for Montaigne,
Rousseau, and Voltaire, modern times being to him what classical
antiquity was to them.

As for the century of his birth Shaw possesses it entire. Like
Nietzsche, he rails at romanticism, but it is evident that what they
both mean by the word is the clichés of second-hand romance.
Historic romanticism is in fact the ground-work of their philosophy.
The quality of drama, of many-sidedness, of antithesis, in Shaw's
thought is of the highest and best romantic strain: witness his fusion
of scientific scepticism with religious faith, of individualism with the
sense of collective discipline, of the primacy of the will with the use
of reason, of a taste for heresy with a taste for legalism—dialectical
oppositions which are the mainspring of his intellectual energy as
well as the source of the misunderstandings he has suffered. Taken
piecemeal, his opinions are easily misfiled; but there can be no doubt
that Shaw himself belongs to the neo-romantic revolt against mid-
century materialism, realism, and determinism, *not* to the revolt
against the generation preceding these. He is with Samuel Butler,
William James, Nietzsche, Tolstoy and Henri Poincairé, not with
Spencer, Darwin, Huxley, Wagner, and Marx. And his robust strain of
aestheticism constantly pulls him back to the visions of Shelley,
Beethoven, Turner, and Blake.

Because he was a man of action, Shaw worked for the "new
ideas" of the nineties. But he criticized from within what he stood
for without. He never invested his whole moral capital in a man, a
book, or a cause, but treasured up wisdom wherever it could
be picked up, always with scrupulous acknowledgment: Henry
George, Dickens, Stuart Glennie, Proudhon, Samuel Butler, Philip
Wicksteed, Mommsen—the full list would be as long as it is unusual.
His eclecticism saving him from the cycle of hope-disillusion-despair,
his highest effectiveness was as a skirmisher in the daily battle for
light and justice, as a critic of new doctrine and refurbisher of old,
as a voice of warning and encouragement. That his action has not
been in vain, we can measure by noting how little Shaw's iconoclasm stirs our blood: we no longer remember what he destroyed
that was blocking our view.

Perhaps an iconoclast is always a man who destroys cheap images
rather than old ones. At any rate, it is one of the oldest of all western
ideas—the idea of Christianity—which is in Shaw the basic and
lasting one. For Shaw is a fundamentalist Christian; only, he in-

sists that the traditional words be compelled to carry an active meaning. For him Sin, Revelation, the Communion of Saints, the Life Everlasting, the necessity of Gospel Love, are truths of experience. But they must be kept empirically true by constant re-embodiment, as time buries the live meaning under the crust of habit. Charity, for example, can no longer mean giving coins to beggars; it must mean making war on poverty. Finding the means to the end is the task of live brains, and to attempt it is to do God's work.

It is a divine mission, first, because God is not omnipotent and needs help, and second, because men can only fulfill the soul's desire through devotion to something greater than their present wants. Hence Shaw's personal puritanism—or what passes for such—his invectives against drink, meat, idleness, and sexual indulgence. He does not forbid these, he grades them, and makes his own choices accordingly. Hence also his war against scientific materialism, which, he argues, leads to moral determinism if logically pursued, and to casual hedonism if not.

When asked why man should resist determinism and refuse to soften an evil lot through reasonable sensuality, Shaw appeals to intuition and will against pessimism and the demoralizing counsels of reason. For Shaw as for Goethe, the obligation to strive is a primary feeling: reason initiates nothing and would stop everything. Its use is to come after the fact and devise helpful justification of action. Culture, humaneness, spiritual grace, are not forced on us by logic: they are either self-evident goods or pointless. There is, Shaw reminds us, no argument in behalf of moral conduct which will not equally well support immoral. But it is clearly impossible (and immoral) to exact moral conduct, cultivation, and grace from those whom circumstances force to lead sub-human animal lives. Therefore society must be reformed.

Reform, to Shaw, means socialism, but as one might expect, his socialism is not of the textbook, or even of the orthodox Marxist, brand. It springs from the steady view of two opposite needs to which he referred ten years ago as the Paradox of Government. On the one hand, society needs a common faith and vigorous institutions with the power to coerce; and on the other, the individual as a human soul or as the bearer of a new and possibly saving heresy, must be free. It is difficult enough to reconcile these two needs, but the problem holds still another hazard: the need of action under the pressure of time. A quarter of a century before anyone had heard of Mussolini, Shaw was discrediting "sham democracy" by pointing out that government being meant for ruling, no regime could long subsist as a postponing-machine. He warned us that since institutions must first of all serve the daily bodily needs of men, obsolescence, inaction and delay were sure to bring about revolution and dictatorships, the dictators acting as responsible rulers in a sense forgotten by the King or Parliament they displaced. Shaw could also foresee that peoples faced with the choice of drifting or accepting martial law would always choose the latter; and rightly, since anarchy and starvation are no choices for the sane. This is the origin, extent and meaning of Shaw's "postwar conversion" to fascism, as well as the reason for his later praise of strong men. Impatient to make his point, he was nevertheless careful to include among them Stalin, Ataturk, and Franklin Roosevelt.

But martial law, as Shaw pointed out in re-editing the Fabian Essays forty years later, can only be a temporary measure, being in truth no law at all. No society can endure without a constitution, just as no government can find stability by prolonging arbitrary power. Now the constitutive principles which Shaw has never departed from in his half century of political theorizing are two: equal incomes and free criticism. In the Preface to *On the Rocks,* which like all his plays properly suggests more diverse "lessons" than its preface, occurs that remarkable dialogue of Jesus with Pilate in defence of "the new idea that may save the Empire." Free criticism is indispensable to the life of civilization, and persecutions mean death for both. This is no mere lip-service to the worth of the individual soul, for it is re-enforced by Shaw's almost maniacal hatred of cruelty. Like his own Androcles, as soon as he hears of man or beast being abused, he sees red and rushes to the defense. A second Voltaire, Shaw could point to a long list of verbal duels he has fought to uphold the creature against the state, from the escaped convict put in chains, to Sir Roger Casement tried on irrelevant grounds, or caned boys, flogged sailors, and vivisected animals.

It is with precisely the same political motive that Shaw wants absolute equality of income: to bring about that identity of treatment without which no society, whether a club or a nation, is worth living in. The religious reason for it, namely that we are members one of another, is supported by the economic reason that modern industry has destroyed the meaning of property in one's own labor; and both together suggest the necessity of common enterprise, common sharing, and a common faith. Shaw thus arrives with very different facts at the conclusions of Rousseau's *Social Contract,* which seems, exactly like Shaw's thinking, to favor alike extreme individualism and complete communism.

The true interpretation would seem to lie in a pragmatic synthesis of the two, which Shaw has tried to expound in his remarks on the observance of law. As individual and critic, said Shaw, Karl Marx has the right to urge the abolition of private property. As a responsible citizen who cannot be allowed to endanger going institutions, Marx must continue paying rent to his landlord and must not instead send in his check to the Treasury. It is characteristic of Shaw to put his problems in legal terms: "the case for the critic-dramatist," "the case for group extermination," "the case for Jesus," and so on. Before the court of intellect everything is arguable, Shaw being too practical a committeeman to suppose that all the good reasons are on one side.

But the weakness of this distinction between legal protest and anti-social agitation, appears as soon as we consult history. Corrupt and antiquated governments can be very tolerant of argumentative critics without ever yielding to their reasons, and there comes a point where violence is the only language intelligible to those who will not hear. History then takes another plunge into the chaos of revolution, civil war and tyranny. If this expresses the nature of human beings as we find them, we must radically change that nature or, trusting in evolution, hope that it will change itself.

These reflections define Shaw's Utopia: a society in which a common faith would inculcate common aims, in which equality of status and income would not blot out the recognition of special talents and higher natures, in which new ideas would be tolerated in the teeth of resentment, but not carried out to the destruction of order; in which, finally, the strivings of the soul of man would be not toward greater comforts but toward more abundant life. Like all Utopias, it is drawn to suit its maker, but unlike Plato's, there is a word in it about the means of bringing it about. On the immediate practical plane, Shaw leaves us with the now familiar schemes of planned economy and the new notion of "eclectic democracy," or the popular choice of certified leaders. For the longer run, as we all know from his longest and worst play, he sees the need of a greatly extended lifespan. He and Swift share the vision of the moral realist: Yahoos call forth Struldbrugs, both equally inhuman. For middling mankind has not yet solved the basic political riddle of how to make the good become the powerful.

The fact that Shaw's indefatigable political thinking on national and international questions has had no perceptible results, coupled with the fact that public opinion has been content to dismiss his views as comically irresponsible, is a measure of his distance from what we are pleased to call the thoughtful man. It can only be small comfort to him that as he approaches the century mark like another

Fontenelle he finds the world living up to the warning predictions he began to utter in early manhood.

v

A fair conclusion from these remarks would be that Shaw is classic in the making. But it is clear that the bogus prince Posterity will not accord Shaw or anybody else the close and catholic attention that a few contemporaries have been giving him for fifty years. Only a disciple or an enemy can keep up his enthusiasm as far as the four millionth word. Yet we can reassure ourselves with the thought that Swift and Voltaire, equally prolific, live in the public mind by one short fiction apiece. A reputation rests on a fisherman's float, not on the Complete Works sunk at the bottom. What will future ages choose from Shaw? It would be rash to guess, and perhaps even worse to assume that he will be known for all time by only one work and always by the same.

This much can be said: so long as there is an art of criticism, it is certain that some of Shaw's eight solid volumes will be read. So long as the broad forms of western society endure, some of Shaw's comedies will survive. Understanding does not require that present conditions of life and those portrayed on the stage be identical. Do we not still enjoy *Figaro* and the *Précieuses Ridicules?* The salt of satire is a great preservative but even a simple piece such as *You Never Can Tell* can hold its own by the magic of sparkling words and spectacle. And with the historical plays, Shaw has got a grip on the imagination of future ages for as long as the memory of Caesar, Saint Joan and the rest continues unbroken.

Dramatic reputations rely, in any case, on a very few samples. Congreve, Farquhar and Goldsmith live by one play each, Dryden, Sheridan and Beaumarchais by two; even in Shakespeare's abnormal position nearly two-thirds of his thirty-seven plays rarely occupy the public. Shaw's hand seems quite full enough. As to the rest of his output, one can confidently rely on the variety of his interests and the vigor of his prose to enlist among our descendants small groups of devoted readers. If we are only now properly editing Swift's pamphlets and discovering consistency in Voltaire's thought, we may safely leave to the historical scholars of the twenty-third century the pleasant task of rediscovering *Doctors' Delusions, On Going to Church* and *Common Sense About the War.*

Meanwhile the thick shades of careless contempt and reasoned scorn will doubtless close in upon the sinewy, diabolonian figure so long familiar to the literate world. Already the tale of Shaw's popularity seems a legend and the profundity of his "gay science" an untenable paradox. His plays, like *Hamlet* to Pepys, are poor things. It is of course a fitting destiny that Shaw should not weather oblivion "better than Shakespeare." But the works are there, glowing faintly under the falling darkness and dust of the century. It is the first twilight; night and morning are still to come.

RONALD PEACOCK

1946

Shaw

For the spectator who is interested in poetry and drama and theatre in their interfusion Shaw is embarrassing. "The poet in Shaw was still-born," writes Eliot. We have all felt again and again an extraordinary deflation as soon as the curtain has fallen. The agility and wit of Shaw's social criticism holds his plays together and casts his spell into the auditorium. The plays do not live as plays beyond the fall of the curtain. As they draw to a close they do not give the feeling of a building being completed; the forces which propel them are indeed bent all the other way, towards demolition. These works do not, after their emergence in time, solidify, as the great dramas do, into a shape for the memory; they leave us without the retrospective vision of form achieved. And yet Shaw cannot be thought out of the theatre by a theory of drama and poetry. It is not so much that he has simply conquered the stage and made it serve his own purposes; he has also, in spite of our reservations, served some of *its* purposes; of that there is as little doubt as of the fact that he has not served all its purposes or its greatest, as Jonson and Molière did.

There is a certain quality of calculation in Shaw's approach to comedy. It may be a wonderful calculation, of which the pleasantest thing to say would be that it is the "instinct of his genius." He has never hidden the fact that he is at heart an evangelist; and he has thirsted for more souls than the pamphlet—"his" form if ever there was one—could procure. He tried the novel. But he is essentially a man of ideas, of agile intellectual criticisms, and the novel, with all its apparatus of description and report, is a bore to him. Moreover, the audience of the novel is the individual; and the object of Shaw's criticism is society. In the theatre he catches three large groups who together make up the whole of mankind except its eccentrics: those interested in entertainment, those interested in ideas, and those interested in art. He catches them, moreover, in their social agglomeration and cohesiveness—his address is to society, and there it is assembled before the stage.

Having turned to the theatre, it was undoubtedly a stroke of personal genius to choose comedy for his form in the conditions obtaining in the theatre and intellectual life generally at the turn of this century. Comedy carries didacticism with a better grace than other kinds of drama. If there are to be ideas and debate in plays, then they offend the intellectual nature of comedy less than the emotional nature of tragedy or "serious" drama. There are reasons for Shaw's eminence that have less to do with the theatre proper than with his person and his ideas; but here is a reason for his eminence that springs from the very conditions of theatre and drama at that time. In an age of "problem plays" comedy, as a form, even though it does lose something, loses less than other forms. Shaw therefore appears as the culmination of an epoch that was opened by Ibsen (Dumas fils was of course a harbinger). He may dominate in part by qualities that would have given him eminence outside the theatre; but he also dominates on grounds of drama alone, in the age in which he wrote. It is a culmination, viewed broadly, of three things: social thought, its application in the theatre, and Shaw's own conviction, aggressively held, that art should always be parable. His work is the *best* effort of all the drama that was inspired by social criticism. It is even superior to Ibsen's, where Ibsen's implications are social.

The novelty of Shaw's comedy called forth inevitably protagonists and antagonists, and it has been defended mainly as a comedy of ideas in contrast to one of manners or situation. That battle is won. We know now that in Shaw's "pamphlets in dramatic form" we have to watch the drama of ideas, of which persons and events are the diagrammatic illustration.

As an iconographer, he has with consistent conscientiousness always given us both the theory and the example, the thought and the illustration, the preface and the play. And no doubt the only proper way of judging his work finally is one that takes account of the unity of preface and play.

This is the tribute that Shaw wrests from us; compelling us to ask the question that has always been asked since romantic criticism taught us to put it: what unique quality of personal experience is he endeavouring to convey?—before we judge his work. Yet matters do not end with this romantic interest in personal messages, and unique ways of stating them. Shaw claims to be an artist and he works in a

well-recognized form; and so it is fitting to recall that art may depend on artists, but artists also depend on art. Artists may revolt;
they also submit. Forms—lyric, dramatic, narrative—admit of extensive variation, they are developed and modified. Yet they are not
without a certain constancy of character, and impose, sometimes
when we are least aware of it, an authority of their own which is
above the single worker. Shaw does not escape. One could write a
lot about him with the merest reference to comedy as an art with
traditions. But he did not create his form out of the void; he selected
it from amongst others for his use, and he owes something to it.
Again, at the moment he entered the theatre, drama had been
given a powerful direction by Ibsen; he owes something to this too.
In the relation between what he owes and what he gives criticism
discovers something both about drama and about Shaw.

Within the limits of the art of comedy he has displayed a striking
originality in two principal directions; first in the point of view he
adopts for his critical attack, and secondly in his adaptation of
comedy to the naturalist technique.

Regarding the first point, Shaw conforms to tradition in the sense
that you must have a fixed point from which to work, to launch your
criticism. In Molière, for instance, the established position is generally interpreted as the rule of the golden mean of reason. Shaw is
also devoted to reason. But whilst Molière takes his fixed point from
the general experience of men as rational and social beings, Shaw
takes his from a rational philosophy of his own. Hence he inverts the
usual method. Instead of isolating the unreasonable character, he
isolates the reasonable one. Molière gives us a series of characters
who offend our idea of rational behaviour: Harpagon, Alceste,
Arnolphe, Argan, Tartuffe are examples. Shaw, on the other hand,
gives us a series that illustrates his own idea of rational behaviour:
Dudgeon, Caesar, Tanner, Dubedat, Undershaft, Shotover, Magnus,
Joan and so on—all characters with a head, with their eye on the
point, piercing illusions and grasping reality.

The difference is accounted for by a difference of interest. Molière
—and we can say Jonson too—feeding on the thought of the Renais-
sance, was interested in a conception of man; Shaw, under the influence of the thought of the late nineteenth century, in a conception
of society. His main attack being on society, his transformation of
traditional comic method is brilliant. Taking an unconventional
character, a person with the gift of insight and freedom, he impinges
it upon a group of conventional social animals, and the impact reveals at every turn stock notions and reactions, prejudices and dis-
honesties, in short the illusionary, the unreal, the irrational. Molière
exposes one character in turn; Shaw the social herd, all together.

And these characters of his are most certainly dramatic conceptions, because they create, by being what they are, startling situations.

It is not necessary to dwell on the remarkable efficacy of this transformation for Shaw's purpose. It shows itself all of a piece with the man, his temperament, his challenge, his message. We accept it as an instrument supremely adapted to its use, and acknowledge the immense talent that could make such an adaptation of a comedic method. But this is the point where, if we cannot detract from the personal genius of Shaw, we can arraign the artist, for the cunning of the method cannot cover the inadequacy of the result, when we apply the standards set by the highest imaginative comedy. Molière's Harpagon and Alceste, Jonson's Volpone and Sir Epicure Mammon, are imaginative creations. You cannot agree or disagree with them; in their simplicity and ideality they *are*. They have an existence and a permanence that are unassailable; and they are, moreover, centres from which moral energy radiates with an operation that cannot be limited by the fall of a curtain. Shaw's principals are not products of this kind of imaginative power. At the most it can be said that his series has a certain force and solidity because each member of it is a reflection of Shaw's own intelligence, and their effect is cumulative. The core of each one of them lies in their critical penetration, a quality of their creator. It is their only real vitality. They are without the vitality of instinct that makes a total living creature and on which the characters of Molière are based. For this reason we remember less what they are than how they talked; and every time we disagree with their opinions they lose some of their power. Each one of Molière's great creations is an image of a human folly, and he leaves us a whole gallery of them. Shaw gives us but one image: of the critical mind acting as a solvent. There is a point outside the drama where the two authors meet, on the ground of philosophy and practical wisdom, or the effort towards it. It would be difficult to decide which is the greater intellect. But it is easy to judge Molière the greater artist, because he gives us forms, against which Shaw can only put a *perpetuum mobile* of critical comment.

The second point about the mutual relations between Shaw's personal aim and the dramatic form concerns the realist convention in which he works. His comedy flowing from his criticism of society, he needs for his purposes the ordinary social milieu, with the sort of crisis that arises from typical bourgeois circumstances. In this milieu he lets his unconventional characters challenge the creatures of habit by word and action, and the rest follows. His material is that of all bourgeois drama since the middle of the nineteenth century, more particularly since Ibsen. One of the things he admired most in the latter was the way he made his audience feel that what they saw on the stage was what went on in their own homes. The direct attack is of the essence of Shaw's intention. His method in fact is to give us a comic version of Ibsen's principal theme, the rebel against society, the true man against the false. Ibsen being swayed on the whole by the Germanic seriousness, by some deep-seated emotional need for tragic crisis, his subjects and treatments were generally the reverse of comic. Here and there, however, he explores this latter vein, and *An Enemy of the People* appears as the embryo of Shaw's comic method. In developing his work from this position Shaw achieves a remarkable feat. For in the first place comedy and wit introduce a compensating element of imagination into the lamentably prosaic waste of bourgeois realist drama; Shaw avoids the mistake of other imitators of Ibsen. And in the second place he liberates comedy from the cruder forms of its long-accustomed artificialities and tricks—the disguises, the eavesdroppings, the mistaken identities, the stock characters and so on. They have been the properties of comedy since Plautus and were made necessary by the demands for concentration and sustained liveliness of situation in the theatre. Having found another source of vivacious movement in his unflagging raillery, Shaw dispenses with the traditional tricks as the main tools of construction, and uses the "realistic" social scheme. Not that he foregoes altogether the prerogative of comedy in the matter of fantastic incident and improbable dénouement. In fact he gains here another advantage over the "serious" social problem dramatist, because he can treat more cavalierly the difficulty of contriving a probable end as well as a probable situation. He may use far-fetched incidents and dénouements, but they are not the part of his material that really counts. For example, the arrival from the air of Percival and Lina Shchepanowska in *Misalliance* is quite fantastic, and so is Lina herself in the circumstances of the play; but the basic situation had become a commonplace one of contemporary social life. The incident in itself adds superficially to the entertainment; no writer of stage comedy, not even Molière, can afford to neglect any source of amusement, and Shaw has the good sense to be as small on occasion as his greatest predecessor. But even so, the real Shavian comedy is independent of the bit of fantasy; for it follows when we see the impact of Lina, an original character, a free woman and true to herself, on the convention-drenched people around her.

These are the two principal features of Shaw's work which make a mutual relationship between him and his form clear. Our first impulse is to say: this is not comedy as it ought to be. Our second is to justify it as the proper mode for Shaw's idea. With our third impulse we look more closely at work that seems to owe no obligation except to its own law, its own subject-matter, and we discover that it does owe something to its genre, to its predecessors, to pre-existent authorities. It illustrates a continuity, not a break. Shaw adheres first to the principle that comedy must have a fixed vantage-point, though he transforms it to suit his own purpose. He retains, too, the prerogatives and tricks of comedy, without, however, the necessity of being chained to them. He also keeps to stock types for comic purposes, but his new social philosophy gives him a new set of types. Even in incidentals he can follow well-worn grooves of the art; the Straker-Tanner relationship in *Man and Superman* rests on the conventional master-valet set-up, given a completely new vitality from the new social background. And his second great obligation is to the dramatic developments that immediately preceded him and in which he was caught up. He uses the natural probable situation of bourgeois life, public or domestic, that focuses a problem of social behaviour. And he acknowledges the debt by originality of treatment; that is, he gives us what no one else gave and Ibsen had only hinted at, comedy.

C. E. M. JOAD

1946

Shaw's Philosophy

NATURE AND SOURCES OF SHAW'S PHILOSOPHY

There are two senses in which a man can be said to have a philosophy or to be a philosopher. First, there is the sense in which a man may seek to present a coherent and comprehensive view of the universe as a whole, of the status of human life within it and of the way in which in the light of that view and granted that status human life ought to be lived.

Secondly, there is the sense in which a man may be the dispenser of wisdom in memorable thoughts and sayings on a vast number of topics of secular importance—on money, God, love, marriage, desire, death, ambition—wisdom which may, as in Shaw's case, spring from and be informed by the coherent and comprehensive view; or, as in that of Dr. Johnson, be unpervaded by any synthesizing conception of the meaning and purpose of life as a whole. (I don't mean that Johnson did not advance such a conception, merely that it has little to do with what he has to say on money, marriage, the navy and so on.) Shaw is a philosopher and has a philosophy in both these senses. In this chapter I shall be concerned only with the first of them, the sense in which he is the exponent and part originator of the philosophical doctrine called Creative Evolution.

Although this philosophy outcrops sporadically throughout the plays, its main deposits are to be found in two places; in the Preface to and the Hell Scene in *Man and Superman,* and in the Preface to and the five plays of the *Back to Methuselah* Pentateuch. Of these the latter is the more important, not only because when it appeared in 1921, Shaw's thought had undergone considerable development since the *Man and Superman* (1903) stage, but also because, as Shaw himself at the end of the *Back to Methuselah* Preface says of the 1903 presentation of his philosophy, "being then at the height of my invention and comedic talent, I decorated it too brilliantly and lavishly. I surrounded it with a comedy of which it formed only one act and that act was so completely episodical . . . that the comedy could be detached and played by itself. . . . The effect was so vertiginous apparently that nobody noticed the new religion in the centre of the intellectual whirlpool."

In what follows I shall rely chiefly on the exposition in *Back to Methuselah*, reinforced by reference on subsidiary points to *Man and Superman*.

THE MATERIALIST SCHEME

I will first say something of the background and sources of Shaw's theory of Creative Evolution. Shaw's thought runs back through Samuel Butler to Lamarck. The view that Butler expounded can best be understood in relation to the doctrine of Darwin. Darwin's doctrine was essentially biological, but it formed an essential part of the comprehensive materialist scheme of the universe which held the field in the latter part of the nineteenth century. Under this scheme the universe was envisaged after the model of a gigantic clock; somebody at some time or other had, so to speak, wound the clock up; in other words the universe had at some time got itself started—the materialist could not, of course, explain how but as nobody else was in this respect in any better position his inability was not a distinctive objection to materialism—and thereafter it functioned indefinitely through the automatic interaction of its parts. Life was one of the parts, a product of the operation of the same physical and chemical laws as governed the behaviour of non-living matter.

Under the influence of certain rather rare physical conditions—materialists were never tired of emphasizing the paucity of the areas of the cosmos in which the conditions favourable to life obtained—matter had become conscious, conscious as it was sometimes put, of itself. Matter's consciousness of itself was life, and life's subsequent development was governed by the same material conditions as had given it birth. One day when these conditions no longer obtained, life would finish its pointless journey with as little significance as in the person of the amœba it began in. Meanwhile, its status in the universe was that of an outside passenger travelling across a fundamentally alien and hostile environment in which what was mindless and brutal conditioned and determined what was spiritual and akin. Causation in other words operated universally from the less living as cause to the more living as effect; within the living organism from the body to the mind and within the mind from the less to the more conscious part of it.

This was the scheme in which Darwin's discovery of evolution, or, more precisely, of the laws of natural selection and the survival of the fittest through which evolution operated, played an integral part; integral, because in the attitude which it adopted to the phenomenon of life, in the explanation which it offered to the elaborate and varied process which beginning with the amœba had culminated in ourselves, Darwin's account postulated the intervention of no spiritual force or agency, no mind, no life and no god, but was content to rely upon the operation of those same material forces as had governed the planet prior to life's appearance.

More particularly, variations in species occurred. Either they were adapted to their environment or they were not. If they were not, they were eliminated; if they were, the variation in respect of which they were adapted and by reason of the adaptation obtained an advantage in the struggle for existence was handed on to their offspring and became stamped into the life history of the species, where it developed and intensified, until at last it represented a degree of differentiation which entitled biologists to say that a new species had emerged. So far, so good; but why did the variations occur? Darwin professed agnosticism; he did not know, although sometimes he attributed them to chance. But the question was, it was obvious, of crucial importance. If there were no variations, if no changes in species occurred, then each generation would be an exact replica of the preceding one and, short of new creations, the amœba and his contemporaries would still be the sole forms of life upon the planet. Variations, then, played an essential part in the machinery of evolution; they were necessary to get it started. Why, then, did they occur? It was here that the followers of Lamarck took the field.

LAMARCKIANISM

Variations in species, they urged, were due to the effects of environment. When the environment changed, living organisms must either adapt themselves to it or disappear. Those who were successful in effecting the adaptation survived and transmitted the adaptation in virtue of which they had survived to their descendants. These adaptations were mainly envisaged by Lamarck in terms of the growth of new organs and the gradual lapsing of old ones. Changes in environment led to new wants, new wants to new habits and new habits to new organs which were formed to minister to the habits. In point of fact, the difference between Lamarck's doctrine, so far as I have stated it hitherto, and Darwin's was not very striking. Why, it was asked, in the contemporary controversies, did the giraffe grow his long neck? According to Darwin's followers long-necked giraffes were born by chance much as children with freckles are born by chance. They enjoyed a natural advantage in the struggle for food— they could nibble the leaves on the higher branches—and, therefore, were better placed in the struggle for existence than their shorter-necked contemporaries. Thus, the fittest survived but they were the fittest by chance; they had not become the fittest by design. According to Lamarck, the giraffes at a certain stage of their history, finding that most of the leaves on the lower branches on the available trees had been eaten, were under the necessity of either growing longer necks in order to reach the higher leaves, or of perishing of hunger. Those who successfully adapted themselves to the changed conditions by growing longer necks survived and transmitted the characteristic of long-neckedness to their offspring. Once again in the struggle for existence the fittest survived, but they were the fittest not by chance but by reason of their success in adapting themselves. But the process was, in Lamarck's view, no less automatic, no less determined than in Darwin's; in fact, it was more so. A change in the external environment, a change, it might be, in the climate determined a change in the living organisms which were exposed to it, or it did not. If it did not, the organisms died out. The scheme was thus so far at one with Darwin's in that it, too, abstained from postulating the action of any informing purpose of plan to account for the changes in and development of species; up to this point it fitted equally well into the prevalent materialistic scheme.

BUTLER'S CONTRIBUTION

But suppose that the changes in living organisms by means of which they adapted themselves to changes in their environment were purposive, in the sense that somebody or something operating independently of the living organism, or perhaps developing in and through it, willed them; suppose, in fact, that changes in living things were not *always* the by-products of prior changes in dead things, but that at least sometimes they occurred independently, as the result of living things' desire to adapt themselves better to dead things and possibly to use dead things for their own purposes. If this were so, causation might sometimes at least operate from the animate to the inanimate, and the vital, in virtue of which animate matter was animated, instead of being merely a by-product of the material, might be in some sense independent of it, and, being independent, might be able to act upon it, use it, even enter into and inform it. Such, in effect, was the assertion of Samuel Butler, an assertion which he proceeded to work up into the sketch of a philosophy. It was of this sketch that Shaw proceeded to fill in the outlines, fully acknowledging his debt to Butler "in his own department the greatest English writer of the latter half of the nineteenth century,"—"when," Shaw wrote in the preface to *Major Barbara,* "I produce plays in which Butler's extremely fresh, free and future-piercing suggestions have an obvious share, I am met with nothing but vague cacklings about Ibsen and Nietzsche,"—and developed into the fully fledged philosophy of *Back to Methuselah.*

So much for a sketch of the background; let me now try and outline the philosophy, as it appears in its fully developed form.

OUTLINE OF SHAW'S THEORY OF CREATIVE EVOLUTION

Shaw postulates a universe containing or consisting of two factors, Life and matter. Admittedly he sometimes speaks of Life as creating matter as when, by willing to use our arms in a certain way, we bring into existence a roll of muscle, but the general view is that matter is, as it were, there to begin with. Thus, matter is spoken of as Life's "enemy." "I brought life into the whirlpool of force, and compelled my enemy, Matter, to obey a living soul," says Lilith at the end of *Back to Methuselah.* Regarding matter in the light of an enemy, Life seeks to dominate and subdue it. Partly to this end, partly because of its innate drive to self-expression, Life enters into and animates matter. The product of this animation of matter by Life is a living organism. A living organism, then, derives from and bears witness to the presence of both the two fundamental constituents of which the universe is composed; it is Life expressed in matter. Shaw suggests rather than explicitly states that Life cannot evolve or develop *unless* it enters into matter to create organisms; they are, in fact, the indispensable tools wherewith it promotes its own development. To put the point in another way, by means of the device of expressing itself in and through matter Life is enabled to enjoy a greater variety of experience, to accumulate more knowledge and greater intelligence and to develop a more intense power of awareness. To develop these faculties, to make these acquisitions may be described as Life's immediate purpose since they facilitate, indeed they constitute, the process of Life's development. Living organisms, then, are the instruments which Life creates to facilitate the process of its own development, and matter, though Life's enemy, is also, as it were, the whetstone upon which Life sharpens itself in order to further its own evolution. This office matter performs by reason of the limitations which it imposes upon Life's powers, thus forcing Life to make efforts to overcome the limitation and so to develop itself by the acquisition of new powers.

Yet the object of Life is to pass beyond matter: to pass, that is to say, beyond the necessity for incarnating itself in and concerning itself with matter. Until this consummation is reached, matter will continue to obstruct and limit life.

Life is also dependent on matter in the sense that each individual expression of Life, being dependent upon the body in which Life incarnates itself to constitute a living organism, terminates its separate existence *as an individual expression* with the death of the body, and, presumably, reverts to the main stream.

When the need for incarnation in matter has been transcended, Life's individualized expressions being no longer dependent upon incorporation in a body for their individuality will, we may suppose, become permanently individualized; will, in fact, be immortal. This conclusion is indicated in the dialogue between the *Ancients* and the *Newly Born* in the last play of *Back to Methuselah*.

The He-Ancient: For whilst we are tied to this tyrannous body we are subject to its death, and our destiny is not achieved.
The Newly Born: What is your destiny?
The He-Ancient: To be immortal.
The She-Ancient: The day will come when there will be no people, only thought.
The He-Ancient: And that will be life eternal.

This, perhaps, is not as clear as could be wished, since it leaves it uncertain whether the immortality looked forward to will be the personal immortality of separate individual units of life, or will be merely the immortality of Life as a whole. If it means the latter—and this is, I think, Shaw's general view—then individuality, the individuality of the living organism, is a function of matter.

THE METHOD OF EVOLUTION

What is the nature of the force or activity which is spoken of sometimes as driving the evolutionary process forward, sometimes as identical with it? We cannot say or, rather, we can define it only in terms of its own activity. It is, to use an expression of Shaw's, "vitality with a direction," expressing itself in the will to create matter or to mould the matter which it finds but has not created. "The will to do anything," he writes, "can and does, at a certain pitch of intensity set up by conviction of its necessity, create and organize new tissue to do it with. . . . If the weight lifter, under the trivial stimulus of an athletic competition, can 'put up a muscle,' it seems reasonable to believe that an equally earnest and convinced philosopher could 'put up a brain.' Both are directions of vitality to a certain end. Evolution shows us this direction of vitality doing all sorts of things."

Now, the need for new tissue to carry out the will and to further the development of the vital impulse leads to the development of new organs in existing species and ultimately to the development of new species of living things. Shaw is here taking over from Butler and the Lamarckians, the view that Life's need for something sooner or later produces that for which the need is felt.

How, to revert to the classical example, does the giraffe get his long neck? "By wanting to get at the tender leaves high up on the tree, and trying until he succeeded in wishing the necessary length of neck into existence." In this quotation Shaw summarizes what he takes to be the doctrine of Lamarck. He proceeds to add in his own right: "You want, consequently, additional organs, or additional uses of your existing organs: that is, additional habits. You get them because you want them badly enough to keep trying for them until they come. Nobody knows how: nobody knows why: all we know is that the thing actually takes place. We relapse miserably from effort to effort until the old organ is modified or the new one created, when suddenly the impossible becomes possible and the habit is formed." The new habit and the new organ to be the vehicle of the new habit, are evolved because in the long run we need them or— for Shaw uses both modes of expression—because Life needs them in us. "If you have no eyes and want to see and keep on trying to see you will finally get eyes."

This, the method of evolution at the pre-conscious level, is still its method at the conscious, is still, in other words, the method of evolving humanity. Man feels a need and gradually wills into existence the faculty or organ which will enable him to satisfy it. The formula for this process is described in the first play of *Back to Methuselah*, as first desire, then imagination, then will, then creation. Here is a summary statement of it from that wonderful dialogue between Eve and the Serpent at the beginning of the first play*:

> The Serpent: . . . imagination is the beginning of creation. You imagine what you desire; you will what you imagine; and at last you create what you will.

* I heard Shaw read this aloud—he had written it during the day—on two successive evenings at a Fabian Summer School—beyond comparison the most impressive, dramatic occasion at which I have been privileged to be present.

Eve: How can I create out of nothing?

The Serpent: Everything must have been created out of nothing. Look at that thick roll of hard flesh on your strong arm! That was not always there: you could not climb a tree when I first saw you. But you willed and tried and willed and tried; and your will created out of nothing the roll on your arm until you had your desire, and could drag yourself up with one hand, and seat yourself on the bough that was above your head.

A point which Shaw stresses is the *abruptness* of the appearance of the acquisition, whether it takes the form of organ or faculty or awareness, in which the new evolutionary advance consists. There is a definite jump from the old level of behaviour and thinking to the new one: "The process is not continuous, as it would be if mere practice had anything to do with it; for though you may improve at each bicycling lesson *during* the lesson, when you begin your next lesson you do not begin at the point at which you left off; you relapse apparently to the beginning. Finally, you succeed quite suddenly, and do not relapse again. More miraculous still, you at once exercise the new power unconsciously."

The process of Life's development, as hitherto described, expresses itself mainly in the acquisition of new bodily habits and physical traits. But the same process continues at the level of thought. We develop new powers not only of the body but of the mind, powers of insight, vision and intelligence because we want them, or because Life wants to develop them in us that we may more effectively implement Life's purpose as it is, or conceive for Life new purposes which it has not yet itself conceived.

Later, however, it appears that Life's entry in and concern with matter is a mere temporary phase of Life's development. Matter is entered into, only that it may be transcended; it is a ladder which must be scaled in order that, having arrived at the top, Life may pass on to something else. Thus, though the Ancients in the last play in *Back to Methuselah* have complete mastery over their bodies, and can create surplus arms and legs at will, though they also possess power over other bodies and can apparently kill with a glance, the exercise of these powers does not interest them. They are bored with the knowledge of matter, bored even with the manipulation of matter. Their attention is directed elsewhere, their interests lie in something else. In what else? Before I attempt to answer this question, there are one or two subsidiary developments of the main evolutionary theme about which something must be said.

DIGRESSION: (1) ON THE RIGHT CONDUCT OF LIFE

As I hinted at the beginning, Shaw is a philosopher in both the senses of the word which I there distinguished. In his capacity as a dispenser of wisdom, he has contrived to let fall a great number of pregnant observations on the secular topics of human interest and concern from Marriage to Moderation and from Greatness to Gambling.

Many of these are collected in the *Revolutionist's Hand-Book* which is printed at the end of *Man and Superman*. All are more or less informed by the underlying philosophy—in the first sense of the word "philosophy"—of which they are the directly deduced corollaries. I have space here to mention only three topics which are of such importance both to the preacher and to his congregation that though, as I have hinted, Shaw's treatment of them is a corollary from his general position and could, therefore, with sufficient insight presumably be deduced from it, what he has to say on them may deservedly rank as an integral part of the Shavian philosophy.

These three topics are, first, the right conduct of life; secondly, women and genius, and, thirdly, art.

If we are instruments created by Life for the furtherance of Life's instinctive purpose, our *raison d'être* will be found in the fulfilment of Life's intentions in regard to us; not, then, in the pursuit of our own purposes. The furtherance of Life's purpose will consist in the being used up to the last ounce of one's energy and capacity in work that seems to one to be worth while for its own sake. Shaw's own talents and energies have been remorselessly used in the spreading of Socialism and the writing of plays. It is by the maximum expenditure of effort in the ardours and endurances of living and thinking that one will develop and improve one's initial endowment of faculty and accomplishment, thus returning them at death with interest—an interest which is to be measured by the degree of the realised improvement upon the initially given potentiality—to the general stream of Life of which we are the individualized expressions, with the result that when Life expresses itself in the next generation of living organisms, it will do so at a slightly higher level than it did before, because of the enrichments of acquisition and accomplishment that we have brought to it.

Now happiness will be found in the furtherance of the purpose for which we were created. Not unnaturally, since life will do its best to ensure the donkey's activity by dangling the carrot of happiness before its nose. Effort and endeavour, then, are the means to the happy and successful life and we shall find the recipe for happiness in not having enough leisure to wonder whether we are miserable or not. It is in the same vein that Shaw bids us "get what you like or else you will grow to like what you get."

Shaw's philosophy enables him to provide a new basis for the moral philosopher's traditional criticism of the life of pleasure-seeking. This, for Shaw, is a perversion of function, since it entails a diversion of effort to the pursuit of one's *own* concerns, and in the indulgence in one's *own* gratifications, when we should be engaged about Life's business. The life of the epicure, the hedonist and the egotist, is, then, a kind of playing truant when we should be at school and Life pays us out for our apostasy by ensuring that, as the direct pursuers of pleasure, we shall miss the pleasure that we pursue. Hence, the aphorism, "Folly is the direct pursuit of Happiness and Beauty."

DIGRESSION: (II) ON WOMEN AND GENIUS

I do not wish to suggest by this sub-heading that women are geniuses or even that women have genius. The intention is to present the genius whom Shaw assumes, by implication, to be essentially male in relation, a relation which is usually one of opposition to women. (Shaw does, incidentally, speak in connection with George Sand of the comedy afforded by the accident of the genius being "himself a woman").

Femaleness, in the creative evolutionary philosophy, is represented as being more primitive, in the sense of being more fundamental, than maleness. Shaw even goes to the length of suggesting that the initial form of life was female. Lilith in *Back to Methuselah* is represented as producing Adam from within herself. In the beginning, Lilith "who came before Adam and Eve . . . was alone: there was no man with her." She "sunders herself in twain" to give birth and is left at the end of the Fifth Play wondering whether in order to supersede human beings she must needs give birth again.

Already latent in the dialogue between Gloria and Valentine in *You Never Can Tell,* this conception is developed in the Hell scene in *Man and Superman.* Here Shaw conceives Life as working through woman to create man to carry Life to higher levels. "Sexually, Woman is Nature's contrivance for perpetuating Nature's highest achievement. Sexually, Man is Woman's contrivance for fulfilling Nature's behest in the most economical way. She knows by instinct that far back in the evolutional process she invented him, differentiated him, created him, in order to produce something better than the single-sexed process can produce."

So far, so good; but unfortunately (for woman) in giving man so small a part in the process of reproduction, she set free his energies for developing his vital inheritance by making acquisitions of which she had no prevision; as, for example, by thinking thoughts that she could not follow, by whoring after beauty that she could not understand, by desiring and pursuing things disinterestedly in and for themselves. For "how rash and dangerous it was to invent a separate creature whose sole function was her own impregnation! For mark what has happened. First, Man has multiplied on her hands until there are as many men as women; so that she has been unable to employ for her purposes more than a fraction of the immense energy she has left at his disposal by saving him the exhausting labour of gestation. This superfluous energy has gone to his brain and to his muscle. He has become too strong to be controlled by her bodily, and too imaginative and mentally vigorous to be content with mere self-production. He has created civilization without consulting her, taking her domestic labour for granted as the foundation of it."

Man also invents "dreams, follies, ideals, heroisms" and, we may add, creeds and causes with which both to amuse and develop himself, thus further diverting his energy and attention from the performance of the purely biological purpose for which woman created him. But since woman is the vehicle of a more direct inheritance from Life, since she is biologically primary and man biologically secondary, woman succeeds in ninety-nine cases out of a hundred in bringing him to heel by turning him back to his specifically biological function, which means turning him from adventurer or visionary first, into the worshipper of herself—hence romance—and, secondly, when the hook of family maintenance has been swallowed with the bait of sexual attraction, into a bread-winner for herself and children. And since getting a job means doing the work which the world is prepared to offer you and to pay you for doing, instead of the work which you want to do, the subsidence of the artist, the idealist, the revolutionary or the scholar into the breadwinner involves a struggle, a struggle between creativity and the thrill of beauty, curiosity and the pull of knowledge and, it may be, the vision of God on the one hand and the power of woman, symbolizing security, conservatism, common sense and earthiness in the interests of keeping the family together and the Life Force's pot boiling on the other. Thus, we are told that for a man "marriage is a heavy chain to rivet on himself." Woman "is born with the chain attached to her, and marriage is the only way open to her of riveting the other end of it into a man." In ninety-nine cases out of a hundred she succeeds. Woman is endowed by the Life Force with the faculty, or rather with the appearance of the faculty, of being able to share man's enthusiasms, respond to his ideals, echo his thoughts. But this apparent sympathy is only the bait on woman's hook. Once it is swallowed the feminine enthusiasms, the shared ideals, the "disinterested" interests, are discarded like a worn-out glove and the young man who would reform society, see visions, talk with God, finds himself reduced by his triumphant mate to the role of a breadwinner for herself and her children.

And so it goes for ninety-nine cases out of a hundred; but the hundredth case is the case of the genius. The genius is the repository of a special "potential" of Life expressly created for the specific purpose of carrying Life to higher levels by giving man a new insight into truth, a new concept of political association and moral obligation, a new vision of beauty, or a new refinement and subtlety of personal relationship. As Shaw puts it, a genius is a man "selected by Nature to carry on the work of building up an intellectual consciousness of her own instinctive purpose." He is, accordingly, the vehicle of as direct and purposeful an inheritance from Life as the woman herself, and will sacrifice woman in pursuance of his purpose as ruthlessly as she sacrifices the ordinary man in the pursuance of hers.

Since the genius is by definition in advance of the existing level of evolutionary consciousness, being, in fact, a biological "sport" on the spiritual and intellectual planes, the work which he feels impelled to do is *ex hypothesi* work for which the world is not yet ready; for which, therefore, it is not prepared to pay. If he is a "sport" in the æsthetic field, if he is a Schubert or a Cézanne, he is usually allowed to starve to death in a garret in the usual way. If he is a "sport" on the moral or political plane, if he is a Blake, a Tolstoy, a Swedenborg, a Servetus or a Bunyan, or, Shaw would add, a Christ, he is usually persecuted with all the rigour of the law. In either event he is not a good husband, precisely because he is not "making good." What is more, he will be prepared without scruple to put his wife to the job of earning for himself and family the money which he is too preoccupied to earn himself. He will risk the stake and the cross; starve, when necessary, in a garret all his life; work his nerves into rags without payment; study women and live on their work and care as Darwin studied worms or Ehrlich bacteria; a sublime altruist in his disregard of himself, an atrocious egotist in his disregard of others. Here woman meets a purpose as impersonal, as irresistible as her own; and the clash is sometimes tragic.

Hence the clash between woman and the genius arises from the directness of the inheritance which each has from Life; or, if the phrase be preferred, the strength of the respective "potentials" at which Life is manifested in them. In the genius, Life's purpose is to lift itself to heights of consciousness not previously achieved; in the woman, to safeguard and maintain the level which has already been attained.

DIGRESSION: (III) ON ART AND THE ARTIST

Shaw's view of art has already, by implication, been touched upon. Art is a device by means of which Life achieves its purpose of lifting itself to a higher level of conscious awareness and the great artist is the instrument which it creates for the fulfilment of that purpose.

The method of Life's advance is envisaged in two stages; first, the great artist appears—an original thinker from this point of view is a special case of the artist—the representative of a new and original inspiration from Life. He embodies his vision in paint or sound or stone or words. Now, precisely because it *is* an original vision, the work of art in which it is embodied breaks the rules of composition, outrages the accepted concepts of form and style and taste, discards the hitherto accepted recipes for the catching and embalming of beauty and is, therefore, held to be a monstrosity of ugliness and disharmony. (Beethoven's Third Symphony, the music of Wagner, and the paintings of the Impressionists are examples especially cited by Shaw.) It challenges prevalent notions, flouts current prejudices, startles, shocks and flies in the face of popular morality. Hence, the life of the genius is usually poor, solitary and brutish and, since he is a genius in respect of only the hundredth part of himself, the remaining ninety-nine hundredths being an ordinary chap with a craving for human sympathy and affection, and a natural desire to win the world's esteem and to bask in the sunshine of popular favour and his wife's approval, the genius is usually the most wretched of men. If, however, his vision does, indeed, embody a new and original impression from Life, others will presently come to see things in the colours of the spectacles which he has tinted for them. The outrageous symphony or painting will be adopted as the accepted standard of orthodoxy and good taste and the heterodoxies of today will be enshrined in the *Home Notes* of tomorrow. This is the second stage, the stage in which the common consciousness of civilised mankind moves up to the level of insight at which the original genius first appeared. Thus, the genius is beauty's midwife. He does not create beauty but he brings to birth in sound or paint or stone the beauty which he has first discerned, so that ordinary men with their duller and grosser senses may presently apprehend for themselves the beauty which the work of art throws, as it were, into high relief. He makes wide and straight for the many the narrow path which he has been the first to follow.

Such, then, is the distinctive Shavian attitude to art and its function. It is a device, one of the most important, for refining and enlarging the awareness of men and women and so lifting Life itself to a higher level of consciousness.

This is a high function and Shaw's attack on romantic art, by which he usually means art directed to the glorification of woman, is the expression of his indignation at its perversion. Art, as Shaw conceives it, is very largely a male preserve. It is, of course, natural that woman should seek to induce the artist to be content to glorify her, instead of going about his proper business of raising the general level of Life's awareness and deepening and refining Life's power of insight. But to do this is, in effect, to use the power of art to stabilise life at the level which it has already reached, instead of raising it to higher levels. It is as if the artist were to rest on the oars of his predecessors' achievements, instead of striking out for himself. Rightly regarded, art should supersede sex and not glorify it. In this sense, *ne cherchez pas la femme,* Shaw tells us, is the clue to the motivation of great art.

But there another attitude is discernible in Shaw's work in respect of which, and in respect of the manner of his advance to it, Shaw's thought curiously reproduces Plato's.

Plato has a twofold attitude to art. He suspects it because it rouses the sleeping dogs of emotion which were better left to lie, strengthens the irrational part of the soul, and makes images of the things of the sensible world and so directs soul's attention away from instead of towards reality. But there is another strain in Plato's thought, a strain that comes out more particularly in the *Phaedrus* and the *Symposium,* which represents art as the medium in which the Form of Beauty is manifested and, therefore, as a window, one of the clearest, through which man's soul may obtain a glimpse of reality.

Whilst Plato tends to move from the first position to the second, the development of Shaw's thought seems rather to have been from the second to the first. In the last play of *Back to Methuselah* we find a comparatively lowly place assigned to art. With love, it is regarded as the staple occupation of the very young; the Festival of the Artists, staged at the beginning of the last play of the Pentateuch is, apparently, supported entirely by the "under fives." "Soon," says the Ancient, "you will give up all these toys and games and sweets."

The He-Ancient belittles art, very much as Plato might have done when advocating the expulsion of artists from the ideal State. "As you grow up," he says, "you make images and paint pictures. Those of you who cannot do that make stories about imaginary dolls." But who, he presently asks, would make statues and images if he could apprehend the originals? Who would want stories if he knew the facts? This thought is developed by the She-Ancient: "Art is the magic mirror you make to reflect your invisible dreams in visible pictures. You use a glass mirror to see your face: you use works of art to see your soul. But we who are older use neither glass mirrors nor works of art. We have a direct sense of life. When you gain that you will put aside your mirrors and statues, your toys and your dolls." Shaw does not here go to Plato's length and treat art as a will-o'-the-wisp leading men away from reality. It is, for him, rather a substitute for reality, a substitute accepted perforce by those in whom Life has not yet sufficiently developed to be able to achieve and sustain a direct view of reality itself.

The suggestion might be ventured that the artist may be regarded as one who has *had* the vision of the soul but been unable to sustain it, and so makes the work of art to serve as a memento of the original, which his vision once glimpsed, but can glimpse no longer. If this were true, the work of art would be an expression not of the inspiration which the artist has, but the inspiration that he had once but has failed to maintain. I cannot find any evidence for this suggestion in Shaw, although it seems a logical corollary of his view of art.

RETURN FROM DIGRESSION. THE PURPOSE OF LIFE

What, then, is the reality of which the artist makes copies, but which the Ancients directly apprehend? Shaw never seems to have made up his mind. His philosophy envisages Life's evolution as the development of an ever more intense and penetrating power of awareness. Now, awareness must be directed upon something, this something being other than itself, and Shaw's thought seems to me to demand the inclusion in the universe of an element of static and immutable perfection upon which the consciousness of a fully developed Life Force might come to rest. Such an element is, indeed, postulated by other philosophical systems with which Shaw's has affinity. Thus, Platonic philosophers attain to a vision of the timeless

Forms which, thereafter, they contemplate. Aristotle's God is engaged, at least in part, in working out mathematical problems, engaged, that is to say, in contemplating the static perfection of mathematical quantities and their relations. The reason for this demand is obvious; thought by its very nature demands an object; there must be something for thought to think about. This something must be other than the thought itself and, since the factor of change in the universe has been appropriated for the developing consciousness of the thinker in whom the ever-changing Life Force is expressed, the object, the thing thought about, must, one would have supposed, be represented as exempt from the changes by which the evolutionary process is itself pervaded.

Shaw comes within striking distance of this position without ever explicitly adopting it. It will be noted that in the quotation cited above, the She-Ancient speaks of a "direct sense" not of reality, but "of life," which suggests that Life's power of cognition in its latest and fullest development is directed upon itself. The speech of Lilith with which the play concludes, while contriving to give a fairly full exposition of Shaw's general view is, on this particular point, singularly uninformative.

What, we want to know, do the Ancients *do* with their developed consciousness? What does their thought busy itself about? What is it that it is the ultimate purpose of Life to know?

Such answer as Shaw gives is contained in the two following passages from Lilith's last speech:

> After passing a million goals they press on to the goal of redemption from the flesh, to the vortex freed from matter, to the whirlpool in pure intelligence that, when the world began, was a whirlpool in pure force. And though all that they have done seems but the first hour of the infinite work of creation, yet I will not supersede them until they have forded this last stream that lies between flesh and spirit, and disentangled their life from the matter that has always mocked it.

> I brought Life into the whirlpool of force, and compelled my enemy, Matter, to obey a living soul. But in enslaving Life's enemy I made him Life's master; for that is the end of all slavery; and now I shall see the slave set free and the enemy reconciled, the whirlpool become all Life and no matter.

These passages embody the following propositions:

(1) That Life was originally a whirlpool in pure force;

(2) that it entered into matter, used matter and compelled matter to obey it;

(3) that by so doing it became matter's slave;

(4) that the object of Life's development is to put an end to this slavery by winning free of or conquering matter. It is not clear whether matter still remains, Life having, as it were, merely disentangled itself from it, or whether matter is ultimately eliminated by Life, so that it ceases to be;

(5) that redemption from the flesh having been achieved, Life will become pure thought.

But if, insisting once again that thought must surely be of something and that that something must be other than the thinking about it, we repeat the question, what, then, does Life in its ultimate expression think about, there is no answer. The system, in fact, in its ultimate consummation seems to deny the truth upon which Shaw has so often insisted in the course of its development. We are told that we must not think about and concern ourselves with ourselves but lose ourselves in what is greater than and external to the self. But if we are Ancients these admonitions no longer apparently apply, for in the case of the Ancients thought, so far as one can see, is directed only upon itself. To postulate that it should be directed upon anything else would be tantamount to introducing into the Shavian universe a timeless, static element whether conceived as God, as Forms, as the Absolute or, even, as mathematical relations, which Shaw's thought, dominated by the conviction that the evolutionary process is all that there is, can never quite bring itself explicitly to admit.

I propose to conclude by indicating first, the respects in which the Shavian philosophy carries the doctrine of Creative Evolution beyond the point at which it was left by his predecessor, Butler, and, secondly, some of its more obvious weaknesses.

LIKENESSES OF AND DIFFERENCES BETWEEN THE SHAVIAN AND BUTLERIAN PHILOSOPHIES

A conscious, creative, immaterial force expressing itself in matter and using and moulding matter in the pursuit of its own purposes is the premise taken as the starting point of both Shaw's and Butler's philosophies. They show a common outlook on many subsidiary matters, for example, each writer is a great adherent of practical intelligence; each sings the praises of common sense. Shaw, like Butler, hates professionals, especially doctors, and tends to look at people from a biological point of view, recognizing in those organisms which are best adapted to the purposes of living the most valuable products of evolution. Moreover, for Shaw as for Butler, such persons are those who, while possessing no culture and few intellectual attainments, nevertheless exhibit a store of instinctive rule-of-thumb philosophy. 'Enry Straker and Alfred Doolittle are the lineal descendants of Mrs. Jupp in *The Way of All Flesh,* and Yram in *Erewhon.* All these very pleasant and amusing people know what to do on all ordinary and extraordinary occasions, but none of them could tell you how they know it or why they ought to do it. Like some fortunate bridge players, they play the right card instinctively, while others after much thought and travail as often as not produce the wrong one.

So far the outlook of the two thinkers is the same; but when we push our inquiries a stage further, a marked difference reveals itself. Butler regards the operations of the speculative intellect as a pedantic futility, and appears to look forward with equanimity to the merging of the practical intellect in unconscious instinct. There is nothing in his writings to show that he does not think man would be better off without the intellect altogether, and that its gradual supersession may be expected as the next stage in human progress towards the goal of evolution. For Shaw, on the other hand, the operations of the intellect *are* the goal of evolution. While for both the Force that animates the universe is a single, unified, unconscious urge, it is, in Shaw, an unconscious urge struggling for consciousness. He admires the instinctively successful and practical man, but only because it is in such as he that Life, by achieving a momentary equilibrium in the present, prepares itself for new achievements in the future. Shaw glories in life; he glories in it to the extent of maintaining that if we are to live properly we must live longer; but he only wants us to live longer, in order that we may think more. Thus the Ancients in the last play of the *Back to Methuselah* Pentateuch, having achieved a relative emancipation from the needs and exigencies of material existence employ their freedom in the unfettered activity of the intellect. What does the intellect do? It contemplates. It is this contemplation, the occupation and the delight of mystics in all ages, that Shaw seems to regard as the object of evolution; it is for this that the whole experiment of life was undertaken. Butler prepared the way for this conception, but he did not share it. He divined the meaning and described the method of evolution, but he gave no hint of its ultimate purpose. The system with which Shaw presents us in *Back to Methuselah* is thus a definite advance on Butler's work. It embodies a constructive essay in philosophy, which was probably beyond the reach of Butler's more negative mind; though it may be doubted whether, if Butler had not lived, such an essay could have been made. In this, as in so much else, Butler was Socrates to Shaw's Plato.

RECEPTION OF SHAW'S PHILOSOPHY

It cannot be said that Shaw's philosophy has won wide acceptance. For this his eminence in other fields is, no doubt, in part responsible. The English find it hard to forgive a man for making more than one reputation, and Shaw has made at least half a dozen. It is easy, then, to play down his claims as a philosopher on the ground that the man who was a great prose-writer, playwright, orator, wit, political thinker and public figure could not also be endowed with the profundity of the original philosopher, apart altogether from the time, energy and industry which the pursuit of philosophy demands. This criticism, the fruit of sour grapes, is, I think, negligible. Shaw's eminence in each of the various departments I have mentioned enhances and does not detract from his eminence in the others; for his thought, as I have tried to show, is remarkably coherent and the doctrine of Creative Evolution informs and unifies his doctrines on every other topic. Another reason for the comparative neglect of the more philosophical aspect of Shaw's work is the contemporary appearance of two divergent developments of the creative evolutionary view, that of Bergson in *Creative Evolution* and that of S. Alexander in *Space, Time and Deity,* which, though they postulate the same metaphysical background as Shaw does, depart in their development of this background in radical particulars from Shaw's. As they were presented to the world in the more orthodox trappings of formal philosophical writings, they tended to occupy the spotlight of philosophical scrutiny and criticism to the exclusion of Shaw. As one who has endeavoured, not very successfully, to provide a formal philosophical setting for Shaw's doctrines,* I can vouch from personal experience for the comparative absence of serious attention which they have evoked. So much having been said by way of explanation and extenuation, it must be pointed out that there are manifest points of weakness upon which serious criticism, if it had, in fact, been accorded, could have fastened.

THE DIFFICULTY OF END OR GOAL

Of these the most important are: (1) The neglect, to which attention has already been drawn, to make provision for any end or goal upon which the developed consciousness of the evolving Life Force

* In *Matter, Life and Value* (Oxford University Press).

could be directed. Shaw presents us with a dualistic universe which contains Life and matter in which Life incarnates itself and through which Life develops. But if we ask, to what end does it develop, there is no answer. There is, that is to say, no element of perfect or changeless reality in Shaw's scheme, the apprehension and realization of which might be regarded as forming the purpose and goal of the evolutionary process. Shaw's cosmic scheme would seem to demand the inclusion of precisely such an element, an element of absolute value. Shaw might have said that Life evolved in matter, through matter and beyond matter to a knowledge of value. He hints as much, but never explicitly says it.

THE DIFFICULTY OF THE RELATION BETWEEN LIFE AND MATTER

(2) No satisfactory account is given of the relation between Life and matter. Life enters into matter, uses and moulds it. But how? We are not told. The traditional problem of the relation of Life to matter, of the spaceless to the spatial, of the animating spirit to the animated medium is not so much solved as begged. Sometimes Shaw speaks of matter as attracting Life. "What was wrong," says Pygmalion in the last play of *Back to Methuselah* "with the synthetic protoplasm was that it could not fix and conduct the Life Force. It was like a wooden magnet or a lightning conductor made of silk; it would not take the current." The metaphor here is that of an electric current running down a wire; different kinds of wire can, presumably, take different potentials of current. More often we are simply told that Life or evolution "must meanwhile struggle with matter and circumstance by the method of trial and error," in order to rise above "matter and circumstance." It may, of course, be the case that the relation is ineffable and can only be prefigured in the language of metaphor and myth; but to many this fact, if fact it be, would seem so intractable and the relation which it conceals so unthinkable, that they would insist on demanding the abandonment of the dualistic scheme which requires it and substitute a monistic explanation either, like the materialist in terms of matter alone or, like the idealist in terms of Life or mind alone. The reflection that the unexplained relationship between Life and matter entails and includes the vexed question of the relationship within the living organism between mind and body, only serves to throw into high relief the enormity of the assumption that Shaw leaves as it were ungrounded. The two loose ends, mind and body, are never tied together, but are left dangling.

THE DIFFICULTY OF FREE WILL

(3) It is never clear how far, for Shaw, the individual is free. Is he merely a vehicle for the canalisation and subsequent development of the Life Force, or can he win some measure of freedom from Life's promptings? In the first event, he is a mere fountain-pen for conveying the stream of Life, no more responsible for what he does than is the pen for what it writes. It is fairly clear that Shaw does not mean this. For if the individual were not in some sense free, the admonitions and exhortations and injunctions of which Shaw's practical philosophy consists would be beside the point. To be told, for example, that success in life consists in being used in pursuit of its purposes by the power that made you, clearly implies that it is open to you to resist being used in this way, open to you to follow your own purposes, in fact, to fail.

This, I have no doubt, is Shaw's view. We are, at best, imperfect instruments of Life's purpose. In particular, we busy ourselves with our own concerns instead of using ourselves up in Life's service, and although Life does its best to point out to us through the instrumentality of Shaw and other wise men, whom it sends into the world "to give conscious expression to its instinctive purpose," the way it would have us go, and encourages us to follow it by contriving that the life of direct pleasure-seeking will be unrewarding even in terms of pleasure, nevertheless, we do in fact all too frequently go astray.

Assuming, then, that we do have freedom, three difficulties arise. (a) First, is our freedom only a freedom to go wrong? Are we, when we go right, when, that is to say, we go about Life's business, mere automata, responding to the promptings and impulses that reach us from Life, whereas when we assert our own wills and go our own ways, when, in fact, we thwart Life's purposes, we are acting as self-determining individuals? This is a depressing view to take of human free will.

(b) If we are free, whence do we derive the energy which enables us to pursue a course divergent from Life's purpose in regard to us? Granted that we are instruments of life, how can the instrument turn against the hand that wields it? Is it, perhaps, the interposition of matter between the main stream of Life and its individual expressions that confers a measure of freedom upon the latter, much as a line of rocks lying athwart a river will diversify it into a number of different streamlets, each of which may pursue its own course, though *the energy with which it pursues* is that of the parent river. This suggestion, perhaps, is not unplausible; but besides making use of a metaphor which may well be inadmissible, it derives the fact of freedom from the interposition of matter which limits the power of Life over its individual expressions. Shaw himself never, so far as I know, tackles this difficulty.

(c) It may and has been urged that Shaw's theory provides a pitiably inadequate expression of the facts of moral experience.

ERIC BENTLEY

1947

Shaw's Political Economy

I

"The love of economy is the root of all virtue."
—John Tanner, m.i.r.c.

Of the fifteen reputations which Shaw has laid claim to, his reputation as a socialist is perhaps the most familiar. Shaw has been expounding socialism for over sixty years, and there would be no excuse for expounding it for him, were it not that ignorance of it is displayed in nearly everything that is said on the subject. Before giving Shaw a careful reading I myself had heard only two things about his politics: that when he was young he belonged to a dreary group of half-hearted socialists who imagined that capitalism could be overthrown by wire-pulling and talk; and that when he grew old he came to admire tyranny and condone violence. I was not the only one to hear things of that sort. Most of Shaw's biographers re-affirm the cliché about the Fabian Society. Perhaps the biographers have read H. G. Wells, who, when the Fabians threw him out, wrote: "If they had the universe in hand, I know they would take down all the trees and put up stamped tin green shades and sunlight accumulators." Shaw's political philosophy is buried as deep as, say, William Godwin's. Digging Shaw up again, as if he were one of those writers whose chief glory is to be rediscovered in academic theses, I propose to discuss three questions: first, what is Shaw's "Fabianism"? second, what are Shaw's views on the prime problems of political philosophy, the problems of the state and revolution, authority and liberty? third, what is the pedigree and status of Shaw's political philosophy? where does he stand in the tradition of European socialism?

The attack on Shaw's politics has taken several different lines: that he has betrayed his earlier Fabianism, that Fabianism was not worth betraying, and even that he never was a real Fabian. Evidently we need light on Fabianism as well as on Shaw. The Fabian Society, founded in 1884, and after a few months opening its doors to Sidney Webb and Bernard Shaw, was a club of Victorian intellectuals whose plan was never either more or less than to influence the public life of their country as much as a club of intellectuals can. Even today, when the Society is larger than ever before, it has not more than 5000 members. It is idle, then, to complain that it is not a proletarian party and it is impossible to sneer at it as a group of intellectuals unless one thinks groups of intellectuals have no right to exist. The Fabian Society differed from a political party not only in its sheer lack of party organization but also in not being bound to have a "party line."* There was in fact wide divergence of opinion on many things. Agreement limited itself to the socialist goal and to certain attitudes concerning ways and means, attitudes which gradually defined themselves in the struggle against capitalism and, perhaps even more, in the struggle with other kinds of socialism, especially Marxism. Not that Shaw, for one, ever concealed his debt to Marx. His socialism began with Marx and Henry George in 1882. The economic basis of history "dawned on" Shaw when he heard George speak; it was clinched by his reading of the first volume of *Kapital*. In later years Shaw would call himself an "old Marxist." Nevertheless, when he declares (*Fabian Quarterly*, April 1944) that "Socialists who are not essentially Marxist are not Socialists at all" he apparently understands by Marxism solely the economic interpretation of history and the uncompromising collectivist stand. It does not appear that Shaw read anything in Marxist literature except the *Communist Manifesto* and *Kapital* I and II. For their part the Marxists denounced Shaw and the Fabians. It is to them even more perhaps than to reactionaries that we owe the legend that Fabianism was academic and futile. Even so moderate a liberal as Mr. Edmund Wilson confesses to having derived his damaging critique of Bernard Shaw's Fabianism from a Marxist source.

Marxist socialism claims to be, not a sentiment of indignation at injustice, but a scientific demonstration that capitalism will give way to socialism. Fabianism begins and ends as an appeal—emotionally

* See *Fabian Tract No. 70* (1896): "It [the Society] has no distinctive opinions on the Marriage Question, Religion, Art, abstract Economics, historic Evolution, Currency, or any other subject than its own special business of practical Democracy and Socialism."

based—for social justice. Negatively stated, it is a protest against social inequality. Though the Fabians were far from knowing it their attitude reached its most highly articulated expression in Shaw's *Intelligent Woman's Guide* in which exact economic equality is called for to provide a basis for the natural diversity—or inequality of men. How such conceptions differ from Marxism became clear in lengthy disputes between the two schools of thought.

The Fabian quarrel with the early Marxists was over two closely connected parts of Marxist doctrine: the labor theory of value and the class struggle. Shaw himself led the Fabians in both disputes. The technical side of his critique of the labor theory of value he derived from the British economist Stanley Jevons who advanced a theory of "marginal utility" identical with that which was independently advanced on the continent in the 'seventies and 'eighties. Following Jevons, Shaw denied that the exchange value of a commodity depended primarily on the amount of socially necessary labor put into it and argued that the value of any commodity is a function of the quantity available. Fearing that this argument would take the teeth out of socialism by denying that the capitalist's profits were stolen from the workmen's earnings, in the sense that the product of labor is in excess of its price, the Marxists clung to Ricardo's labor theory of value. Shaw was more impressed by another side of the Ricardian economics: its description of rent. In rent he finds the diagnostic of capitalism. And in *Fabian Essays* (1889), written before the advent of inductive, historical economics (it was Beatrice Webb who would lead the Fabians into this path later), Shaw proceeds on time-honored Ricardian lines. His account of rent may be read as a parable.

Mr. A seizes the best piece of land in a virgin region and makes $1000 with its products. Mr. B, the next man to turn up, gets inferior land which yields, say, $500. Mr. A may now rent his land to Mr. B for $500, for the latter could not make a higher rate of profit anyway. Mr. A can now retire and live as an idler on rent. So much for the parable. Shaw now extends the use of the term "rent" to the whole area of private profit making. The remedy for the injustice it involves is socialism:

> What the achievement of socialism involves economically is the transfer of rent from the class which now appropriates it to the whole people. Rent being that part of the produce which is individually unearned, this is the only equitable method of disposing of it.

In other words Shaw agrees with Proudhon that "property is theft." Shaw's "rent" is much the same as Marx's "surplus value," but the injustice of the capitalist system is to Shaw all the greater because

commodities do *not* exchange according to the labor that has gone
into them:

> Commodities produced in the most favorable situations, well inside the
> margin of cultivation, with the minimum of labor, will fetch as high a
> price as commodities produced at the margin with the maximum of
> labor. And all the difference between the two goes to the landlord.

Thus from the Ricardian parable follows the Jevonian principle
that "the exchange of the least useful part of the supply fixes the
exchange value of all the rest." From this principle follows the
Shavian definition of humanity under capitalism.

In a society of buying and selling the vast mass of the population
has nothing to sell but itself. If there were only one workman in
their settlement, Mr. A and Mr. B would have to pay a good deal
for his services. But, the supply of workmen being in excess of the
need, their value falls to nothing. To nothing, not to their wage
level. For a wage is only the feeding and stabling of the animal.
Wherever horses are to be had for the asking, at no cost save their
maintenance, their value is not the cost of maintenance: it is nil.
Capitalism ought thus, says Shaw, to be called proletarianism,
which again is but a polite word for prostitution. Mrs. Warren's profession is only the most dramatic example of proletarianism. That is
why Shaw, the dramatist, chose it to illustrate the nature of modern
society.

Shaw's theory of value, then, was, like Marx's, the hub of an
analysis of capitalism. Where it differed from Marx, other than
verbally, it differed in being less of a "scientific" demonstration on
the one hand and less of a metaphysic on the other. And this meant
not only that Shaw's economic essays are infinitely smaller things in
intention and effect than Marx's but that Shaw is much less of a believer in fixed laws both in economics and nature. He seized on
Jevons because the latter seemed to leave a loophole for human will
and effort. In Jevons there was no "law of motion of capitalism," no
historical inevitability. Shaw fought the Marxists whenever, like the
Darwinists, they seemed to be determinists.

The discussion of value was opened and closed in the 'eighties.
The matter of the class struggle needed a lengthier airing. (Again
Shaw's chief antagonist was the contemporary English champion of
Marx, H. M. Hyndman.) Shaw's argument in this battle was not in
the least the argument of classical economy—that there is a harmony
of interests as between capital and labor. He fully agreed with Marx
that there was no such harmony. He fully shared Marx's wish for a
classless society. He did not agree however that present antagonisms
of interest would automatically induce the proletariat to struggle for

power. Again it is the law of history, the historical necessity, the inevitability, that Shaw objects to. He fears that reliance on them is as futile as reliance on God and that to wait for History to produce socialism is to wait forever. When the Marxist replies that if the workers are not class-conscious they must be made so he is of course appealing from historical necessity to the will of a minority. Shaw is not averse to this. He merely concludes that, so prompted, the struggle for socialism will have lower and upper class people on both sides and is therefore not accurately described as a *class* struggle.

The present absence of class consciousness is not the only thing. There always will be an absence of proletarian class consciousness on the part of those whose customers are the rich:

> The line that separates those who live on rich customers from those who live on poor customers: in other words, which separates those interested in the maintenance of Capitalism from those interested in its replacement by Socialism, is a line drawn not between rich and poor, capitalist and proletarian, but right down the middle of the proletariat to the bottom of the very poorest section.

Thus the class struggle of the Marxists—the struggle between those who pay and receive wages—is cut across by another struggle—the struggle between those whose customers live on interest and those whose customers live on wages.

To the Marxist all this is ineffably bourgeois: the Fabians fail to see the historic mission of the working class. Naturally. For the Fabians deny that such things as historic missions exist. And—it is true—they are unique as post-Marxist socialists in putting no more faith in the proletariat as such than in any other group. Less, if anything. Shaw has always held that if the poor were already wiser and better than anybody else that would be a reason for keeping them poor. His socialism resembles D. H. Lawrence's in that he wishes to do nothing with the proletariat except abolish it. At this point the Marxist abandons his argument of necessity and appeals to pure sentiment, to that praise of the poor as poor which is the essence of demagogy. Theoretically the Marxist should not believe in the superiority of the poor or in the villainy of the rich. Actually very much Marxist propaganda does posit these things. The Fabians offered a much less dramatic program: that of permeating the liberals, of using parliamentary methods, of gradualness. What could be more disgusting to the political salvationist? To this day our scorn for the Fabians unconsciously echoes the indignation of the outraged revolutionaries. The defense of the Fabian position should be two-fold. First, sanity is often less exciting than insanity.

Second, permeation and gradualness were the beginning, not the end, of Fabian policy.

That Fabian policy was sane is shown by the astonishing measure of success which attended it. No group of *philosophes* since the Benthamites had known so well how to get results. It would be impossible to account for the social legislation of England in the twentieth century without the work of preparation performed by such people as the Webbs. That most of it was enacted by Liberal and Conservative regimes is a tribute to the policy of permeation. Meanwhile the Fabians themselves had taken a new stand. They were one of the most solid bodies of informed support that went to the making of the Labour Party (1900–1906). The reconstitution of the Labour Party in 1918 was the work of Sidney Webb as much as any one man. At this date the kind of people who earlier mocked at the Fabians for their academicism and remoteness from the political struggle began to shift their ground. They noted with glee how the purities of theory are contaminated by the impurities of practice. They pointed to the number of Fabians in the Labour governments of 1924 and 1929 not to show the success but the failure of Fabianism. But can the vacillation and pusillanimity of Ramsay MacDonald's cabinets be blamed upon the doctrines of Fabianism? One should recall that Sidney Webb was the first to denounce MacDonald's treachery, that Beatrice Webb was at this time proposing a new Reform Act more revolutionary than that of a century earlier, that Shaw was suggesting a new set of Fabian Essays to bring Fabianism up to date with schemes for a new kind of government.

Mention the Fabians and someone will bring up "the inevitability of gradualness." It can be brought up here, however, only to be dismissed. Coined as late as 1923 by Sidney Webb, deplored by Beatrice as early as 1932, the phrase was never a summary of the Fabian mentality and never meant what it is generally supposed to mean. It meant, not that gradual socialism possessed the same kind of historic inevitability as is claimed by Marxist communism, but only that deep social changes take time. In the first flush of youth the Fabians had believed that socialism could take effect in a fortnight. Later, as Shaw put it, they realized that though you may nationalize the railways in an afternoon, it will be a long time before all your first-class and third-class carriages become second-class carriages. Thus in reviewing Russian history between 1917 and 1924 Shaw rebukes Lenin for being insufficiently Fabian; the latter, trying to introduce communism at a stroke, had subsequently to acknowledge the "inevitability of gradualness," and beat a retreat. Webb's famous phrase is therefore no blanket endorsement of parliamentary methods.

In fact, the anti-parliamentary animus was nothing new to British collectivism, as readers of Carlyle and Dickens can testify. If the Fabians were willing to make use of parliament it was never because they were all parliamentarians on principle but because they could see no other practical path to reform. They were not pacifists. Their difference with the advocates of violent revolution was based on the conviction, not that violence was wrong, but that it was inappropriate at the time. Fabius was chosen as their patron not because he waited but because he waited *before he struck.* H. G. Wells's taunting observation that Fabius waited and *never* struck may have been pertinent as applied to some of the Fabians—but it was especially inapplicable to the socialism of his chief antagonist, Bernard Shaw, who in *The Clarion* (21 October 1904) had already protested against the idea

> that there are two courses open to us: parliamentary action and physical force, each of which excludes the other. That is not so: Parliamentary action is usually the first stage of civil war. It brings the issues before the man in the street; it works up public feeling; and when the reactionary party is not prepared to fight, and the advancing party is, it settles the question without bloodshed. It is of course possible that Capitalism will go under without a fight; but I confess I should regard any statesman who calculated on that as an extremely sanguine man. The mistake made by our wildcat barricaders is not in believing that the revolution will be effected by force, but in putting the fighting at the wrong end of the process. It will take many more years to make the questions burning ones; and it will take more years still before the burning works up a single Englishman to the point of firing on any other Englishman—if necessary—sooner than tolerate the status quo. The Marxists believe that the whole thing will be done by "historical development," which the Liberals (Marxism being only an intellectually pretentious form of proletarian Liberalism) call Progress with a large P.

Passages like this have been forgotten by those who think that Shaw began to talk this way only under the influence of Stalin. But we must not pretend that Shaw and Fabianism never changed with the times. They would have been stupid not to. The changes, however, were adaptations and adjustments, not betrayals and conversions. The major adjustment concerned this very question of violence. The First World War and the Russian Revolution opened Shaw's eyes to many things. Perhaps now he fully realized what Engels had meant by describing war as the midwife of social change. In 1904 he had said that the situation was not yet revolutionary. From the 'twenties on he was not so sure. He began to think it high time the Englishman *was* ready to shoot:

I am afraid our property system will not be settled without violence
unless you make up your minds that, if it is defended by violence, it
will be overthrown by violence.

These words were spoken a few months before the Nazis defended
property by violence and were met, not by counter-violence, but by
a disunited left weakened by years of propaganda against the use of
force—weakened, many Marxists said, by the German equivalent of
Fabianism, recalling how Eduard Bernstein had Fabianised the
Social Democrats after his association with the Fabians in London.
But I hope I have shown with what doubtful propriety one equates
Fabianism with the perennial wishy-washiness of labor's right wing.

"Shaw, then, began by attacking the non-Fabian socialists for
their bellicosity and ended by attacking them for their pacifism"—
so say his critics. There is no inconsistency in Shaw's two positions.
In each case he was opposing a strategy that could not succeed. An
armed insurrection led by Hyndman would simply have shocked the
British gentleman without doing socialism any good. Was it not preferable, so long as no more drastic action was feasible, to win the
sympathies of as many British gentlemen as possible? After 1919,
however, came a change. A peaceful Social Democracy led by Ramsay MacDonald would inveigh against capitalism in vain. The time
for drastic action had come. In the earlier situation Shaw believed
that a "showdown" would be premature: the socialists would get
more by asking for less. In the later situation Shaw believed the
avoidance of a "showdown" would be missing a chance of socialist
victory and giving capitalism a new lease of life: asking for a little at
this stage would be to get nothing at all. As for militarism and
pacifism they are abstractions and superstitions. In politics there are
only ends and the means—now "militaristic," now "pacifistic"—by
which ends are reached.

Probably few of the Fabians were as clear-headed as Shaw about
all this. The Webbs seem to have harbored for a long time the un-
Shavian illusion that capitalists can be talked into socialism. But we
should not imagine that the Webbs always led the way in Fabian
thinking. In this matter of violence it was Shaw who led, and the
Webbs who came to his conclusion much later. It is the same in the
related question of leadership. The Webbs had always believed in
the expert but they had imagined him wholly as servant (the servant, they said, is our noblest functionary) and not as leader. Shaw
did not leave it to Lenin or Stalin to give him a belief in the active
leader who does much more than merely carry out the expressed
will of the masses. One need hardly cite his *Caesar and Cleopatra*,

his prefatorial praise of the Bismarckian man of action who will sweep away all humbug, or his doctrine of Superman. The most acute analyst of Shaw's socialism in the early days, Max Beer, saw in it all the things that would later offend the liberals. Writing in 1904 from the Marxist standpoint, Beer said Shaw was the victim of relativism:

> Having no objective guide, no leading principle to go by, Shaw necessarily arrives at hero-worship—at the hankering after a Superman to guide mankind. I have noticed the same mental development in several continental critics like Harden, Bahr, Ernst, etc. They began with Social Democracy, passed through the Ibsen period, worshipped *The Enemy of the People*, finally becoming adherents of Nietzsche in theory and of Bismarck or some other social imperialist in practice. Marxism is the antithesis of all that. It has a body of doctrines; it regards theory as the guide in practical life; and it destroys all heroism in history. In the place of the heroic factor it sets material and economic factors as the motor power of historical development. . . . The Revisionists, or Fabians, say: "Socialism is, before all, an administrative problem; it is not a class struggle, but a clever management of public affairs! It is the Superman in local government."

Discount the weighing of certain words with Marxist emotion and what Beer says is perfectly acceptable. Once dispute the adequacy of "material and economic factors" to make revolutions on their own, and you do have to appeal to human will and hence to "heroism." Max Beer makes the alternatives very clear and surely his position is more convincing than that of liberals who too lightly assume that we can do without the assistance alike of History and the Superman.

Beer is also right in his assertion—however sarcastic—that the Superman doctrine is implicit in the Fabian expert. He saw deeper than those who found in the latter nothing more than a dreary bureaucratic mediocrity. And he saw it long before the Webbs did. The first inkling that the Webbs had of the real needs of leadership seems to have been in the 'twenties when Beatrice called for a "dedicated Order of Socialists" resembling the Society of Jesus. At the time she was anti-soviet. A decade later, after visiting the country which Shaw was already overenthusiastic about, she was to praise Soviet Russia for having—so she alleged—made leadership a vocation.

The Webbs learnt from Shaw, and Shaw learnt from the Webbs. It is impossible to make out, as some have tried to do, that they made a merely freakish trio. They were complementary. The Webbs' weakness was an oversimplification of human nature. They regarded people as more tractable than they really are. Shaw, on the

other hand, was an artist and therefore, as he said, "a specialist in
human nature." The Webbs had much to learn from him about the
intractability of the human animal, about the necessity of conflict
and of leadership. Shaw had to learn from the Webbs the large-scale
facts, the statistics, the manifold particulars of sociology. In a sense
the combination of the Webbs and Shaw *is* Fabianism. This combination gave us the Fabianism of the early tracts and of the *Fabian
Essays* (1889); it gave us also the Fabianism of the Minority Report
and the standard history of trade-unionism. It gave us the Fabianism that "permeated the Liberals"; it gave us also the Fabianism
that helped to shape and guide the Labour Party.

Between wars (1919–1939) the Fabian Society was relatively
dormant; and when it woke up—how impressively!—with the out-
break of the Second World War it was in younger hands. The inter-
mediate years, however, had a special importance in the unfolding
of Fabian theory and in the development of the remarkable collab-
oration of Shaw and the Webbs. That the "Old Guard" did not intend to rest content with their very successful permeation of the
Liberal Party, or even with the Labour Party which they had done
so much to create, is already clear from a letter of Shaw's dating
from before the First World War. He wrote to his French translator
that the earlier objectives of the Fabian Society were now achieved:
the notion that socialist societies can reform the world by enlarging
their membership had been killed; a large part of socialism had
been translated into parliamentary measures so that respectable
Englishmen could now be socialists as easily as Liberals or Con-
servatives; and, finally, the working class had been detached from
the Liberal Party by the founding of the Labour Party. As for the
future, the important thing, says Shaw, is to realize that the Labour
Party is not a socialist party but only a radical wing of the trade
unions:

> The Labour Party is good in that it represents labour but bad in that it
> represents poverty and ignorance, and it is anti-social in that it supports
> the producer against the consumer and the worker against the employer
> instead of supporting the workers against the idlers. The Labour Party
> is also bad on account of its false democracy, which substitutes the
> mistrust, fear, and political incapacity of the masses for genuine political
> talent, and which would make the people legislators instead of leaving
> them what they are at present, the judges of the legislators.

Fabian policy, Shaw suggests, must be to "detach the socialists
from the Labour Party" and make them into a compact group of
experts and leaders which will show the way to all radical parties.

This last suggestion is either merely a proposal to continue the

Fabian Society or a proposal to found the kind of political party which would never succeed in getting into parliament. One is not surprised therefore that after the war Sidney Webb preferred to put his energies to reorganizing the Labour Party itself as a socialist party. It was of course a hazardous task. Even today it is not clear how far the Labour Party's socialism goes. In 1924 and 1931 it scarcely seemed socialist at all.

The most pertinent criticism of the earlier Fabians was that they left too many things out of account. Shaw himself has complained that they shared too many of the prejudices of Victorian "advanced" people such as anti-clericalism and anti-militarism. Consequently they neglected to study—to give three outstanding examples—trade unionism, foreign affairs, and much of the machinery of government.

Gradually the leading Fabians managed to cover the neglected areas. Beatrice Webb was the great pioneer in the first. She and her husband became the historians of trade unions and cooperatives, thus not only filling a gap in their knowledge, but establishing a new empirical approach to sociology. What Shaw derived from their study was, as might be expected, an idea, an interpretation. Trade Unionism was, he declared, the "capitalism of the proletariat." When the workers banded together to defend the principle of selling in the highest market and giving as little as possible for their money, Proletarianism was complete. Since, moreover, the union leader's ideal was capitalism with himself getting the profits Shaw saw that the unionists were joining with the capitalists to form what the Fabians had not seen the possibility of: State Capitalism, Moralised Capitalism, a "socialism" of production, not distribution. Against this trend Shaw puts a case which is now termed "Stalinist" but which he probably derived from the American radical Edward Bellamy: one should fight, not for a "right to strike," but for the nationalization of unions (as of all other concerns) and compulsory labor for all "with death as the final penalty."

It was Shaw who first induced the Fabians to work out a more intelligent attitude to foreign affairs. When war was declared against the Boers, British liberalism, led by the young Lloyd George, was pacifist. To Shaw the pacifist position has never been convincing and, since nowadays he is accused of jingoism or muddle-headedness, it may be well to explain why. As a matter of fact Shaw himself explained why in the pamphlet "Fabianism and the Empire" and, more directly perhaps, in a letter he wrote to Hyndman at the time. Shaw's position is that once a war has begun, there being only two sides, it is usually advisable to back the lesser evil against the greater. Later, during the First World War, he went so far as to argue that you fight even for a pirate ship if you happen to be on board when it is attacked; in the letter to Hyndman he more moderately argues that the pacifism of the liberals helps the Boers to win and that this is undesirable because the Boers are less likely to do good in South Africa than the British. True, he concedes, the British Empire stands for sheer Mammonism. But it is easier for the British to pass from Mammonism to a socialist transformation than for the Boers to pass from Kruger's Old Testament fanaticism to any good thing whatsoever.

Whether Shaw's view of the Boer War was correct or not, it should be clear that his analysis was much more hardheaded than that of other radicals of the day. He saw the futility of war. He also saw the futility of liberal pacifism. In the First World War he proclaimed that he found no more ethical content than in the collision of two trains, yet once the war started he thought British victory much preferable to the alternative. He was therefore equally abhorred by reactionaries and pacifists. Both groups laughed at Shaw after the war too when he consistently supported the League of Nations, which he and the Fabian Society had done not a little to start. It is characteristic that Shaw, who clearly saw that a League without power would never stop war, supported the League *faute de mieux,* and advertised its less spectacular functions. One might sum up his attitude to foreign affairs as a passionate desire to end the international anarchy linked to a sharp awareness of the power factors, political, economic, military, and psychological that stand in the way. Beside, say, H. G. Wells's proposals, Shaw's statements on international relations are tentative and few. They are also more realistic. Wells, the "scientist," generated vast, windy schemes as a boiler generates steam. Wells's thinking was nothing if not cosmic. Shaw, the artist, is more easily affected by hard facts, by brute obstacles, like nationalism, like capitalism, like the human love of dangerous illusions.

As to the third great omission in Fabian thought—the omission of a theory of government—Shaw and the Webbs have devoted a large part of their later careers to it. At the same time as they were supporting every actual and immediate step towards socialism, they were working out on paper their most systematic critique of the present system and their most sweeping proposals for reform. After the First World War the Webbs wrote (and Shaw revised) their only full-length analysis of modern life: *The Decay of Capitalist Civilization.* They also published a plan which went far beyond the mere demand for socialism: *A Constitution for the Socialist Commonwealth of Great Britain.* This book was the starting point for all

those suggestions for a new kind of government which have filled
Shaw's political essays since the 'twenties. It is an attempt to sketch
the institutions of a socialist society.

In her very fair-minded biography of Beatrice Webb, Mrs.
Margaret Cole pooh-poohs the *Constitution* as badly written and
impractical. Badly written it is. But let us hope it will not always
seem impractical. Socialist literature is weak on the institutional side
because socialists have too often assumed that such things will take
care of themselves. The Webbs' book is important because it tries
to give the socialist idea the solid content it so often lacks. It is
based, like all the later books of the Fabian Trio, on the assumption
that twentieth-century civilization is beyond repair, and that socialist reconstruction will have to cover every institution, economic and
political. Like Shaw, the Webbs when young were thought very
mild and conservative socialists; like him they are thought impractical extremists, even renegades, in their age. Yet there was no reversal of former principles. The whole development was summed up
in advance in *Man and Superman:*

> All who achieve real distinction in life begin as revolutionists. The most
> distinguished persons become more revolutionary as they grow older,
> though they are commonly supposed to become more conservative
> owing to their loss of faith in conventional methods of reform.

II

A Constitution for the Socialist Commonwealth of Great Britain
is nowhere lengthily quoted by Shaw or even paraphrased. He en-
dorses its main proposal—that the British government should be
replaced by a new bicameral system consisting of a Political and a
Social Parliament—and adds to this his own ideas. Sometimes what
is peripheral for the Webbs is central for Shaw. The abolition of the
Party System, cautiously hinted at by the Webbs in a footnote, is a
main plank in Shaw's platform. (Perhaps he has been to school to
his debating antagonist, Hilaire Belloc.) Instead of nineteenth century parliamentarism Shaw wants occupational franchise and the
building of a vast hierarchical state.

The Shavian state differs from most hierarchical schemes in that
power proceeds from below. It is "in touch with the people and
must satisfy them." It differs from most democratic schemes in removing the higher functions of government from direct popular
control. Shaw has sometimes advocated making the franchise
dependent on passing tests in political science and public affairs,
the tests to be harder for each level of the hierarchy; but it seems

that even those who have passed no tests will be able periodically to pass judgment on the government as a whole. The public is like the purchaser who can tell whether the shoe pinches though he would not be able to make shoes himself. The doctrine that he *can* make his own shoes Shaw calls the "mock democratic folly of pretending that the intellectual and technical work of Government can be dictated, or its ministers directly chosen, by mobs of voters." That democracy needs leadership every bit as much as any other system of government is presupposed in the following plan:

> You can conceive the new state getting a basic representative Congress to keep it in touch with its subjects. This Congress would have sufficient local knowledge to elect the local chiefs of industry throughout the country. These local chiefs can elect provincial chiefs who can elect national chiefs. These national chiefs—you may call them if you like a Cabinet—in their turn have to elect the national thinkers, for a nation needs two cabinets: an administrative Cabinet and a thinking Cabinet.

Although this plan is designed, Platonically, to make the philosopher a king and the king a philosopher, it is unPlatonic in that the base of the pyramid is a democratic franchise. It is in fact radically different from any form of aristocracy or democracy (the only two forms of government Shaw respects) that has ever existed. Only those who prefer mud-slinging to meaning could call it fascist.

Indeed it should provide the context for a more accurate account of Shaw's attitude to Mussolini and Hitler. A touchy subject, but one that should be faced: to say it should not be taken seriously is to make too large a concession to those who always laugh Shaw off. Shaw should always be taken to mean something even if he cannot always be taken to mean simply what he says. He can always be taken seriously; he cannot always be taken literally. People with no sense of humor find him a Mass of Contradictions. And before even the best-disposed of us can appraise Shaw's approach to fascism we must take note of the special nature of his approach to politics in general.

Shaw has never really set out to be a systematic and objective political scientist. That was the Webbs' job. Shaw's function—there is no accurate name for it—was to prod, to irritate, to enliven, to push and pull in this direction or that as the situation demanded. He was a special sort of propagandist: an artist in propaganda. He converted the trade of the Northcliffes and the Hearsts into a special craft or mission. He was not providing blueprints. Even his lengthiest political work purports only to bring out points which the political scientists have neglected, not to state an alternative political philosophy. And Shaw was entirely selfless. He didn't care if you thought him a fool provided his barbs shot home. He didn't care if you thought him a fascist if only he had undermined your own liberal complacency. The important thing was not the reputation of Shaw but the history of the world.

All Shaw's statements are "slanted." What he says is always determined by the thought: what can I do to this audience? not by the thought: what is the most objective statement about this subject? In political discussion Shaw's audience—since he became famous—has been a very large part of the British public. Consequently one can scarcely exaggerate his preoccupation with the British. Certainly his most notable limitation is his ignorance of other peoples. Certainly his most noble characteristic is his passionate and lifelong attempt to reform the country in which he pretends to be an aloof foreigner. If Shaw finds something to admire in one of his quick trips abroad (Russia is the obvious example) he uses it as a stick to beat England with. If he finds something in a foreign country to dislike he is quick to add that you mustn't imagine England is any better: for British publication he changed the title of *The Future of Political Science in America* to *The Political Madhouse in America and Nearer Home,* adding a preface to rub in the last phrase. "The Inquisition," Shaw tells us elsewhere, "was a liberal institution compared to the [British] General Medical Council. The Inquisitor who condemned Joan was bad but he was "far more self-disciplined and conscientious both as priest and lawyer than any English judge ever dreams of being in a political case in which his party and class prejudices are involved." And so on. The formula has been exploited *ad nauseam.* In any hands but Shaw's it would always have seemed callow, and even in his it has become trite. It is the formula of an exasperated idealist. And it is exasperation that has driven Shaw into his most dubious declarations.

Twenty years ago Shaw entered into controversy with the eminent liberal professor, already a refugee, Gaetano Salvemini. In many ways Shaw got the worst of it. Salvemini knew Italy and Shaw did not. I doubt if he really knows any country except England. In the whole tiresome dispute he made only one good point—surely his lowest score in any controversy—but since it was his main point, for the sake of which he had provoked the whole discussion, and since none of his liberal opponents has ever tried to understand it, one may be excused for re-iterating it here. The point was that nineteenth-century liberalism was bankrupt, and that British socialists might wake up to that fact, if only they could lose their inferiority complex, if only they could stop talking as men in perpetual opposition. Shaw seems to anticipate the outsmarting of the Labour leaders at the hands of Baldwin and Simon in 1926 and of Baldwin and King George in 1931:

> Of course if you compare Italy with a Mazzinian Utopia, it is full of abuse and tyrannies. So is America, so is France, so is England, so is Russia. . . . Because I face the facts in the full knowledge that the democratic idealism of the 19th Century is as dead as a doornail, you say that I come dangerously near to the point of view of the British ruling class. But are you not delighted to find at last a Socialist who speaks and thinks as responsible rulers do and not as resentful slaves do? Of what use are Socialists who can neither rule nor understand what ruling means?

Of course anyone who represents Mussolini as relatively good and British Labour as relatively bad will simply remind American liberals of Charles Lindbergh and the isolationists, for whom the moral was: leave Britain to be trampled on by the fascists. For Shaw, however, the moral was: let Britain wake up, let Britain take thought, and let Britain do what he has spent his life urging her to do—adopt a socialism without Ramsay MacDonalds.

It should by now be plain that people who know nothing about Shaw except that he several times complimented Mussolini, and with so many liberals, never regarded Hitler as a moron, must have a very eccentric picture of Shaw's politics. The Shaw the public knows and the Shaw the critics know is always the man who says outrageous things in the press, never the man who writes solid books. What Shaw actually says about fascism when not playing advocate to Mussolini's devil has been much less heeded. Here is an extract from his *Everybody's Political What's What:*

> Nowadays the Capitalist cry is: "Nationalize what you like; municipalize all you can; turn the courts of justice into courts martial and your parliaments and corporations into boards of directors with your most popular mob orators in the chair, provided the rent, the interest, and the profits come to us as before, and the proletariat still gets nothing but its keep."
>
> This is the great corruption of Socialism which threatens us at present. It calls itself Fascism in Italy, National Socialism (Nazi for short) in Germany, New Deal in the United States, and is clever enough to remain nameless in England; but everywhere it means the same thing: Socialist production and Unsocialist distribution. So far, out of the frying pan into the fire.

Shaw adds that Fascism is a short name for State Capitalism, that it has produced a world war, that in this war the issue was confused because Russia fought alongside "the western fascists," but that in the end the belligerents will "fight for their own sides, plutocracy against democracy, Fascism against Communism." This analysis may oversimplify the issues by identifying Stalin's regime with democracy and communism. It can scarcely be taken to be favorable to fascism.

To some extent the Shavian analysis of fascism is Marxist—in its description of fascism as State Capitalism, for instance. Where Shaw parts company with the Marxists is in his assumption that fascism—in Italy and Germany—was supported by the masses. This assumption does not seem as unwarranted to many of us today as it did to the optimistic zealots of the 'thirties who told us that the majority of Germans (they scarcely dared say of Italians) were hostile to their Leader. No less than the opinion of the zealots, Shaw's opinion was based, not on information alone, but on a presupposition about human nature. "The average citizen," the optimists said to themselves, "is a liberal." "The average citizen," says Shaw, out loud, "is a fascist."

This was no quip. Shaw has always contended that the evils of capitalism must be blamed not on the capitalists who only do what everybody would like to do but on the workers, who through ignorance, stupidity, or cowardice, let the capitalists get way with it. This acquiescence is the most fatal failure in all modern civilization. Now fascism is only a capitalism further consolidated, and further acquiesced in. The tendency of the average man to hand over responsibility to others was never more fully pandered to. It is with bitter irony that Shaw describes fascism as typically democratic, and that he says: "I do not believe in democracy."

Shaw is against fascism for the same reason he is against nineteenth-century liberalism: both are doctrines which relieve us of responsibility, of controlling and planning our own communal life. That is to say, they are anti-socialist doctrines. Fascism pretends to be socialist. It introduces some measure of socialist production but cannot practice socialist distribution without removing its lynchpin: capitalism. The nineteenth-century liberal prides himself on the equation: liberty = free enterprise. In short, says Shaw, liberalism and fascism are rival masks of capitalism, and fascism is in some ways the better of the two. It sometimes benefited the proletariat, it gave bureaucratic status to functionaries who were formerly only casual employees, it tightened up the public services, it assailed individualism and preached putting the community first. To that extent it prepared the way for genuine socialism. Liberalism seems less apposite in the present world. It has discredited itself by preaching an abstract and negative liberty. Its characteristic modern forms are the economic doctrine of free enterprise and the political doctrine of anarchism:

The cry of Liberty is always on the lips of the propertied classes who own the lion's share of land and capital and have nothing to fear but nationalization of these resources, because it implies that the less government activity there is the more free the people are, and because it helps to elect the thoughtless who always support the status quo because anything unusual shocks them.

Liberalism can only cease to be mockery when Liberty is a concrete possibility for the masses, that is, under socialism. Liberalism was born too early. It is really "a post-Communist and not a pre-Communist doctrine and therefore it has a great future before it when the world is full of Communists who will be at leisure for the greater part of their lives." For there is no liberty without leisure.

All of this is rubbing the liberal cat the wrong way. Shaw has always taken it as his role to do precisely that. "He is never so happy," Hyndman wrote over forty years ago, "as when he is running a tilt at the party with which he is, at least nominally, associated." All the most ridiculous people in his early plays, as in his late ones, are the advanced people, liberals like Roebuck Ramsden, suffragettes like Mrs. Clandon and Gloria, "disciples of Bernard Shaw" like Dubedat, whereas the capitalist and the conqueror are shown to be comparatively sane. One of Shaw's best essays is called "The Illusions of Socialism." In it he shows that socialists have carried liberal illusions to an extreme. It is not only Marxism proper but almost all forms of non-Fabian socialism that Shaw regards as "intellectually pretentious forms of proletarian Liberalism." In the course of his essay Shaw specified two major socialist illusions: the religious illusion of the day of revolution as a millennium and the dramatic illusion, "the crude Marxist melodrama of 'The Class War: or the Virtuous Worker and the Brutal Capitalist.'"

It may be that the trick of showing the enemy to be a much more sensible person than your friends is less appropriate when the enemy is Hitler than when he was Wilhelm II. (At least it is easy for us to say so, overlooking the fact that, in America and England at least, the hatred of "the Kaiser" was much more virulent than hatred of Hitler ever was.) To stress the dangers of liberalism when civilization is threatened by illiberalism is perhaps the most suspicious item in Shaw's long political career. If we cannot quite agree with Max Beer who long ago classed Shaw with the continental intelligentsia which in such large numbers turned from Marx to Nietzsche and from Nietzsche to simple imperialism, we can see that he cast at least one look in that direction. A constant danger for the radical is that he may come to hate his rivals so much that he will join with the enemy to op-

pose them. In recent years we have been confronted with the spectacle
of communists hating Hitler less than Churchill, and of liberals hating Hitler less than Stalin. I do not think Shaw was deeply involved
in these ignominies. His championing of the rightist against the
liberal is the old-fashioned devil's advocacy of a Victorian debater
rather than the real diabolism that is so common today. Moreover,
if Shaw's solution of the problem of power seems too Machiavellian,
it is at least a resolute attempt to escape pious liberal platitude. His
leftist opponents are still where they were sixty years ago—appealing either to historical necessity or to the assumed political superiority of the masses.

Actually Shaw is closer to Rousseau than to Machiavelli. Like
Rousseau, Shaw seems to the casual modern reader an anarchist, a
sheer rebel. Like Rousseau, Shaw seems to the more knowing reader
precisely the opposite—an authoritarian. We do not really understand either Rousseau or Shaw until we see that for them liberty is a
paradox, since it is achieved through its opposite, restriction. Both
philosophers would agree with present-day American Republicans
that a government interference means nothing if not interference
with someone's liberty. Only they would add that liberty is in general achieved after this contradictory fashion.

III

Doubtless the both/and approach of a Shaw, no less than of a
Rousseau, is alien to the either/or thinkers of today. Yes. Although
Shaw has offered a brilliant analysis of fascism, upon the whole he is
very old-fashioned. His Victorian education has limited his understanding of the twentieth century. So little has he tried to know as
much about us as he knew about our grandfathers that, when he
speaks of "today," we sometimes have the impression that he means
1910. He sometimes seems remote to those of us who were born into
the twentieth-century melee because almost everything he knows
was learnt in the nineteenth century. Yet the old-fashionedness is in
most contexts less of a limitation than a merit, and we can go back
to Shaw with as much pleasure and profit as to any other Victorian.
He is old-fashioned but he is not obsolete. His knowledge of particular areas of contemporary fact may be faulty but his analysis of the
modern world in general is valid now if it was ever valid; for the
events of the twentieth century amount to tumult much more than
to change, let alone progress. The classic analyses of our age are still
nineteenth-century analyses.

Shaw is a Victorian socialist. Aside from the Webbs his political
teachers were Henry George, Karl Marx, Stanley Jevons, and

Edward Bellamy. They at least are the giants. If we were to watch
Shaw learning a fact here, acquiring an attitude there, picking up an
idea in another place, we would have to list a score of other Victorian socialists—most important among them William Morris and
Belfort Bax, Stuart-Glennie and Henry Salt. Insofar as Shavian
socialism is in a broad tradition that goes back beyond the Fabians
I would say it is neither in the French "Utopian" line nor the German "scientific" line nor the Russian "anarchist" line but in the
British "aristocratic" line. Behind Shaw is Ruskin, and behind Ruskin
is Carlyle.

Calling himself a communist, "reddest also of the red," Ruskin
preached order, reverence, and authority. He believed in some such
hierarchy as Shaw was to advocate (though he was not so sure it
could not be hereditary). It was Ruskin who before Jevons—and by
a much simpler reasoning—argued that economics is not a realm of
impersonal laws but a realm of human regulation, potentially a
branch of human welfare. It was Ruskin who taught Shaw that
there are only three ways of procuring wealth—working, begging,
and stealing—and that capitalism condemns many to beg by allowing a few to steal. The corollary—that the good social order is one in
which everyone works—is a cornerstone of Shavianism. The point is
for Shaw not only good economics (his kind of socialism, as we
have seen, finds the essential contradiction of capitalism in the co-
existence of worker and idler, not worker and capitalist), it is also
good philosophy. It is the philosophy of Goethe and Carlyle,
summed up by Nietzsche's Zarathustra: "I labor not for my happiness, I labor for my work." Ruskin has it: "Life without work is rob-
bery. Work without art is brutality." And the whole body of Shaw's
political writings might be regarded as an expansion of the best of
Ruskin's dicta: "Government and cooperation are in all things the
laws of life; anarchy and competition the laws of death."

What Shaw has in common with Carlyle is no less extensive than
the main theme of Sartor Resartus: human ideals, not being eternal,
must, like other kinds of clothing, be constantly discarded and replaced. Even the ideal-monger, the philosopher himself—that tailor
of idealists—must be re-tailored if the dignity of man is to be assured, if the purpose of human life is to be unfolded. In the specifically social sphere Carlyle prepared the way for the Fabians in
two ways. In Sidney Webb's words he was "the first man who really
made a dent in the individualist shield" by subjecting his age to a
point by point attack. Second, he looked forward to a collectivism
which would be produced neither by historic inevitability nor by the
wisdom of the populace.

The socialism of Carlyle, Ruskin, Shaw, of what I have called the

British "aristocratic" line, is not scientific; it is ethical. Their belief in humanity is not faith in the common man but in the gentleman. For the gentleman is a synthesis of the democrat and the aristocrat, the follower and the leader. He is a living symbol of the fact that aristocracy is not something to be superseded but to be included in democracy, that the nobleman, if he has ceased to be a robber baron, is welcome in the new age, that we, as much as Louis XIV or George III, need men of light and leading. Moreover the gentlemanly ideal is the golden mean between two rival types—the priest and the soldier, the Pope and the Emperor or, in more recent jargon, the yogi and the commissar. That is why the British genius, which is for temperance, did not wait for Shaw before it formulated this ideal. Not only Carlyle and Ruskin, but such contrasted doctrinaires as Burke, Newman, and T. H. Huxley were spokesmen for it. In some unprepared remarks addressed to the National Liberal Club in 1913 Shaw said:

> What is the ideal of the gentleman? The gentleman makes a certain claim on his country to begin with. He makes a claim for a handsome and dignified existence and subsistence; and he makes that as a primary thing not to be dependent on his work in any way; not to be doled out according to the thing he has done or according to the talents that he has displayed. He says, in effect: "I want to be a cultured human being; I want to live in the fullest sense; I require a generous subsistence for that; and I expect my country to organize itself in such a way as to secure me that." Also the real gentleman says—and here is where the real gentleman parts company with the sham gentleman, of whom we have so many: "In return for that I am willing to give my country the best service of which I am capable; absolutely the best. My ideal shall be also that, no matter how much I have demanded from my country, or how much my country has given me, I hope and I shall strive to give to my country in return more than it has given to me; so that when I die my country shall be the richer for my life." . . . The real constructive scheme you want is the practical inculcation into everybody that what the country needs, and should seek through its social education, its social sense, and religious feeling, is to create gentlemen; and, when you create them, all other things shall be added unto you.

In all this Shaw was ratifying a British tradition. He was also giving it a new turn. He was giving the idea of the gentleman an economic basis. A capitalist is not a gentleman, because his ideal is to sell dear and buy cheap. A proletarian is not a gentleman, because, as the theory of value made clear, he has no value. He is a prostitute. His fate is what Shaw elsewhere calls the "only real tragedy in life: the being used by personally minded men for purposes which you recognize to be base." The capitalist economy of rent, idleness, and waste is "uneconomic" and therefore unfavorable to virtue. The capitalist idea is to get more than you give. The socialist idea, the "economic" idea, the gentlemanly idea is to give more than you get. This is the core of Shavian ethics.

The problem is how to create the civic virtue of the gentleman in the modern world. To some extent—perhaps in 5% of the population, Shaw once suggested—it already exists. If so, the credit must go to Nature which cannot be prevented from creating at least a few Fabians in every generation. For the capitalist system, far from encouraging civic virtue, encourages only the pretense of it that our politicians so eloquently flourish, and discourages the real thing by making it extremely unrewarding. It is barely possible to be a good citizen in a world where uncharitable behavior is necessary to success and even to survival. The civic virtues, Shaw concludes, are not likely to be widely practiced until capitalism is abolished. That is one reason why socialism is the necessary next step in the history of civilization.

Shaw has been criticized for his unusual definition of socialism: "equality of income and nothing else." The definition has been dismissed by many socialists as "extreme rationalism," as indicating a predilection for inhuman, mechanical, abstract order. Shaw's Marxist critics have been the severest, their main point being that, if you socialize production, exactly equal distribution is neither necessary nor desirable; distribution will be either according to the amount of work done ("socialism") or according to the needs of the worker ("communism"). Yet, if Russia is an example of "socialism" in this sense, everyone who is prepared to criticize Russia at all must wish that socialism in Shaw's sense had not been so entirely overlooked. "Society," says Shaw, "is like a machine designed to work smoothly with the oil of equality, into the bearings of which some malignant demon keeps pouring the sand of inequality." Though Shaw himself does not seem to realize it, the malignant demon has been busy in Soviet Russia. He did recognize the demon's handiwork in Germany, Italy, and America. Though he praised the fascists and the New Dealers insofar as they socialized production, he condemned them in the end because they drew the line at socialist distribution. Every kind of socialism so far tried has been at best incomplete and at worst spurious. To those who point to any of them as a model Shaw's definition of socialism is a sufficient rebuke.

If inequality is the chief barrier to civic virtue, equality is its chief prop. When no privileges are conferred by wealth or birth, the Fabian 5% can find their natural level: and they may turn out to be more than 5%. The democratic paradox of Equality—hitherto a sly deception, meaning that people are called equal but are not treated equally—begins to bear fruit when natural authority and subordination take the place of the caste and spoils systems. The democratic paradox of Liberty begins to bear fruit when equal pay guarantees to all that sufficient subsistence without which there can be no free behavior and when universal compulsory labor shortens the workman's hours, leaving him with the time in which to behave freely. The democratic paradox of Fraternity begins to bear fruit when one man's gain is not necessarily another's loss, when, though you may have "superiors" at your job, you have no "betters" in society, when human unity means, not that you confer your unwanted love upon your neighbor while pushing his face in the mud, but that you and your neighbor are at one in a common enterprise. ("You *are* your neighbor," says Shaw, observing that the murder of Marat by Charlotte Corday was really suicide: Marat killed by the spirit of Marat.)

It may seem from all this that Equality is Shaw's maid-of-all-work, one of those emotive words which enable the reformer to substitute spell-binding for sense. Yet, on the contrary, Shaw is one of the very few socialists who are candid about the limitations of socialism. "A socialist state," he says, "can be just as wicked as any other sort of state"—a remark of a very different temper from the Marxist account of the disappearance of the class struggle, the sudden cessation of dialectical conflict (unless on a purely spiritual plane), the withering of the state, and the advent of the stateless society of the free and equal. Shaw makes no promise that the state will ever wither. He knows that the socialist state will be very powerful and that all power is for evil as well as good. This is no reason for preferring irresponsibility. We must simply stop thinking of socialism as an endless good time, as unqualified freedom, an escape from the human condition. It will not change human nature overnight; there is probably a large part of human nature that it will not change at all. In some ways the capitalist's idea of socialism as a system of bureaucracy, regimentation, and tyranny is more realistic than the socialist's, always granting that by bureaucracy the capitalist means state control, by regimentation order, and by tyranny that responsibility without which there can be no real freedom.

Much of the liberal yearning of the past two hundred years has been a yearning for more freedom and more happiness than the human creature is capable of. And democracy and socialism are the causes the liberals chose for the attainment of their impossible ideals. In this sense Shaw is not a liberal. He believes in socialism because socialism will remove what have been in the past centuries the most dangerous and effective inducements to anti-social behavior and will encourage social impulses which under capitalism have existed only in spite of the system. Thus socialism offers some opportunity to men to bridge the gap which they have created between their real and their imagined world, between Pragma and Dogma. Under socialism they should be able to regulate their affairs better. They should be able to create a finer and more honorable way of life.

When Shaw is told that the poor are happy poor he need not, like other socialists, deny it. He can reply that he wants to make them, not happier, like contented pigs, but better, like the discontented Socrates. And when the idyllic picture of the withering of the state is dangled before his eyes he is not more impressed than by the "capitalist utopia" that is supposed to come from letting things slide —laisser faire, laisser aller. Anarchism and Capitalism are dreams of irresponsible bliss. Shaw prefers to admit that socialism will not bring as much freedom as many would like or even as much as a few people already have under capitalism. The liberal who thinks Shaw's socialism goes too far in asking equality of income is likely to think it does not go far enough in the direction of freedom and democracy. Yet we have seen that, according to Shaw, liberalism has a future. In fact the function of socialism is precisely that it allows liberalism to come into being as something other than a dream. But while the socialization of an economy is a relatively speedy affair, the progress of liberalism is necessarily slow, since it involves a radical change in the general attitude to life, a change from apathy to responsibility, which includes a change from ignorance to knowledge.

You do not have democracy until the whole population understands politics and accepts responsibility for them. In this sense no population has as yet come anywhere near to democracy. Compared with us, the first generation that attains to democracy will be a race of Supermen: and this was always the chief application which Shaw made of Nietzsche's term. The creation of Supermen is the greatest task that lies ahead of us, a longer and more arduous task than the socialist revolution. For, though the natural aristocracy of Shaw's socialist state will solve many problems, the awful problem of power before which we all tremble today can be adequately solved only by a moral improvement in the whole race. Words which Shaw wrote thirty years ago have been rendered more impressive by the invention of the atomic bomb:

The one danger before us that nothing can avert but a general raising of human character through the deliberate cultivation and endowment of democratic virtue without consideration of property or class is the danger created by inventing weapons capable of destroying civilization faster than we produce men who can be trusted to use them wisely.

Democratic idealism with a vengeance! Shaw has no belief that any social upheaval, even socialist revolution, is enough. There is nothing for it, as he said fifty years ago (and repeated with a sinking heart in *Geneva*), but "to convince men of the immorality of abusing the majority power and then to make them moral enough to refrain from doing it on that account." There is no hope, that is to say, but that the passion for social justice which has always been at the root of British aristocratic socialism should spread to the whole population.

If Shaw believes in nobility, it is chiefly because *noblesse oblige*. The cardinal virtue in the Shavian scale, as perhaps we have already gathered, is responsibility. Every creed Shaw has attacked he has attacked on grounds of irresponsibility. The liberal economists shift the responsibility on to laws of supply and demand, the Marxists on to laws of history, the anarchists on to laws of nature. The Darwinists—we shall find Shaw maintaining—assign responsibility to mechanical causes, that is, to pure luck. The Christians—or many who regard themselves as such—get God to bear the burden. And when it comes to making a whipping-boy of Jesus, Shaw says:

> You will never get a high morality from people who conceive that their misdeeds are revocable and pardonable, or in a society where absolution and expiation are officially provided for us all. If there is to be no punishment there can be no forgiveness. We shall never have real moral responsibility until every one knows that his deeds are irrevocable and that his life depends on his usefulness.

This stern doctrine is something more than the "protestantism" and "puritanism" which so many have found in Shaw. It is a tough, lean naturalism without illusions. If, as Chesterton said, Shaw is the first idealist who is not also a sentimentalist, might one not add that he is the first unsentimental *naturalist*? For him life is a Promethean adventure which may entail Promethean tortures to be borne with Promethean fortitude.

Shaw's politics lead us to Shaw's philosophy. Indeed everything in Shaw leads to everything else: we have had many vaster and many more scientific thinkers but few whose thinking was at the same time so manysided and so much of a piece. Shaw's views are all firmly based on a Baconian faith in human control. Like Bacon, and unlike many Baconians, Shaw includes control of the human as well as of the external world. Eschewing alike the supernaturalist myth of a God who will shield us from responsibility and the materialist myth of laws which will shield us from responsibility, man must take the burden upon his own shoulders. A perilous enterprise, rendering every problem infinitely more difficult than it is to panaceists!

STARK YOUNG

1948

Heartbreak Houses

I remember how Mr. Edmund Wilson and I, some years ago in a convivial literary moment, agreed that *Heartbreak House* was probably the best of the Shaw plays. We wondered, I remember, whether in twenty years it might not be the shining light among them. Through the removal of limitations in probability, and through the opening thereby for extravagance, *Heartbreak House* is farce rather than comedy. Nor is that anything against it unless you object to the possibility that farce allows for the poetic or fantastic. The question was whether or not we had begun to be impatient with this larding of social theory and significance on to what essentially was farce, however talented, and would remain so. Mr. Wilson and I must have been thinking that *Heartbreak House* offered a more complete unity of tone than most of Mr. Shaw's plays, and that perhaps the constant effect of assertiveness which was so peculiar to Shaw, and which could get very tiresome elsewhere in his other work, was especially suited to the tone of this particular play. In *Heartbreak House* perhaps this general tone in itself effectively expressed the theme, which is the state of things that was "the cultured, leisured Europe before the War."

It must have been an impression of some different sort that had done the work, for all these reflections went flat on me when I saw *Heartbreak House* produced again these many years after. I had looked forward to seeing the play again not only from curiosity about a work of art, but also, in a way, autobiographically—which is to say curiosity about myself, as to what my state of mind and change might be. For a while, on thus revisiting this drama I took it to be the production at the Mercury Theatre that was at fault. Presently

I saw that the production was fair enough—if slightly blurred—with some good performances, especially Miss Phyllis Joyce as Lady Utterwood, but that the play itself was garrulous, unfelt and tiresome.

Evidently the impression from the Theatre Guild production of *Heartbreak House* that had remained so strongly in my mind as the years went by came from the terrace scene and the company talking there in the moonless blue night. It was a long time ago and I had forgotten nearly all they said, but not that haunting tone composed of the scene, the voices, the vibration of characters, the impending blind ruin. And presently there at the Mercury I saw that I had lost even such a response. I was sufficiently concerned to take the book down afterward and read the whole play again, the long preface included. Very likely Mr. Welles' production lacked emphasis to some extent, parts of the play needing to be speeded up, parts slowed down, the pressure lightened here, increased there, for the sake of a more distinct pattern. But at that, the design of *Heartbreak House* proved on this rereading to be no more marked than it is in the production, if as much. Gradually I concluded that there was something very amiable about the willingness of a theatre company to memorize so many lines, and to heed, or seem to heed, so much rather wilted opinion, half point and half patter. An astonishing sort of inner monotony, as it were, was apparent, and had to be coped with. Except for the different voices, you could have shut your eyes and believed not that several people were there, created and expressing themselves, but that one person was describing several people.

Since Mr. Shaw himself goes to some length in the preface to invite more or less comparison of *Heartbreak House* with Chekhov's plays, we may sketch at least the beginning of such a comparison. Chekhov, he says, had produced four dramatic studies of *Heartbreak House,* of which three, *The Cherry Orchard, Uncle Vanya* and *The Sea Gull,* so far as England went, had got as far as a couple of performances by the Stage Society. The audiences had stared and said "How Russian!" To Mr. Shaw on the contrary it seemed that these intensely Russian plays fitted all the country houses in Europe in which . . . et cetera. Such a remark as that seems to me incredibly wilful and silly. The thesis of blind chaos and selfishness and of following the part of comfortable income and securities is a definite thesis. It may readily fit into the motif of a rotting Europe. But Chekhov would have been surprised to learn that his plays were a declaration in advance of all this. The Russian world of Chekhov can be only partially compared to the England that Mr. Shaw has diagrammed in *Heartbreak House.* A great difference arises from the fact that the expressiveness of the Russian temperament, with its gift and power of outpouring the far recesses of the heart, is a far more difficult matter for the English. This is not to say that either one or the other is better, but only that they are different. Where Tolstoy, Mr. Shaw says, was no pessimist and believed in the efficacy of violent measures, Chekhov, "more of a fatalist, had no faith in these charming people extricating themselves. They would, he thought, be sold up and set adrift by the bailiff; and he therefore had no scruple in exploiting and even flattering their charm."

What a patness and charm of persuasion this Mr. Shaw has! But the mere use of the words "flatter" and "charm" give away the British rubbish, or Teutonic conception, behind the idea. The references here are plainly to *The Cherry Orchard*. But no person in it wants to be flattered as to his special idiosyncrasy, nobody in this play is talking with that self-consciousness and varying degrees of egotism or no egotism so common to modest Englishmen. The charm of these people in *The Cherry Orchard*, and often of the Russians we meet is that nobody is thinking at all about being charming; nobody is self-conscious, nobody is affected. That sentence of Mr. Shaw's is a whole commentary on the difference between Chekhov's world and that British world which Mr. Shaw so pugnaciously caters to, rebukes so entertainingly, severely and sincerely, and makes a fortune out of.

The more you know of Chekhov's writing and of him and his life and friends, the more absurd Mr. Shaw becomes on the subject. It is all very well to use a man or a work of art to hit something or somebody over the head with; and certainly the sport is an old one. But nobody could be more astonished than Chekhov would have been to hear of his having no scruples about exploiting the people whose words and little ironic, tender or mad acts, and droll or dark life-patterns he put into plays and stories or left jotted down in his notebook. To "flatter" anything about them would not fit anything in him. What he did with his people was to turn them into theatre, just as Mr. Shaw in *Heartbreak House* turns Chekhov into a sort of literary Hyde Park soapbox dialectic for the theatre.

That such a man as Mr. Shaw could use the life that is presented in Chekhov's plays in Chekhov's way, and even some of Chekhov's ideas and attitudes, is obvious. In spite of the unsuccessful translations of the Chekhov plays into English, a great deal of him comes through; and I should think it possible enough that Mr. Shaw regards his own *Heartbreak House* as being technically related to the three Chekhov plays that he mentions, *The Cherry Orchard* especially. Whether he does so or not, the comparison is inevitable and the relationship plain. On that subject we should have to say that either he boldly exercised his usual independence in the way of doing things, or else he was blind as a bat to Chekhov's technique, stage-effects and spirit. We should be brow-beaten indeed to accept the idea that in *Heartbreak House* there is more than the merest hint or tiny reflection of Chekhov's true method, none of that pure, painstaking economy and drawing, none of that humility of vision, none of that shy certainty of intuition. And Mr. Shaw's play has none of the variety in emotional rhythm that Chekhov's has, either in tone or in profound self-revelation among the characters.

Chekhov sees his people as rooted in something, which means that he begins with what they are, their quality, and from this he derives what they will express. Mr. Shaw, for all his prattle about their class, clichés, bogies, culture and complacent, urgent or ironic circumstance, sees his people in the light of their opinions. Such a course makes for certain effective dramatic patterns, for distinct *dramatis personæ*, real or not real, and for straw men, to be set up or knocked over at will. But it is, I think, his greatest and his final weakness as a creative artist. And it provides the reason why no intelligent member of the traditional British ruling class has ever needed to fear Mr. Shaw very greatly. Nobody could ever take one of Mr. Shaw's magnates or autocratic ruling class characters as the real thing. They may be arresting or provocative, but—for a while at least —it is their author, not themselves, that is so articulate. The portrayal, however, could be dangerous only when it came from the centre of the character himself. It is this quality of the centrifugal that makes Chekhov different from Mr. Shaw, though centrifugal seems a word too strong for that delicate, moving security and expressive freedom that Chekhov achieves for his people, and the matrix of gentle humor, like that of a wise doctor, within which he sees what they say or do, and for which he brings no compelling benefit or reform.

Taking a work of art as a kind of biological whole, which is the only way it makes any sense, I should say that nothing Mr. Shaw presents in *Heartbreak House* to prove his case could be a better evidence of the decay, if you like, of the English scene than this play itself is, with its lack of any organic unity or exciting technique, its fuzzy lack of power, its exhibitionistic self-assertion, its futile chatter in coquettish monotone about what the first bomb could obliterate or the first ism could make stale.

STEPHEN SPENDER

1949

The Riddle of Shaw

When I was a child, we had a cook who was strongly opposed to our not finishing a pudding. Whatever we left on our plates she would serve up the next day, but frozen, under the pretext that it was ice cream. Two recent books* of Bernard Shaw's opinions in his extreme old age inevitably give the impression of frozen left-overs.

16 Self Sketches are mostly remnants rescued from the past, written at various periods over the last thirty years. *Days with Bernard Shaw*† is a volume of carefully recorded conversations with him, written down by his neighbor Stephen Winsten, during the last years of the war and the first year of the peace.

Shaw is certainly one of the most puzzling case histories in modern literature. He evidently considers himself, and he may well be, the greatest living reputation. Yet his works have scarcely been discussed by modern critics. The various essays devoted to him have been by enthusiasts of his biography and his personality rather than of his works. Apart from one interesting essay by Edmund Wilson, I can think of no serious criticism of his many volumes. The aggressive Shavian self-assertiveness has perhaps frightened off the critics, who like to get their teeth into something massive, soft, and yielding, like Henry James.

These two volumes emphasize that Shaw considers himself a poetic dramatist, a social reformer, a Socialist who has revolutionized the social conditions of his age. He admits though to being an "irrepressible mountebank," so perhaps these claims are not altogether serious. Yet they must in some sense be serious, or they would not be funny: it would be merely silly for anyone except Shaw to

Reprinted from *The Nation*, April 30, 1949.
* *16 Self Sketches.* Bernard Shaw.
† *Days with Bernard Shaw.* Stephen Winsten.

make them. Rather magnificent in Winsten's book, is the portrait of the vain old man. The fear that he will be forgotten, that the young do not read him, that, after all, history has passed him by is grandiose and defiant, like Shaw's passion for money. At times he takes his place beside Yeats in his old age, or beside the magnificent last pages of *Finnegans Wake*. Only the Irish are capable of such a glittering ruinous splendor. This makes it all the odder that Shaw seems to have regarded Yeats as a poet who "went wrong" because he "could not spell and had no sense of number"; and James Joyce as a writer of pornographic plays. (What plays does he mean, incidentally?)

The only contemporary poet whom Shaw admired was W. H. Davies, unless one counts also Gilbert Murray, whose translations of Aeschylus and Euripides Shaw regards as masterpieces.

Perhaps Shaw is a two-dimensional giant moving in his own two-dimensional world. According to the rules of this two-dimensional existence, he never errs. In public life, he believes that it is far more important that men should change society than that they should improve themselves. For to Shaw the individual is like a sentence within the book which is written by social conditions. For him, in literature, the difference between poetry and prose is that poetry rhymes and has "number," prose doesn't. He found rhyming tedious; so he wrote his plays in prose. In private life, every problem should be solved by the kind of good sense which operates on the heart of the problem, reducing it to an abstraction dealt with by the intellectual will. Thus sex is the problem in marriage: all right, marriage must be without sex. This precept might seem to be Shaw at his least serious, but apparently it is the one which he acted upon in his own marriage. Meals must be without meat, and clothes without linings, not for the kind of reasons which would move Christ or Gandhi, but in order to reduce these problems of actuality to levels of theory.

In his plays Shaw develops artistically in the same two-dimensional way. Edmund Wilson has pointed out—what Shaw himself draws attention to—that there is musical art, borrowed largely from Mozart, in Shaw's plays. That is to say, he has learned from music the secret of external form and progression and sequence: movement of pattern within a mood which could be determined by a musical direction; the art of instrumentation by which dialogue is interwoven, like wood wind with strings. But while Shaw has learned the external tact of musicianship and applied it to drama, he has not learned the inwardness of Mozart. His art is the direction of dialogue from the outside, not the creating of character from within. When he tries (as in *Heartbreak House*) to model a play on

Chekhov's "inside" creation of character, he becomes, as when he tries (in *Saint Joan*) to be poetic, self-conscious and almost embarrassing.

Thus Shaw's great achievement has been to stand outside and above the struggle with words, the struggle with the "blood and mire" of personal experience, which is the lot of other contemporary writers. He has conducted brilliant arguments with his generation in which his dialectical method has consisted in shifting the argument, constantly and with great skill, so that his opponent is left with the feeling that the ground, changed so often, has been cut from under his feet. Shaw all his life has defended socialism and even called himself a Communist. At the same time he has fought against all direct taxation of his own earnings, and is proud today to call himself a millionaire. One wonders what ground Shaw stands on in his fight for socialism. The answer seems to be contained in a recent letter to the *New Statesman and Nation* in which he explains that while he has always believed in complete equality of income he has always assumed that this income should be raised to five thousand pounds a year for everyone. To have an income below this is, apparently, not to be a Socialist but to indulge in the crime of poverty.

Shaw, of course, can be forgiven everything, because he is a great entertainer. To my mind, entertainers are the only people entitled to claim as much as they want of everything from their contemporaries, because they are the only ones who have an immediate and obvious public value. Politicians, inventors, and saints do at least as much harm as they do good, and poets and philosophers must wait on posterity to decide their worth. But the entertainer has immediate worth and therefore should be immediately accepted and rewarded. Shaw deserves to be a millionaire.

However, Shaw is more than entertainer, and this is where the difficulty for the critic arises. What is the central passion of his work? The answer is, I think, a kind of fanatical good sense, prepared to sacrifice feeling and enjoyment to good sense, and therefore sometimes fraying at the edges into vegetarian and anti-vivisectionist nonsense. Here, in conversation with Winsten, is an example of this passion:

> When things look very black, G. B .S. said, it is well to remember that public evils are not millionfold evils. What you yourself suffer is the utmost that can be suffered on earth. If you starve to death, you experience all the starvation that has ever been or ever can be. If ten thousand others starve with you, their suffering is not increased by a single pang; their share in your fate does not make you ten thousand times as hungry

nor prolong your suffering ten thousand times. You should not therefore be oppressed by the frightful sum of human suffering. There is no sum. Two lean women are not twice as lean as one nor two fat women twice as fat as one. Poverty and pain are not cumulative, and you must not let your spirit be crushed by the fancy that it is. . . . Do not let your mind be disabled by excessive sympathy. At present nobody can be healthy or happy or honorable; our standards are low, so that when we call ourselves so, we mean only that we are not sick, nor crying, nor lying, nor stealing.

This is a noble message, merciful both to those who suffer and to those who are oppressed by the thought of their suffering, and justifying happiness. It contains the best of Shaw, a kind of serious laughter, a refusal to be discouraged, and at the same time a refusal to adopt the aesthetic pose of the creative artist, of Yeats for instance, dancing over the destruction of a civilization.

Shaw reveals in the *Self Sketches*, and again in his conversation, what he plainly considers the biographical clue to his own psychology. His father was a drunkard, a fact which must have frustrated his relationship with his children long before they became conscious of it. His mother resolved the problem of living with her husband by living according to a program of determined good sense, at the price of completely destroying all affection and need of affection in herself. She took into her home her singing teacher Lee, who was not, Shaw insists, her lover, but who became a substitute father to the Shaw children. In short, the key to Shaw is that he feels himself to have been unloved when he was a child. His life and work have been a heroic, intellectually willed solution, a compensation for this psychological lack. That its effects have always persisted in him is curiously shown, I think, by the examples quoted in these books of his extreme imperturbability in the presence of the deaths of those very close to him. To be completely "reasonable" about the deaths of others shows, I think, a very deep repression of feeling and also a reliance on the force of one's own separate life which arises from a lack of confidence in affection.

Shaw's vanity is obvious, but there is also humility in the way he reveals the lovelessness which is the source of his deepest self-reliance and also of a certain weakness. Our own generation has many reasons to be grateful to him. Future generations will judge whether or not his best work triumphs over the lovelessness in his nature and attains that charity without which literature cannot survive.

G. B. S: 1856–1950

Methuselah is dead. In Shaw goes the last of the Victorian prophets, the last of the long line of young beards who became the great, bearded old gentlemen. Yet, in important ways, Shaw had no connection with the nineteenth century at all. He was really a man of the eighteenth century, closer to Voltaire and Swift than to Marx and Morris. The Anglo-Ireland of 1856, when he was born, was an ossified eighteenth century society. It was elegant yet genteel; it was ruled by the blistering aristocratic candor and the simple aristocratic naivety; it was naturally irreverent, as aristocratic societies are; it was libertine in word, but preserved the trite, conventional and charming copybook morality of the eighteenth century in action. When he died, Shaw was really a hundred years older than his admitted age, as sweet and prim and gentle as anyone out of Goldsmith.

Inside this prosaic moral crust, the Anglo-Irish have always carried a defiant spirit. The high point of the Irish genius is reached in pure, disinterested destructiveness, and of that Shaw was the supreme intellectual embodiment in his time and the eager heir of Swift. It is important to note, however, that this destructiveness is mainly directed at sitting birds; the war of 1914 may have come at an awkward time in Shaw's life as an artist—he was fifty-eight—but once the world began to destroy itself, Shaw's destructiveness was outdone, he made crazy and unhappy attempts to outpace it, and as an artist or teacher ceased to have much to say. Assimilated by the middle-aged, he had no spell for the young in politics and as an artist he influenced no one. There remained only his *réclame*, perhaps his most remarkable achievement—his unique stage personal-

Reprinted from *Time*, November 13, 1950.

ity remained sharp, sagacious and dazzling; the delightful vanity of his genius kept the limelight till the last.

Shaw had an inspired instinct for success; innate prudence combined shrewdly with presumption in getting it. Emigration to a duller and richer civilization than his own he saw was the only safe thing for a man who found destructiveness so exhilarating. It was the only sure escape from Irish melancholy and cynicism. In Victorian England, the young Shaw found enough to last him a lifetime. As a middle-class individualist of the highest power, who believed that poverty was a crime, who married a rich and intelligent wife and made a fortune which could be compared with that of any Undershaft, Shaw was an ambiguous socialist: his intellect was totally engaged; his whole life (as Trotsky suspected) was not. The device of the Superman, the super-intellect, the Life Force, was his escape from the determinism of Marx and it coincided with his native, eighteenth century taste for despots.

The charm of it all for Shaw himself was that the English always survived his attacks and came back for more. They earned his lasting respect by paying him handsomely for it and then, by turning Fabian as he had urged, diddling him out of his savings and earnings at the rate of 19/6 in the £, plus the Death Duties. In Ireland, he might have been reduced to the alcoholism which had frightened him as a child in the life of his father. And there was a second strain of Irish genius which can be developed to a higher pitch outside that country: the role of the stage-Irishman. Whenever that genius has submitted to the discipline of the theater, it has been irresistible. Behind Shaw the dramatist were Goldsmith, Sheridan and Wilde.

The early danger in Shaw's career was that he would become a dilettante—the famous jaeger suit, the Norfolk jacket and knickerbockers, the diabolical twist to the eyebrows and, later on, the dinner jacket into which he changed every evening during the war, when no one wore such a garment, are obdurate vestiges of dandyism. But the shocking London of the 'seventies was too much for the genteel and moral Irish Protestant, who had worked as an accountant and claimed to be a kin to a baronet. He heard the Biblical and warlike voice of Marx. Its despotic sound, its subversiveness, its talk of the continuous war of classes, its protest against poverty, the passion of its economics, lastingly moved Shaw, for he was poor, came from an oppressed nation, had lost his religious faith, and was in need of a weapon and a role.

The great Irish evil, which all Irishmen fear, is romanticism; Shaw's conversion was real enough, but common sense, sanity, shrewdness, the practical were the Shavian aims. He was neither a visionary nor a crank; but rather, in the manner of Swift—though far more successful in his mission to the English—a negotiator. By eloquent attack, irony, laughter, bounce, by the intrigue of words and a wit that cut everything to ribbons, in a prose so clear, fast and pure that it was like a charmer's music to the snake, Shaw hypnotized England. People became Socialists without knowing it even while they were denouncing Shaw as a mountebank and a playboy. Trotsky lamented that Shaw was a good man fallen among Fabians. But Shaw knew his Englishman and loved him, as the stinging fly loves the thick hide it farsightedly chooses as a safe home for its eggs.

What Trotsky really lamented was that Shaw was not a crusader or a fanatic. Others have complained that he was neither a philosopher nor a political thinker of any substance. Shaw's great vanity as an artist—and he was an artist above all—enabled him to agree with double-edged modesty with his critics. He often spoke, truly, of his poor education. He observed with real humility the learning and the passion of the Webbs, whom he worshipped. It was a kind of modesty when he boasted of his brilliance and genius; because (if it can be put this way) brilliance and genius were all he had. And he knew their nature: he had the penetrating comic genius. He was expert, as the comic genius is, in absurd juxtapositions and *non sequiturs*. His prose is made of sentences which have less and less to do with the preceding ones; each is a fresh beginning, fresh with new, vivid effrontery and traveling away from the point, like the words of an incurable but dazzling talker who is intoxicated by his own flow.

The result is that the reader or audience sooner or later falls into the boredom of the over-stimulated. If *Arms and the Man, Candida, The Man of Destiny, John Bull's Other Island, Major Barbara, Pygmalion* and possibly *You Never Can Tell* are excepted, the law of diminishing returns begins to work halfway through his plays. There are wonderful moments in *Man and Superman* and *St. Joan,* but comedy, or in the last case, tragedy, degenerate into the *longueurs* of debate; farce becomes crude. Devastating in his ability to talk on both sides of the question and to cap or sink his own arguments, Shaw damps us because he talks his way back to the status quo, and leaves the impression that all he has had to say has only verbal importance. We are back where we started.

The failure in feeling was noticed by the earliest critics of Shaw. William Archer said of his characters that instead of blood "a kind of sour whey" flowed in their veins. The fact is that anger and indignation—the most intellectual of our emotions—were alone portrayed successfully; the laughing anger of Shaw must be compared to Voltaire's. The brief poetical passages in *John Bull's Other Island* are the poorest sentimentality; even the saintly figure of Father Keegan in that play occasionally arouses shyness. In *St. Joan* the pathos is commonplace and the mysticism embarrassing. Shaw hardly goes deeper than the sentiment—pure though it is with the curious Irish purity—of the philanderer; and philanderers of either sex make the mistake of crediting the opposite sex with their own characteristics. Shaw's lovers do not test each other's hearts, but only their wills. They are adroit in the campaigns worked up by the mental affections; they are trained in that military sense of love one sees also in Sheridan, in seeking out the strategy of character. There is no hate in this love and no fear either; it is neutral.

All this was a brilliant device for dramatizing feminism and the new women—one might say Shaw emancipated women and Wells emancipated men—but the emancipation soon appeared to cover a superficial part of life; the doctrine was to lead to a serious nutritional deficiency when he described the spiritual passions, as in *St. Joan* and in his religious theorizings. On these he is as dry and flat as a biscuit.

Chesterton accused Shaw of the gloom of a general Puritanism, and this naturally rankled. The weakness of the Puritan, especially of the Shavian kind, is his dangerous levity and cheerfulness, the merry, practical streak which evades the ungovernable tumult of feeling. The theory that the Life Force was driving on and on was felt by his audiences to be an escape from the crucifying emotional matter of the gains and losses. One more dazzling Irishman had talked himself out of life into the heavens like a whizzing rocket and had come down dead and extinct like the stick. One more superbly agile lizard had lived off its own tail, consumed itself and come back to exactly what it was before.

Exasperated critics frequently took the failure of feeling further and said that Shaw's characters were unreal, that they were no more than walking arguments. This is a half-truth, though it is a fact that Shaw did not believe in character for its own sake. Few Victorian writers did. His eye for the middle-class milieu was perfect. He knew exactly the values beneath the humbug and was only rash in assuming that men and women can live without it. Candida is an excellent portrait of a woman and so is the delightful Major Barbara. The theater, and comedy above all, has always dealt in types; the sentimental Englishman and the disillusioned Irishman in *John Bull's Other Island* are brilliantly observed. The political characters in *St. Joan* are a triumph of irreverent dialectic and penetrating understanding.

The economic view was as rewarding an approach to the anatomy of character itself as the now fashionable psychological approach. His young men have the assertiveness of youth itself, their vanity is perfect. His masterful or stupid middle-aged women are a special excellence, and so are his pompous fathers. Undershaft is convincing as a human being. A very vain man, Shaw was a connoisseur of vanities and his collection is not wounding or disheartening—as it is, say, in smaller writers like Maugham—largely because Shaw is warmed by the fire of a natural affinity. Only a clumsiness of plot— Shaw was not a natural plot-maker, but a reckless piler on of the grotesque for satirical reasons—distorts the focus in which character is seen. The clear failures are his Cockneys; they are a Dubliner's caricatures of a character too subtle for him.

In his public career Shaw continued the art of saying the last word, which was his making as a supreme pamphleteer. As a music critic his levity maddened and refreshed. In dramatic criticism he was more solid, went down to fundamentals, and this part of his work, dense with experience, is bound to survive, however fashion affects the plays.

The 1914 war was a profound shock to Shaw's comic genius and his optimism. *Heartbreak House* appeared to many as a confusion. The disillusion with the failures of the Labor government, in which the Webbs and many of his Fabian friends served, turned Shaw back to his own inherited responses. The old eighteenth century taste for autocrats revived. So Mussolini was admired, Hitler was given a hand and Stalin was exalted. Their virtue was that they were practical. Shaw appeared to agree with the scientists that what succeeds is good and he had been careful, as a Marxist, to say that capitalism had been good in the days when it succeeded. Failure, like poverty, had always been the Shavian crime. The only failure he seems to have been proud of was his own failure to earn more than £6 by novels and casual writing before he was forty. To the hostile, Shaw's trotting to Moscow and his defense of tyrants seemed a mixture of cynicism, contemptible prudence, and an old mountebank's determination to keep in the limelight; a degeneration from the noble pages of *The Intelligent Woman's Guide.*

More virtuous than Voltaire—he was the good man's Voltaire— Shaw was no more free than the Frenchman from the irresponsibility of a chaotically lucid mind which changed the focus too fast for his own eye. The age of Swift, to which Shaw historically and spiritually belonged, believed in authority; it believed that the moral was the practical; it was worldly, though without huge wealth; it believed in the beatitude of the conventional. It managed to believe in these things and at the same time to preach revolution in the name of Liberty, Equality and Fraternity. Victorian practicality meant the

practical man's ruthless advantage; Shaw's was the older practicality of a fundamental fairness and goodness. Romanticism made him
believe that autocrats could distribute this. He believed, like Wells,
like everyone who matured before 1914, in the superior person.
Shaw romantically imagined in his heart that the new despots, like
the old, had both the good sense and the sense of honor of the old
kind of gentleman. But those died with the machine.

It has been truly said that Shaw's anger never made enemies. Irish
evasiveness, sociability and energy made him wish resolutely to cut
the best figure on the thinnest ice. He kept up his stage role to the
last. He was sometimes petulant in the publicity he delighted in. His
great age was his last great turn, which could hardly conceal an appalling loneliness. All his contemporaries were dead. His wife had
gone. He recognized how poor his contacts with human beings were,
now he was without intermediaries. He was, in a sense, unhuman.
He depended on servants whom he hardly knew. He came close at
times to that terrible condition of the old in contemporary England,
who discover that there is no one to depend on and for whom the
mere mechanics of living have become tragically difficult. At the
illness of a servant during the blitz, he and his sick wife had been
obliged to leave the famous, ugly old Rectory at Ayot St. Lawrence
and live among the bombs in London.

He was not friendless, but he was manifestly apart from his
friends, a lonely figure with bright eyes and ceaseless tongue, going
for walks. The handwriting was still firm and bold and beautifully
formed on the famous postcards; the soft and beautiful voice was
still firm and ready when he spoke on the telephone. His mind was
still large and showed only the normal sense of persecution felt by
those in contemporary England who have been relieved of so much
of their property by the State. With the shrewdness of an afflicted
banker he protested against the threat of capital levy. Like Samuel
Butler he had a profound respect for capital.

The brain still worked fast and though frail the body was resistant.
Only his legs weakened. His laughter still rescued him from the
melancholy of his race. He ended as a testimonial to the value of his
famous quirks: teetotalism, vegetarianism, his theories about health
and hygiene. He ended as a kind of saint of prudence, a saint known
for his good sense rather than his sufferings, for his chronically
topsy-turvy advice rather than his visions. He became the Gandhi of
economics.

The vein of compromise, the failure to carry anger for very long,
the tendency to become too clever for wrath, weakens him when he
is compared with Swift. Compared with Voltaire's, his imagination
is drier, lacks picture and lacks nature too. A kind of middle-class

gentility preserved him from the great disgusts, the unspeakable horrors which greater imaginations could grasp. The prose is, however, a superb vehicle for the pamphleteer and any page of it is a model of the art of conducting unfair arguments. He was a highly original artist and the art lay in the transmuting of disruptive debate into a kind of classical Mozartian music. The plays date most seriously when they are debates, yet the verbal wit is perennially irresistible. There is no writer who so conspicuously and largely holds the whole social and political and intellectual life of a long, rich period of heresy and revolt in his hands, a revolt against everything from marriage to God—and back.

From William Morris until the dictators, he holds everything. The England which gave him little recognition until he was known on the Continent and in America—which for years he refused to visit— has dropped him again; even the revolutions of the last thirty years have been made by war, not by Shavian gradualism, even in England. But he was the indefatigable showman at the door for more than half a century who, until the wars came, stole the show. It was war which established the final Fabian victory.

JOHN MASON BROWN

1950

Caesar and Cleopatra

When in 1898 Shaw decided to invade Egypt, to come to grips with the mighty Julius, and as a vegetable-fed Puritan to run the risks of Cleopatra, he had something very much his own to say, which, as usual, he managed to get said in his own way. He was the first to admit the value of what he had written. The fact that Walkley and the critics who originally reviewed *Caesar and Cleopatra* had described it as *opéra bouffe* did not depress Shaw. To him prophecy is routine employment. "In 1920 *Caesar* will be a masterpiece," he wrote in 1908. Readers have long since agreed with him.

Shaw, being Shaw, did not hesitate to offer *Caesar and Cleopatra* to the public as an improvement on Shakespeare. "Better than Shakespeare" was the title he chose for his preface. By this, he pointed out with surprising modesty, he did not mean that he professed to write better plays than Shakespeare. He did, however, claim the right to criticize Shakespeare, to discard and discredit his romantic notions of passion and history, and to substitute new ideas and a new approach born of a new age.

The first change, an inevitable one in Shaw's case, was that where Shakespeare had written a tragedy Shaw wrote a comedy. The side of Shaw which is John Bunyan pretended to be shocked by Shakespeare's Cleopatra. He dismissed her as a Circe who, instead of turning heroes into hogs, turned hogs into heroes. He would have nothing to do with the mature woman, a tawdry wanton as he saw her, whose lustfulness had transformed a world leader into a strumpet's fool. For that matter, he would have nothing to do with the youthful Cleopatra who, according to history, had a child by Caesar. In her place he preferred to draw, and drew delectably, the portrait of a kittenish girl who under Caesar's tutelage flowered into a queen. His Cleopatra's youth was more than a puritanic evasion. It was a Shavian device by means of which superstitions could be mocked and Caesar, the conqueror, humanized by being seen through the irreverent eyes of a child. In other words, it was Shaw's characteristic way of taking the starch out of the stuffed-shirt approach to history.

As for Shakespeare's Caesar, Shaw had only contempt for him. His contention was that Shakespeare, who knew human weakness so well, never knew human strength of the Caesarian type. Just why Shaw, also a man of words, felt that he had a greater claim to understanding the inner workings of a man of action, is something he did not bother to explain. But that he succeeded with his Caesar where Shakespeare failed with his, few would deny.

In his preface to *Caesar and Cleopatra* G. B. S. described himself as a crow who has followed many plows. Surely none of these had led him down stranger furrows than his flirtations with the dictator principle. The champion of the superman, who was fascinated by Napoleon and who has had kind words to say about Stalin and even Mussolini, was bound sooner or later to be drawn to Caesar.

The major source of his Julius was not Plutarch. As he confessed, it was Mommsen, the nineteenth-century German historian. He liked Mommsen's account of the Egyptian visit and agreed with his estimate of Caesar. Shaw also admitted his debt to Carlyle for his concept of the historical hero capable of bearing "the weight of life" realistically rather than suffering from a passion to die gallantly.

The Caesar Shaw drew would not have been recognized by Suetonius or Plutarch, neither of whom liked him. But the man who wrote *The Gallic War* would have recognized this Shavian Julius— with gratitude and relief. The clemency and statesmanship, the largeness of mind and spirit, which for the sake of the record he had been careful to establish as his, are qualities that shine in Shaw's Caesar. Caesar's self-love could not have been greater than Shaw's almost romantic infatuation with the benevolent despot he depicted.

But there was a difference—an immeasurable difference. Where Plutarch was dignified, Suetonius scurrilous, Caesar determinedly official, and Shakespeare rhetorically athletic, Shaw was Shavian. This in itself represented a complete abandonment of the orthodox ways of writing not only history but historical plays. It meant that, more than upsetting an apple-cart, Shaw had brought about a one-man revolution in the theatre and in literature.

He approached the past unawed, anxious to see it in contemporary terms, eager for a laugh, and with a wit which, though impudent, was wonderfully humanizing. The effects of his innovations are still with us, though in lesser hands they have never achieved the same dimensions and have sometimes been downright sophomoric. Quite rightly, it has been pointed out that what is widely thought of as Lytton Strachey's method was something for which Shaw prepared the way. But what is often overlooked is that G. B. S., regardless of his impertinences, was never a debunker. His spirit was always too positive for that, his intellect too superior.

Caesar and Cleopatra is a proof of this. However flippant or hilarious its means may be, its concerns are serious and sizable. For Shaw's real interest, so gaily presented in a very funny play, is nothing less than a study of the anatomy of earthly power and greatness. Although his Caesar may laugh and be laughed at, he is palpably a great man misunderstood by those around him and even by the Cleopatra he has instructed in queenship. If in delineating this greatness Shaw deliberately substitutes colloquial prose for what he had once condemned as the melodious fustian and mechanical lilt of Shakespeare's blank verse, he is nonetheless able in speech after speech to rise to a glorious eloquence of his own.

Caesar's apostrophe to the Sphinx is a sample. Other samples are the wisdom of Caesar's "He who has never hoped can never despair" and his "One year of Rome is like another, except that I grow older whilst the crowd in the Appian Way is always the same age." Or the beauty of his leave-taking of Cleopatra, when he describes Mark Antony to her in these words, "Come, Cleopatra: forgive me and bid me farewell; and I will send you a man, Roman from head to heel and Roman of the noblest; not old and ripe for the knife; not lean in the arms and cold in the heart; not hiding a bald head under his conqueror's laurels; not stooped with the weight of the world on his shoulders; but brisk and fresh, strong and young, hoping in the morning, fighting in the day, and reveling in the evening." In almost every instance the organ plays full and strong, only to be interrupted by a jest. Even so, the sense of greatness is not lost. *Caesar and Cleopatra* makes the past provocative, history human, and greatness gay.

THOMAS MANN

1951

"He Was Mankind's Friend"

Les Dieux s'en vont—"The Gods pass." With George Bernard Shaw
another of Europe's old guard has departed, the Nestor of that great
statured generation, gifted with enduring vitality, productive to the
last, leaving behind what must be called in comparison, a race, not
without interest but frail, sombre, endangered and withered before
its time. He was preceded in death by Gerhart Hauptmann, of whom
G. B. S. scarcely took note, though plays like *The Weavers* and *The
Rats* should have greatly pleased him, and by Richard Strauss,
whom he knew quite well and in whom he admired the great tradition as well as the brash, revolutionary efficiency of a man born
under a lucky star.

Still among us are the octogenarians André Gide, Shaw's kinsman
in capricious genius and protestant morality, and the aged Knut
Hamsun, now merely vegetating, a man broken by politics, though
still the quondam creator of highly discriminate narrative works that
.yield nothing in richness and charm to Shaw's dramatic works. Shaw,
judging by his writings, was sublimely unconcerned with this com-
peer and it is true that in many respects the two of them were
counter-poets, especially in the matter of socialism. The brunt between them in the personal sphere was a sense of obligation towards Germany, well founded in either case, though it spelt
Hamsun's political doom, while in the more intelligent Shaw it
maintained the character of a well-tempered gratefulness, which, for
the rest, laid little claim to any very extensive intimacy.

There is a certain meaningfulness in allowing a German to speak
in Shaw's honour, for Germany—and more particularly the Austrian
cultural dependency of Germany, in the person of Siegfried Tre-
bitsch, who, with curiously unerring instinct, staked his cards on

Reprinted form *The Listener,* January 18, 1951. Used by permission of the author.

translating Shaw's plays into German—Germany recognised his importance to the modern stage, indeed to modern intellectual life as a whole, earlier than the English-speaking world. His fame actually reached England only by way of Germany, just as Ibsen and Hamsun conquered Norway, and Strindberg Sweden, by the same roundabout route, for London's independent theatre fell short of doing for Shaw's reputation—soon to grow to world-wide dimensions—what men like Otto Brahm and Max Reinhardt and their actors, and with them Berlin's dramatic criticism, were able to accomplish, for the simple reason that at that time the German stage was ahead of its British counterpart. Moreover, less frozen in the bourgeois mould, more receptive to new things, better prepared to view the Anglo-Celt as the new spear-shaker, the great dramatic, intellectual and mischief-maker, the mighty wielder of words, twinkling with exuberance, the creative critic and dialectician of the theatre of our age. He never denied his indebtedness to Germany, and repaid it in a highly amusing essay, *What I Owe to German Culture,* going so far as to declare that his own culture was to a very considerable degree German. This is a vast exaggeration, at least regarding the influence of German literature on him, which was meaningless. He himself very humorously described the fragmentary and casual nature of his knowledge of this sphere, which indeed enjoys a great popularity anywhere. In his childhood, he relates, he had once read a story by a certain Jean-Paul Richter and *Grimms' Fairy Tales* as well, adding that he still regarded Grimm as the most entertaining German author. Strange that he should not have mentioned Heine or Hoffmann, usually accounted the most entertaining Germans. Stranger still that he should have regarded Grimm as a single individual, possessed of the unGerman quality of being entertaining. He seems to have been unaware that this Grimm consisted of two persons—the brothers Jakob and Wilhelm, romantically inspired lovers of German antiquity, who listened to their fairy tales from the lips of the people, and collected them conscientiously. This, apart from the fact that the two planned a gigantic etymological dictionary of the German language, with which they were never done, and which German scholars are now again engaged in rounding out. In point of fact, this work of many volumes makes the most entertaining reading in the world for anyone as interested in the German tongue as Shaw was in the English.

"Everyone ought to learn German," Shaw said, and he himself was determined to do so. But since he was only fifty-five there was no hurry. He never did learn it, and when Germans who knew no English visited him he would let them talk until they ran out of breath. Then he would put his hand to his heart and say, "*ausge-*

zeichnet." He did not quite know what this word meant, he said, tongue in cheek, but it always made the Germans happy. I myself would have been quite apt to speak a little English with him, but I never visited him, for purely humanitarian reasons, for I am convinced that he never read a line of mine and this might well have been a source of some embarrassment to him. True, we might have avoided that plight by shunning literature altogether and turning at once to a subject that concerned us equally—music. It was German music Shaw had in mind, and nothing else, when he spoke of German culture and his debt to it. He made that very plain, and declared frankly that all the western culture he had acquired was as nothing compared to his intuitive grasp of German music from its birth to its maturity.

Shaw, the son of a mother who was a singer and singing teacher, left a body of dramatic writing that is the epitome of intellectuality. Yet the music of words is part and parcel of it, and he himself stressed that it was constructed on the model of thematic development in music. For all its sober brilliance, its alert and derisive critical judgment, it strives deliberately for musical effect. No reaction to it pleased the author more than that of a British colleague whom he held in high esteem—Harley Granville-Barker—who exhorted the actors at a Shaw rehearsal: "For God's sake bear in mind that this is not a play but an opera—deliver every speech as though you expected to give an encore." In truth, Shaw, like every important dramatist before him, created his own idiom. The language of the theatre at bottom, as unrealistic as the chanted passion of the opera—exalted, exaggerated, pointed, terse and striking, no wit less rhetorical than Corneille's verses or Schiller's iambic measures, and, strange as it may sound, no less pervaded with pathos, a term not here meant to imply unctuousness and bombast, but the ultimate in expression—an eccentricity of speech, steeped for the most part in humour, full of *esprit*, challenge, effrontery, the reigning paradox.

In his preface to *Saint Joan*, which is so good that it almost makes the play superfluous, he stripped bare the scientific superstition of our times, insisting that the theories of our physicists and astronomers and the credulity with which we accept them would have dissolved the Middle Ages in a roar of sceptical merriment. That sets the style. Yet not only does Shaw, the essayist, speak in this way. He often, indeed for the most part, has his characters speak in similar fashion, and it should be noticed in passing that his figure of speech about "dissolving an audience in a roar of sceptical merriment" precisely describes his own effect on his spectators.

RADICAL SOCIALIST—AND APOSTLE OF WAGNER

When William Archer, in 1885, first met the young Dubliner, only recently come to London, in the library of the British Museum, he found Shaw preoccupied with two works which he studied in turn for weeks on end. They were *Das Kapital* by Marx, and the score of Wagner's *Tristan und Isolde.* Here you have the whole of Shaw— here is Shaw, the radical socialist, zealously addressing meetings, going beyond the teachings of Henry George, who aimed only at the reform of land holding, demanding the nationalisation of capital in every form; Shaw, the guiding spirit of the Fabian Society, who wrote *The Intelligent Woman's Guide to Socialism and Capitalism,* a book Ramsay MacDonald went so far as to call "the world's most valuable next to the Bible"; Shaw, beginning his career as a playwright with *Widowers' Houses,* a tract about middle-class pseudo-respectability, about the social evils of slum ownership; Shaw, who remained forever a man of social contentions, who called his plays, sometimes a little condescendingly, "dramatic conferences," and Shaw, the born Thespian utterly lacking Wagner's sultry eroticism, with its out-heavening of Heaven, yet Wagner's true pupil as a maker of intellectual music and also as his own apostle and tireless commentator. He wrote a book about Wagner, *The Perfect Wagner-ite,* a work of shrewd lucidity that compares most favourably with the burrowing flim-flam of German Wagner exegetists, nor is it mere coincidence that close beside this book stands another treatise of critical gratitude and homage, *The Quintessence of Ibsenism,* for Ibsen, about whose trait, his kinship to Wagner, I once attempted to write, was Shaw's other teacher and his case is an interesting demonstration of the extent to which an altogether different temperament can utilise, for its own purposes, like-minded experiences, once they had been fully encompassed; creatively melting them down into something totally new and personal.

Ibsen is supposed to have said once that each of his plays might just as well have become an essay. Shaw, for one, never forwent the essay, which inhered in his every play—letting it stand beside the play, or rather embodying it in a preface often as long and as eloquent as the play itself, calling things by their names with a critical directness unfitting in the play proper. I, for one, find fault, for example, with the unhappy scrambling of essay and drama that allows Cauchon and Warwick, in the fourth scene of *Saint Joan,* to concoct the terms "protestantism" and "nationalism," in definition of Joan's heresy and of heresy in general. Factually, these terms may not have been anachronisms in the fifteenth century, but as formulations they have an anachronistic effect which breaks up form and style. They belong to the essay, where indeed they are to be found. The play should have shunned them, should have been content with an interpretative formulation. Neither this, nor even the fact that in *Saint Joan*, as in other plays of Shaw, the aria sometimes turns into an editorial, can keep this dramatic chronicle from remaining the most fervent thing Shaw ever wrote—the play that is poetically the most moving, that comes closest to high tragedy, a work inspired with a truly elating sense of justice; a work in which the mature rationality of an *esprit fort* that has outgrown the confines of the eighteenth and even the nineteenth century, bows before sanctity; a work fully deserving its world fame.

There is but one other play I would put beside it, or perhaps even ahead of it. That is *Heartbreak House*—creative fruit of the first world war—a play of which neither Aristophanes nor Molière nor Ibsen need have been ashamed; a play that belongs in the foreground of comedy, a play of sparkling dialogue and a fanciful cast of characters, supremely humorous, yet filled with things cursed and condemned, pitched in the mood of a doomed society. When all the one-act plays are included—enter among them such as *Great Catherine* and *Shewing Up of Blanco Posnet*—it turns out that Shaw wrote more plays than Shakespeare, and if they are of uneven weight, like those of his great predecessor, against whom he liked to match himself so gaily, if some of them have withered, their problems growing outdated, as he foresaw, they do include, beside those already named and singled out for praise, such things as *Caesar and Cleopatra; Man and Superman; Androcles and the Lion,* and the stunningly clairvoyant political satire *The Apple Cart,* things that have withstood and will long continue to withstand the onslaught of time, in part because of their wisdom and their profoundly edifying message; in part because of the winged wit of their poetic idiom. When we add the floodtide of essays, commentary, and amplifying criticism, embodying an all-embracing encyclopaedic knowledge that draws equally on the natural sciences, theology, religious and general history, and especially the social economic sphere, always artistically leavened, full of aesthetic charm and unfailingly entertaining—when we add all this we find ourselves face to face with a lifework of astonishing scope, apparently the fruit of continued inspiration, unceasing merriness, and of an indefatigable will to work.

Like Ibsen and Wagner, Shaw was first and last a hard worker. In the words of Zarathustra, "His goal was not his happiness, but his work." To him, idleness was, above all, a crime against society and utterly foreign to his nature. He said once that he had never been young in the sense that the average person sows his wild oats. For that very reason he remained everlastingly youthful in his work, frisky as a colt, even in his old age. Anti-bourgeois to the core, a Marxist fond of a revolutionary slogan, "Enemies of the bourgeoisie —unite," he was yet in his own moral convictions and mode of life middle-class through and through, indeed puritanical. He could have retired from literature tomorrow, he said, and become a respectable cheesemonger, without changing one iota of his domestic habits. For him, the counterpart of the bourgeois was not the bohemian, but the socialist. The world of people, he said, who spent their evenings over champagne suppers, with actresses, models and dancers—that world was unknown to him, and he wondered how its hapless victims endured it, indeed, he often doubted that it actually existed, for all the actresses and dancers he had known were decent, hard-working women. He himself was a man of rigorous and sensible work habits. He did not burn the midnight oil, tossing off his plays on the spur of inspiration: he performed his intelligently planned literary labours between breakfast and the noonday meal, and he went to bed regularly before midnight, so that he might tackle them in the morning with freshness, lucidity and poise.

NO USE FOR DISSOLUTE BOHEMIANISM

Dissolute bohemianism revolted him—he simply had no practical use for it. Vice bored him, and as for intoxication, he put these words into the mouth of the old captain in *Heartbreak House:* "I dread being drunk more than anything in the world. To be drunk means to have dreams; to go soft; to be easily pleased and deceived; to fall into the clutches of women." Clearly, intoxication was meant to include pre-eminently erotic ecstasy, an experience unknown to Shaw. This does not mean that he was a misogynist. On the contrary, like Ibsen, he may well be described as an extoller of women. The women in his plays are generally superior to the men, in common sense, and sense of humour, usually at the expense of the men. But he was fond of quoting Napoleon, who said that women were the business of idlers; adding, on his own, that no man with any serious mission in the world could spare time and money for affairs with women. St. Anthony he was not, for that saint was beset by temptations, while Shaw, with his vitreous nature, evidently found continence of the flesh as easy as abstention from meat. He made no dogma of vegetarianism; one man's meat, he said simply, was another man's poison. But, the rebellion against the tyranny of sex— his own expression—was part of his social, moral and aesthetic credo, and there is nothing in his plays of passion, infatuation, sensual abandon, that *Come può esser ch'io non sia piu mio* of Michelangelo, and indeed these qualities would seem strangely out of place there.

One is tempted to ask him, as the prince importunes the queen in Schiller's *Don Carlos, Sie haben nie geliebt?* ("Have you then never loved?"). The answer would probably have been a laughing "No"—laughing, but a "No," none the less. Of that same vitreous character, a Marienbad elegy, with its passion-brimmed sorrow— indeed, anything like the experience of the septuagenarian Goethe underwent with Ulrike von Levetzow would have been unimaginable in the case of Shaw, and he prided himself more on it than do we on his behalf. His was a magnificent durability, yet it somehow lacked full-bloodedness, so much so that, despite the grandeur of his life, it detracted from his stature.

I am quite fond of the massive meals that delighted Luther, Goethe and Bismarck, and I rather fancy Churchill's drinking and smoking as well. In the picture of Shaw, not merely his physical presence, but also his intellectual stature, I find a certain quality of gauntness, vegetarianism and frigidity that somehow does not quite seem to fit my idea of greatness. That idea implies a degree of human tragedy, of suffering and sacrifice. The knotted muscles of Tolstoy bearing up the full burden of morality, Atlas-like. Strindberg who was in hell; the martyr's death Nietzsche died on the cross of thought; it is these that inspire us with the reverence of tragedy; but in Shaw there was nothing of all this. Was he beyond such things, or were they beyond him? He called one of his own plays *A Light Play about Difficult Things*—he might well have given that title to all of his writings, and I am not so certain whether this very definition will not apply to all art to come, and whether Shaw may not turn out to have been the smiling prophet of generations, emancipated from tragedy and gloom. Yet I ask myself whether his facility was perhaps not a little too facile; whether he was ever the man to take grave matters with their full gravity. Let the future determine his weight in the scales to the last ounce. This much is certain—his sobriety, like his diet of greens, was necessary to his particular brand of clear-headedness and constraint and liberating ebullience, and nothing could be more erroneous than to mistake his coolness for an actual incapacity for love. He may have laughed at everyone and everything, but he was anything but a Mephistophelian nihilist —thrusting the Devil's chill fist in the face of the powers of creation.

Again, it is his Captain Shotover in *Heartbreak House* to whom he gives these words to say: "Old men are dangerous: it doesn't matter to them what is going to happen to the world." Shaw did care what was to become of the world, right down to the age of ninety-four. The clergyman who intoned the prayers at his death-bed was quite right when he said, "This man was surely no atheist." He was no atheist, for he reverenced the vital force that is conducting so noble an experiment with man on earth, and was sincerely concerned lest God's experiment become a failure.

Convinced that the aesthetic element, creative joy, is the most effective instrument of enlightened teaching, he tirelessly wielded the shining sword of his word and wit against the most appalling power threatening the triumph of the experiment—stupidity. He did his best in redressing the fateful unbalance between truth and reality, in lifting mankind to a higher rung of social maturity. He often pointed a scornful finger at human frailty, but his jests were never at the expense of humanity. He was mankind's friend, and it is in this role that he will live in the hearts and memories of men.

INDEX

ABOUT THE AUTHOR

BY A strange coincidence, Louis Kronenberger, author, anthologist and drama critic, was born in 1904, the year in which George Bernard Shaw scored his first playwriting success with *John Bull's Other Island*. Mr. Kronenberger entered the University of Cincinnati in 1921. He had already decided to become a writer, and in 1924 he went to New York where he landed a minor job on the *New York Times*. In 1926 he got an editorial job with a publishing house and remained in book publishing until 1934, when he went abroad and afterwards to work for *Fortune* magazine. In 1938 he became drama critic of *Time* magazine, a position which he holds at present. During this period he has also written drama criticism for other publications.

He is the author of two novels, *The Grand Manner* and *Grand Right and Left*, a book on English stage comedy, *The Thread of Laughter*, and a volume on eighteenth-century England: *Kings and Desperate Men*. He has written introductions to the work of Johnson, Boswell, Pope, Byron, Fielding, Jane Austen and others.

He lives with his wife and two children in New York City.

DATE DUE

MAR 4 MAY 5		
MAR 18 JUN 5		
APR 11 NOV 12		
MAY 16 NOV 30 MAR 30		
JUN - 1 NOV 11		
OCT 6 NOV 30		
OCT 24 DEC 14		
NOV 9		
NOV 28 MAR 18		
RENEW APR 1		
DEC 12		
DEC 15 DEC 10 2001		
MAR 17		
MAR 3-1		
APR 15		